D0090334

Praise for
Will Your Next Mistake Be Fatal?

"Will Your Next Mistake Be Fatal? *is a compelling and highly readable source book for any CEO navigating through the risks of today's business environment. Robert Mittelstaedt provides a wealth of insights into what can go wrong in any business—even a 'successful' one—and how to recognize and prevent the ensuing chain of mistakes which could take you down.*"

> Ronald D. Sugar
> Chairman, Chief Executive Officer, and
> President Northrop Grumman Corporation

"*We all believe mistakes are unavoidable. This book will teach you, through memorable examples, how to avoid the most common mistakes which can severely impact outcomes in the business world.*"

> Lewis E. Platt
> Chairman, The Boeing Company and retired
> Chairman and Chief Executive Officer,
> Hewlett-Packard Company

"*Bob Mittelstaedt does a wonderful job of explaining, through well-known examples from the Titanic to the Columbia and many other well-known companies, that many 'accidents' are really 'incidents' with a long chain of mistakes, often going back many years and rooted in the institution's culture. This is a book well worth reading by those guiding business enterprises.*"

> Michael D. Zisman
> Consultant to IBM Corporate Strategy, former
> IBM Vice President for Corporate Strategy, and
> Chief Executive Officer of Lotus Development
> Corporation

"*Failure—what leader hasn't been there? The trick, as Bob Mittelstaedt's insights illustrate, is that you can and must avoid the type of unseen failures that drive you and your company off the proverbial cliff.*"

> Craig E. Weatherup
> Former Chairman and CEO of the Pepsi-Cola
> Company

Will Your Next Mistake Be Fatal?

Avoiding the Chain of Mistakes That Can Destroy

Ideas. Action. Impact.
Wharton School Publishing

In the face of accelerating turbulence and change, business leaders and policy makers need new ways of thinking to sustain performance and growth.

Wharton School Publishing offers a trusted source for stimulating ideas from thought leaders who provide new mental models to address changes in strategy, management, and finance. We seek out authors from diverse disciplines with a profound understanding of change and its implications. We offer books and tools that help executives respond to the challenge of change.

Every book and management tool we publish meets quality standards set by The Wharton School of the University of Pennsylvania. Each title is reviewed by the Wharton School Publishing Editorial Board before being given Wharton's seal of approval. This ensures that Wharton publications are timely, relevant, important, conceptually sound or empirically based, and implementable.

To fit our readers' learning preferences, Wharton publications are available in multiple formats, including books, audio, and electronic.

To find out more about our books and management tools, visit us at whartonsp.com and Wharton's executive education site, exceed.wharton.upenn.edu.

Will Your Next Mistake Be Fatal?

Avoiding the Chain of Mistakes That Can Destroy

Robert E. Mittelstaedt

Wharton
UNIVERSITY *of* PENNSYLVANIA

Wharton School Publishing

A CIP record of this book can be obtained from the Library of Congress

Publisher: Tim Moore
International Marketing Manager: Tim Galligan
Marketing Manager: Martin Litkowski
Managing Editor: Gina Kanouse
Senior Project Editor: Kristy Hart
Compositor: Jake McFarland
Manufacturing Coordinator: Dan Uhrig
Cover Design: Anthony Gemmellaro
Interior Design: Meg Van Arsdale

© 2005 Pearson Education, Inc.

Ideas. Action. Impact.
Wharton School
Publishing

Publishing as Wharton School Publishing
Upper Saddle River, NJ 07458

Printed in the United States of America

First Printing

ISBN 0-13-191364-6

Pearson Education Ltd.
Pearson Education Australia Pty., Limited
Pearson Education Singapore, Pte. Ltd.
Pearson Education North Asia Ltd.
Pearson Education Canada, Ltd.
Pearson Educación de Mexico, S.A. de C.V.
Pearson Education—Japan
Pearson Education Malaysia, Pte. Ltd.

Ideas. Action. Impact.
Wharton School
Publishing

C. K. Prahalad
THE FORTUNE AT THE BOTTOM OF THE PYRAMID
Eradicating Poverty Through Profits

Yoram (Jerry)Wind, Colin Crook, with Robert Gunther
THE POWER OF IMPOSSIBLE THINKING
Transform the Business of Your Life and the Life of Your Business

Scott A. Shane
FINDING FERTILE GROUND
Identifying Extraordinary Opportunities for New Ventures

To Mary Ellen, the love of my life, who has saved me from making more mistakes than I care to count over the last 38 years.

Contents

About the Author
Robert E. Mittelstaedt

Robert E. Mittelstaedt Jr. is Dean and professor of the W. P. Carvey School of Business, Arizona State University, and former, Vice Dean and Director, Aresty Institute of Executive Education, The Wharton School. He has consulted with organizations ranging from IBM to Weirton Steel, Pfizer to the U.S. Nuclear Regulatory Commission, and is a member of the board of directors of three corporations in electronics and healthcare services businesses.

Mittelstaedt's research interests have included executive learning, corporate governance, IT, and strategy. He formerly directed the Wharton Innovation Center and the Wharton Applied Research Center. Mittelstaedt founded Intellgo, Inc. He served as an officer in the U.S. Navy in nuclear submarines at the height of the Cold War. He is also a licensed commercial pilot with multi-engine and instrument ratings.

Introduction

What, Me Worry?

What do the failure of Enron, the Watergate scandal, the nuclear accident at Three Mile Island, and most airline crashes have in common? Quite simply, it would be almost impossible to make each of these things happen without a serious sequence of errors that goes unchecked. Whether it is a physical disaster, a political blunder, a corporate misstep, or a strategic mistake, as the investigation unfolds, we always find out that it took a unique set of compounding errors to bring the crisis to front-page status.

In many cases, these blunders are so complex and the impact so serious that we find ourselves saying, "You couldn't make that happen if you tried." The difference between organizations that end up on the front page of a national newspaper in a negative light, those you never hear about, and those that end up on the front page in a positive light, is the process of *Managing Multiple Mistakes (M³)*.

It has long been known that most man-made physical disasters are the result of a series of mistakes. In most cases, if one can find a way to "break the chain," a major catastrophe can be avoided. This recognition of failure chains in operating aircraft, trains, nuclear power plants, chemical plants, and other mechanical devices has led to an emphasis on understanding causes and developing procedures, training, and safety systems to reduce the incidence of accidents and to mitigate damage if one does occur. Strangely, there has been little emphasis on extending this process to help avoid business disasters—whether operational or strategic.

Enron, WorldCom, and HealthSouth are now widely known as major business disasters. Enron might even be classified as a major economic disaster given the number of employees, pensions, and shareholders affected at Enron and their accountants, Arthur Andersen. As investigations unfolded, we learned that none of these was the result of a single bad decision or action. Each involved a complicated web of mistakes that were either unnoticed, dismissed as unimportant, judged as minor, or purposely ignored in favor of a high-risk, high-payoff gamble.

This book is about the avoidable traps that we set for ourselves as business people that lead to disasters. It is about what we can learn from the patterns of action or inaction that preceded disasters (sometimes called "accidents") in a variety of business and nonbusiness settings in order to avoid similar traps and patterns of mistakes. This goes beyond kaizen and six-sigma on the factory floor to M^3 in the executive suite and at all operational levels of companies.

This is not a book about crisis management. It is not about managing public relations, the victims, the lawyers, or the shareholders. It is about discipline, culture, and learning from the experiences of others to improve the odds that you can avoid the things we label as accidents, disasters, or crises altogether. Even if you do not totally avoid such situations, knowledge of the typical patterns that occur should help you create an organization that is observant enough to intervene early and minimize damage. Learning and implementing the lessons described here will not mean that you throw away your plans for handling problem situations. But it could mean that you will never have to manage the aftermath of an unpleasant situation.

There are lessons to be learned from looking at the mistake patterns and commonalities in other organizations, especially since most organizations do not do a very good job of evaluating their own mistakes even though they have the most information. We miss learning opportunities by not being curious enough to look deeply at our own failures, but we also miss a very rich set of opportunities when we do not look at the mistakes others have made, especially when they have been well documented. We often miss these opportunities to learn from others because we believe, "Their situation was different—we don't have much to learn from them."

The reality is very different because studies show that while the specifics may be different across industries and situations, the patterns of mistakes preceding accidents are quite similar. Learning doesn't always come from the sources you expect, like your own experience, your own industry, or very similar companies. It takes a bit of extra effort, but you can often learn more by looking at examples in an industry or situation that is markedly different from your own and recognizing that there are great similarities in the patterns of actions and behaviors. This is because without the burden of a set of assumptions around what you "know" is the right or wrong way to do something, it is easy to observe the salient facts, absent all the distracting details, and quickly say to yourself something like:

- Didn't they know water would boil if they lowered the pressure? (Three Mile Island)
- Why did they fail to follow the procedure and fly into the ground? (Korean Air)
- Didn't they know customers would want a replacement for a defective chip? (Intel)
- Don't they know that customers are often more loyal if you admit a mistake and fix it? (Firestone)
- Didn't they know the leverage and/or fraud might kill the company? (Enron, WorldCom, HealthSouth)
- Didn't NASA learn anything the first time? (Columbia)
- Why is J&J legendary for its handling of the Tylenol crisis over 20 years ago?
- How did a United Airlines crew minimize loss of life with a crash landing where "everything" went wrong? (UA-232 at Sioux City, Iowa)

In each case of a crisis with an adverse outcome, there is a very common pattern:

- An initial problem, often minor in isolation, that goes uncorrected
- A subsequent problem that compounds the effect of the initial problem
- An inept corrective effect
- Disbelief at the accelerating seriousness of the situation
- Generally, an attempt to hide the truth about what is going on while an attempt is made at remediation
- Sudden recognition that the situation is out of control or "in extremis"*
- Finally, the ultimate disaster scenario involving significant loss of life, financial resources, or both, and ultimately, the recriminations

We will explore a number of famous and not-so-famous disasters or near disasters from the perspective of the mistake sequence and where it might have been broken to change the outcome or was broken to minimize the damage. We will call your attention to the mistakes so that you might think about the signals that were present and how you, in an ideal world, might have acted differently.

The mistakes identified are usually the result of direct action or inaction by humans. In many scenarios, the mistake sequence was initiated with equipment malfunctions that were known but not taken into account in decision-making. In other situations, the mistakes may have been in the design of systems or business procedures that were based on faulty assumptions. Sometimes there were significant, uncontrollable initiating or contributing factors, such as equipment failure, a natural weather occurrence, or some other "act of God." These initiating factors must be considered in decision-making when they are present because, although they are not always human in origin, they are a part of the chain of causes that leads to disasters where humans have an opportunity to intervene effectively or ineffectively.

---

* A term from the nautical rules of the road indicating that a collision is virtually unavoidable and the most extreme actions possible must be taken to minimize or avoid damage.

In the past, you may have looked at the occurrence of disasters or recovery from near-disasters as a matter of passing interest in the news. We are suggesting that you look a little deeper, learn a little more, and stretch a little further for the implications that you can use:

- Is there a disaster waiting to happen in my organization?
- Will we see the signs?
- Will we stop it soon enough?
- Do we have the skills to see the signals and the culture to "break the chain?"
- Are we smart enough to realize that it makes economic sense to care about reducing or stopping mistakes?

Learn from the mistakes of others and envision business success without mistakes, because your future may depend on your ability to do just that. To aid in this quest, we will identify some "Insights" linking common themes that come out of the study of mistakes across industries and situations. These will appear appropriately in each chapter and will be summarized in a broad way again in Chapter 10, "Making M^3 Part of Your Culture For Success."

Getting The Most From This Book and Its Concepts

Each of us comes to any book with our own unique set of experiences as a context for reading and learning. Our personal background will affect how we perceive and learn from the all-too-real situations described in this book. Each person reading this will find different ways to relate the concepts to his or her professional and even personal situations, and those differences in learning are desirable. From a process standpoint you will get more out of the lessons imbedded here if you keep a few points in mind:

- Think broadly and do not dismiss an example because it is outside of your industry or interest. The patterns of mistakes are similar and know no boundaries.
- Keep asking yourself, honestly, how you might have felt and what you might have done under similar circumstances to those the executives, managers, and other staff you will hear about who, in most of our examples, really messed up badly.

■ Ask yourself if you have what it takes to rise to the occasion and
  "break a mistake chain" as the heroes or unsung heroes did in the
  few successful mistake management scenarios you will read.

■ Think about the importance and economic implications of avoiding
  mistakes and how you will help your whole organization learn to
  make mistake-free quality a goal, regardless of your business.

■ Ask how you can create better warning systems to help you detect
  and minimize the impact of mistakes in your organization. Concepts
  like an Executive Information System (EIS) or Digital Dashboard are
  not new, but they are still being refined as tools to help managers
  understand what is going on in their organizations.

■ Never forget that much of the information that you need to know to
  understand what is going on inside your business resides outside
  with your customers, suppliers and business partners. Ask how a
  broad range of stakeholders fits into the desire to run mistake free
  effective businesses.

While this is a book about avoiding mistakes, do not forget that the
only sure way to avoid mistakes is to never take a risk, and that is the
ultimate enemy of success. If you feel too conservative about risk after
reading about the messes created by incompetence, go back and reread
the last section in Chapter 10 entitled "The Need for Mistakes" over and
over again until you understand that a competitive capitalistic system
only rewards those who take risks and there is value in learning to
manage risk, minimize failure and learning from both success and
failure.

There are many different learning styles. I have done well with
structured learning, but ever since I was a kid taking apart clocks and
other mechanical devices I have really loved learning by doing. Some
who read this will be like me and just want to jump into the stories and
examples. You might prefer to form your own thoughts about the broad
learning points we can glean from the stories and examples I have
chosen, before I burden you with my model of the relationships and
application of principles.

Others might prefer an early description of a model or framework to
help you see how the cases fit together to form a set of learning points
that can be applied in your situation. If you are in the latter category,
continue with this introduction for a brief description of the model

that I work toward in the final chapter. If you prefer to develop your own mental model as you go along it is time for you to jump right to Chapter 1.

A Framework for Managing Multiple Mistakes: The Business Flywheel

We will explore a variety of operational and strategic mistakes in business and other situations as we progress through the book. In Chapter 10, "Making M3 Part of Your Culture for Success," we summarize the learning points from the cases discussed to point out that business is like an engine, requiring energy to get a flywheel rotating to help a vehicle or other machine produce work in a desirable direction. Once the flywheel is rotating, inertia tends to keep the flywheel and the machine it is working for, moving in the right direction, but mistakes are the equivalent of braking or even shifting into reverse and moving backwards.

Many things help or hinder the rotation of the flywheel. The broad categories of inputs, processes, resources and external uncontrollable factors are illustrated in Figure 10.1, and are discussed and evolved as organizing categories with implications as we go through the examples in the book. Keep this structure and set of relationships in mind as you explore some of the most interesting mistakes man has made in business and physical systems over the last century and then see if you agree with my conclusions in Chapter 10 as to how to apply the principles learned to your business or personal situation.

I

The Power of M³ and the Need to Understand Mistakes

"Anything worth doing is worth doing right."

—My dad and others of his era

Doing things right in business has gotten a lot of press in recent years. We seem to have finally discovered that just having ideas is not enough. Results are what really matter, and results come from both ideas and execution, but the biggest enemy of great execution is mistakes.

I learned many things while serving as an officer in U.S. Navy nuclear submarines in the late 1960s, but one of the things you heard from the beginning was the saying, "There's no partial credit in the fleet." Win or lose in battle—there is no in-between—something that is especially true in the unforgiving environment hundreds of feet below the surface of the ocean and thousands of miles from home.

The problem with mistakes is that they creep up on you—individuals do not get up in the morning and say, "Boy, this would be a great day to make some mistakes." They just find themselves in a place they do not want to be, fighting to survive a crisis and, if they do not survive the crisis, wondering how it all happened.

There are places, like the world of sports, where your mistakes are very visible. For baseball fans, and especially for Boston Red Sox fans, the seventh game of the 2003 American League Championship Series was a lesson in making mistakes.

Boston was ahead in the eighth inning with a two-run lead. The pitcher, Pedro Martinez, had pitched a very good game, and everyone thought this was the year that the "Curse of the Bambino"* would be broken. Martinez had thrown nearly 120 pitches (a lot) and was no longer pitching perfectly, resulting in runners at second and third. The manager, Grady Little, went to the mound and decided to leave his star pitcher in the game. Fans in the ballpark and watching on TV all over the world were saying, "This guy looks tired—are you crazy?" It was very late in the game, the tying run was at the plate, the game was on the line, the chance to go to the World Series was on the line, Martinez was looking weak, and Little decided to stick with the plan.

The rest is history and is now part of the lore of "The Curse." A double by Jorge Posada drove in two runs to tie the game, which went to extra innings. The Yankees won in the eleventh inning. A series of small mistakes built up to cause a disaster (for Boston fans). There were chances to break the chain of mistakes, but Martinez was not able to do so, and Little, uncertain about the alternative path (replacing the pitcher), was unwilling to take any action, sticking with what most people watching the game considered to be a high-risk strategy.

There's no partial credit in the Fleet. There's no partial credit in championship sports—you win or lose. You may not die physically from a sports mistake, but your career might, as Grady Little found when he was fired within a week of his team's loss.

But isn't this true in business as well? Many people are uncomfortable with the stark reality of winning and losing. My wife always roots for the underdog in the World Series, the Superbowl, or the Academy Awards, but she has learned how to win in local politics and business. Especially in the United States, we would like to believe there "is enough to go around," whether it's food or market share. The reality in a globally competitive world is different, however—win or lose. Deliver value or be shunned. Grow or die.

---

* Boston fans believe Boston has not won a World Series since 1918 because the legendary player, Babe Ruth, was traded to the New York Yankees.

We learned as kids to compete for grades, approval, awards, a spot in the school play, entrance to college, or a place on a team or in a club. As individuals, we compete for jobs. When there are enough, we compete for the best jobs. If there are not enough, we compete for any job. In groups, we compete as teams for causes or recognition. What makes the difference between winners and losers on a personal basis? Sometimes it is raw intelligence. But often it is mistakes: in choices we have made along the way, in how we present ourselves, or the way in which we view the world. We often rationalize personal failures by saying, "Everybody makes mistakes." While this may be true, it may also be a point of differentiation that changes lives—or businesses.

Most industries in developed countries have consolidated or will soon. Developing countries are becoming more competitive. In most industries, one or two top players emerge who will do better than others, at least for some period. True differentiation is hard to find. The top players look a lot like each other, and the real difference boils down to the ability to execute. Execution, according to one recent book on the subject, boils down to leadership, culture, and people.[1]

In my experience, the top players know that execution is important and are working hard on leadership, culture, and people. But some don't get it right, and then a winner and a loser emerges. Why don't they get it right? Mistakes—big ones, medium ones, and small ones.

Winners, whether in business, sports, or geopolitics, learn that getting near the top is really tough, but once you get near the top, mistakes are usually the difference between base camp and the peak. Winners learn this quickly and learn how to avoid mistakes—at least the big ones. Losers do not learn this as quickly, and in some cases, they make the same mistakes over and over.

The mistakes and mistake chains or sequences that we will discuss in subsequent chapters are primarily human mistakes. There are often mechanical failures, environmental circumstances (such as weather), technology changes, competitive moves, or other initiating actions that create a situation that requires response. It is in these situations that the ability of individuals to make decisions and cope with the circumstances is tested, and it is where mistakes do or do not occur.

Even the situations that are the initiating events may have their origin in human mistakes. For example, not all mechanical failures of equipment are random. Some are the result of poor design, choice of materials, or manufacturing quality, each of which was likely a human mistake. Some actions by competitors occur because you allow them an opening or indirectly give them a clue as to how to compete more effectively.

Business books have enjoyed great popularity in the last 20 years. One of the biggest in 1994 was *Built to Last*[2] in which the authors identified companies they considered "visionary" and used words like "icon" to describe these leaders. Just 10 years ago, among the 18 companies they classified as visionary were Boeing, Ford, HP, Merck, Motorola, Sony, and Walt Disney. Each of these has fallen on harder times since and, while highly respected for past contributions, is seeing questions raised about its future. Are these venerable names in American and global business just going through a rough patch, or have their positions changed in ways that will prevent them from ever achieving their former prominence in their industries? I have opinions about each, but I don't have a crystal ball for the future. What I can say definitively is that a number of these companies have made serious mistakes or a chain of mistakes that accelerated their fall from the pedestal of business admiration.

In many ways, these are the most challenging times for business in a generation. We have all been awakened to the need to look beyond the comfort of our day-to-day existence, to the need to synthesize the implications of external events, including heightened competition. That, in turn, leads to the need to focus not just on execution but on flawless execution. There is no partial credit in the Fleet.

Patterns of Mistakes and Exponential Growth

At some point in your secondary education, you learned about something called an "exponential." You may have thought this was an abstract mathematical concept, but the reality is that it has all sorts of real-world implications. At the simplest level, the most important thing to understand about anything that involves exponential movement is that it grows (or declines) *really* fast. Whether you are talking about an ant colony multiplying, the magic of compound interest, or the increase in the number of components possible per integrated circuit (Moore's Law), changes happen very rapidly and in a nonlinear fashion.

Exponential growth in severity of damage is often descriptive of a business crisis. The damage may be in the form of lost customers, lost sales, higher costs, liability costs, employee morale, or physical assets. If we make a mistake in business and brush it off, it probably was not too severe. If we start making estimates of what the cost was or will be, it was probably quite damaging financially, if not in other ways.

Whether it is physical, financial, or strategic, phrases such as "things went to hell in a hand basket" do not come close to describing what occurred. This can happen in any business. Geography, culture, and business size are irrelevant. Mistakes happen and businesses that were otherwise successful suddenly suffer a change of direction. This is rarely simply fate. In business, most things happen for a reason, not because a deity willed them to happen—and, aside from natural disasters, when bad things happen, people and their flawed judgment are usually involved.

The objective is to learn to recognize the patterns of mistakes that precede most business disasters and take actions to eliminate the threat or to reduce the incident to something that does not require full-scale crisis management. These patterns of mistakes and potential responses are surprisingly similar across physical and business disasters and across industries. This should make it easier to learn how to deal with dangerous situations, but we rarely take the time to see the parallels in what appear to be unrelated experiences. If we did take the time, it might help us learn and change our behavior. We can learn to see patterns, and patterns can help us anticipate, prevent, minimize, or control the potential exponential downside for most crisis, accident, or disaster scenarios.

Mistakes in business are pervasive, but we do not always witness them unfolding as visibly as we do in physical disasters. We see reports of a chemical plant disaster or an airplane crash on the news within minutes of its occurrence. For business disasters, we do not get blow-by-blow accounts of the decision-making process as we did during Three Mile Island. No, business mistakes, except for the very largest, are hidden from view. They are hidden for many reasons including protection of competitive information, protection of employees and management, potential legal exposure in a variety of ways, and finally, the desire to not upset "the street." Additionally, some "mistakes" are quite clear very quickly, but some may not be seen as mistakes in the eyes of all who examine a situation at a given point in time.

Strategic mistakes are rarely black and white until well after the fact, so there are times when the time frame is relevant for classifying an action or lack of action as a mistake in business. It is also common for some companies to have such a long string of explanations regarding one-time charges that it is hard to figure out if they are making mistakes or have just been hit by a string of bad luck. For years, AT&T booked restructuring and other "one-time" charges, giving the appearance that they were doing well when they were not.

But this is not about how you can become a more effective analyst of a company's mistakes from the outside. The real question is whether or not, as an insider, you are capable of recognizing that a chain of mistakes is underway and are willing to take action to prevent or mitigate damage.

The biggest reason you do not hear much about corporate mistakes, unless they are so colossal that some government entity forces an investigation, is that most companies do not put together blue-ribbon investigative committees to find causes of failures and recommend improvements. No one would accept a statement that an airliner "just crashed—we're not sure why, but we'll try not to do it again." Yet in business, we see all kinds of failures that are not investigated in any serious depth unless laws were violated or people were physically injured.

Physical disasters, things like plants blowing up, are usually investigated in depth because companies have visible and usually costly incentives to understand them. Big physical events can affect public safety, insurance costs, and liabilities related to injury or death. But management mistakes that do not "hurt anyone" except perhaps shareholders, employees, and communities are rarely investigated with the same fervor as physical disasters.

While not as visible, I would argue that strategic and management blunders are likely to be more costly to a corporation and its stakeholders than almost any physical disaster. They thus deserve the same level of inquiry, learning, and improvement to avoid repetition and future damage. I have also observed that many physical disasters have root causes that are similar to management blunders. The specifics are different, but the human behaviors, biases, and blind spots are similar. For this reason, we will examine both physical and management disasters as we explore the commonality of causes and the potential for learning one from the other. The word "accident" is often used to convey the impression that an undesirable event was unavoidable. This is rarely the case. Business accidents, blunders, incidents, crises, or disasters are usually no different than a child who has an "accident" spilling grape juice on a beige carpet, which is then cleaned with an incorrect cleaning compound that leaves a permanent spot.

The damage was avoidable if we had given the child water instead, had not let him go into the carpeted room, or had put a restrictive top on the cup. Mistakes are made in not thinking through situations ahead of time, in not anticipating the possible range of consequences, or through incorrect remedial actions. Regardless of what we call such an occurrence, the idea is to focus on the occurrence and what we can learn from the pattern of mistakes that led to the it and the resulting damage to prevent similar situations or to minimize damage in the future.

The concept of Managing Multiple Mistakes (M³) is based on the observation that nearly all serious accidents, whether physical or business, are the result of more than one mistake. If we do not "break the chain" of mistakes early, the damage that is done, and its cost will go up exponentially, as illustrated in Figure 1.1, until the situation is irreparable.

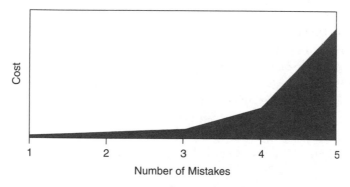

Figure 1.1 Mistakes and costs.

This applies to all types of human endeavor: physical systems for transportation or manufacturing, business decisions from the front line to the boardroom, healthcare delivery, the structure or operation of our electricity grid (or lack thereof), personal relationships, and even politics.

In fact, the Watergate scandal may be one of the best illustrations of failing to manage multiple mistakes. It took some time to understand, but when it was all done, it became clear that this was a case where the initial mistake, the decision to burglarize Democratic Party offices to obtain information that was of little value, was compounded severely by subsequent attempts to cover up earlier mistakes. This is a classic case of what Joseph Grundfest, a Stanford law professor and former SEC Commissioner, calls "crimes of upholstery"—where the damage done by the cover-up was far worse than the original crime. Would Richard Nixon have finished his second term if he and his colleagues had admitted immediately that they had done something stupid and had not attempted to cover it up with unbelievable stories of accidental tape erasure and other fabrications? We will never know, but the pattern of multiple mistakes involves sins of both omission and commission in nearly all the stories you will read in this book.

Understanding accidents of one sort or another has become an organized activity of government and academic study, especially over the last century as industrial and transportation systems became more complex. Most countries have special boards to study accidents and incidents that affect public safety in transportation or potentially dangerous industries. The public visibility of investigations of one sort or another has changed with technology and society over time. Investigations of mine, maritime, and train disasters were in the public eye 50 to 100 years ago, but in the last two decades, we have heard more about nuclear power, airplane crashes, chemical plant problems, carcinogens left behind from industrial activity, failures in space, and Internet worms.

This shift in focus of the types of investigations that get public attention is not surprising given the growth and implementation of new technologies. Investigating agencies worldwide are formed and focus on improving public safety, usually with a goal of zero accidents. Yet there are some, such as Charles Perrow in his book *Normal Accidents*[3], who believe that some level of very significant accidents is "normal" because today's systems are so complex that, as we attempt to build in more sophisticated safeguards, we actually create new categories of accidents that were previously unanticipated. In fact, as a sociologist, he questions what our reaction will be to accidents that we realize we cannot control with better management and training.

In some ways, recent corporate disasters, especially Enron, seem to support Perrow's hypothesis, namely that bigger, faster-acting, technology-driven businesses and systems simply have the opportunity to spawn larger disasters more rapidly. Enron was a man-made disaster, but the availability of systems for rapid and complicated energy trading, the complexity of financing vehicles, and a wide range of businesses all increased complexity beyond any individual's ability to completely comprehend and control the business.

While Perrow's hypothesis is understandable, there are many of us who believe that, while accidents in physical systems and businesses are inevitable, it is possible to understand them and find ways to reduce such events in both frequency and severity. In fact, even though accidents still occur, their incidence in a number of very visible areas (such as aviation) has been reduced over the years, something that we will discuss in later chapters.

Deadly Business Mistakes– Strategy, Execution, and Culture

Some years ago, Peter Drucker wrote an article[4] describing "Five Deadly Business Sins" that have driven many companies into deep strategic and financial trouble. His characterization of these "sins" included:

- "Worship of high profit margins and premium pricing"
- "Mispricing a new product by charging what the market will bear"
- "Cost-driven pricing"
- "Slaughtering tomorrow's opportunity on the alter of yesterday"
- "Feeding problems and starving opportunities"

These, and others we will discuss, are primarily examples of longer-term cultural mistakes that companies make with regularity. Damage does not occur overnight; it occurs slowly and consistently until someone or something breaks the chain and fixes the problem. Breaking the chain for these types of mistakes is difficult because the decision criteria and mindset are hard-wired into the brains of company managers and executives as a result of past successes.

As we will discuss later, the U.S. auto industry has been guilty of many of these mistakes and is trying to change, but serious remedial action was delayed for years until their market share and profitability was decimated by competition from Japan and Germany. Sometimes the initial recognition that a problem exists is the biggest hurdle.

In other cases, individual companies, such as IBM, have made one or more of these mistakes but have realized it early enough, changed, and recovered. But for every company that has detected its mistakes and taken action in time to survive, there are many more that never saw the danger that was coming until it was too late.

Strategic mistakes, particularly those affected by the organization's culture, are among the most difficult to deal with because, at any given point in time, it may not seem like there is a huge crisis. In cultures not known for rapid change, it is too easy to feel comfortable with the way things have always been done until there is a huge crisis that wakes you up to the need for change. This is analogous to an individual's problems with weight control. The problem does not result from a single bad decision or action but from a thousand small bad decisions over a period of time. Just as with weight control, however, if allowed to go too far, these types of business mistakes become life threatening.

Other cultures make it difficult to expose and deal with mistakes of strategy or execution even if they are detected early. Organizations that are paternalistic, hierarchal, consensual, or family dominated all have unique characteristics that may make them inept, defensive, or slow to act on bad news. Many organizations do not even understand what their culture is, much less think about how to take advantage of its strengths and design around its weaknesses, which is necessary to avoid mistakes.

Most execution mistakes are related to operations but may have strategic implications. Execution mistakes usually revolve around tangible actions that are more visible than strategic blunders. They happen more rapidly and are usually measurable in customer dissatisfaction, lost sales, warranty returns, or other shorter-term measures. They have immediate consequences and are thus easier to see and understand.

Culture-driven mistakes, especially around strategy, are usually colossal and fairly permanent in their damage. AT&T attempted to enter the computer business by acquiring NCR—a colossal cultural mistake chain that took years to clean up and cost both companies dearly. While this was a strategic mistake, it affected operations directly with confused product offerings, angry customers, and conflicts over resource allocation and resulting poor financial performance. It eventually resulted in spinning off NCR, which should never have been acquired in the first place.

Execution mistakes can be fatal as well but are more often just very expensive, unless they continue so long that they become cultural. There are many categories of execution mistakes, from not following procedures, as in many airline crashes, to not understanding markets enough to bring out the right product, to bad timing with good products. The dustbin of product development is filled with things like the RCA Videodisk. Introduced in the early 1980s, it was actually a decent product in a clumsy format that was inconvenient for the market at the time. This product was the result of a series of mistakes related to market understanding, technology, product design, and pricing.

Subsequent chapters will deal with the impact that culture can have on the likely success or failure of organizations in avoiding multiple mistakes. A common theme that runs through all the cases we will explore, whether strategy or execution related, is that in most cases it takes three, four, or five mistakes that must occur in sequence to create a serious failure. We will also look at the dramatic effect that organization culture has on affecting a positive or negative outcome.

The reality is that the business world, and perhaps life in general, is more forgiving than we realize. More often than not, you have to mess up a number of times and pretty badly to get a really bad outcome.

Can Technology Change the Odds?

An important question is whether we can use technology to automatically prevent accidents in complex systems, and if so, are these measures a net positive force? Technology is being used for operations in more businesses every day. Common examples include automation of production processes, automation of customer service functions, call center support systems to help make operators "smarter" and more effective salespeople, and information systems that monitor key variables constantly and warn managers when limits are exceeded.

We want to believe that if we program operations and response, we can ensure standard quality and minimize or prevent mistakes. The reality is that business, broadly speaking, is not as far along in this regard as those businesses that must use technology to operate at all.

For example, Airbus Industries pioneered "fly-by-wire" and first introduced it in commercial passenger aircraft in the A320. Historically, the pilot's yoke (or stick, depending on the aircraft) was physically connected, via cables, to the ailerons and elevator, the primary control surfaces for roll and pitch of the aircraft. As airplanes grew larger and heavier, hydraulic actuator systems (something like power steering in automobiles) were connected to the cables to make it easier for the pilot to control the airplane. Even with a hydraulic system, pilots physically feel a direct relationship between the movement of their hands and the response of the aircraft.

Fly-by-wire removes the physical connection, with a joystick generating an electronic signal that is sent to actuators that drive the movement of the control surfaces. Fly-by-wire makes controlling a large passenger aircraft akin to playing a video game, literally using a joystick to control the aircraft attitude and direction. For pilots, this was a major technological leap that was not necessarily welcome since the "feel" of the aircraft is artificially induced in the stick by electronics and the response of the airplane may be limited by algorithms and parameters set in software.

For aircraft engineers, this technology simplified construction and maintenance and potentially enhanced safety. It meant that a computer could be put in the loop to limit what the pilot can command the airplane to do. This is an attractive capability providing engineers the ability to actually limit what the airplane will do rather than just writing a manual that warns operators not to exceed certain parameters. To improve safety, Airbus aircraft with fly-by-wire are limited in ways that change under different conditions. Parameters such as angle of attack, bank angle, roll rate, and engine power, among other things, are monitored, managed systemically, and limited, no matter what the pilot does with the stick. This has the effect of making it impossible to stall* the airplane, and it simplifies the number of things a pilot needs to remember to do in response to certain emergency situations.

Boeing held steadfastly to the mechanical control model until the 777, which is Boeing's first fly-by-wire passenger aircraft. The reason for being late to adopt this technology was explained to me by a retired Boeing senior engineering director, "You just don't know what's going to happen to those electrons between the front and the back of the plane. I like a direct connection better."

---

* A "stall" in an airplane is not what the layman might think—the engine doesn't quit. This technical term means that the aircraft wing angle of attack is so steep that the wing ceases to produce lift (because airflow is disrupted over the upper surface). This is dangerous because it can lead to uncontrolled descent, especially a spin. The angle of attack in a stall is always the same for a given aircraft, but the stall speed varies as a function of many variables including weight, density altitude, and bank angle.

For a time, the old view seemed the safest as Airbus worked out its fly-by-wire bugs in a very public fashion at an air show in France in 1988 with the crash of an A320 into a forest while performing a low-altitude, low-speed fly-by. There were a few other related crashes*, but in recent years the technology has been improved, proven in commercial service, and incorporated into all Airbus aircraft developed after the A320.

When Boeing adopted fly-by-wire on the 777, it came with a big difference—the ability for the pilot to override the computer's limits. Boeing argues that the pilot should be the ultimate judge of whether an emergency requires going beyond standard operating and safety parameters. As an example, a Boeing spokesman[5] cited a China Air 747 incident in 1985 where the crew recovered from an out-of-control dive with a recovery that stressed the airplane at up to 4g's, something that Airbus fly-by-wire would limit to 2.5g's, perhaps limiting its capability to recover from some unusual attitudes.

Those who advocate unlimited pilot control believe that fly-by-wire limits are akin to saving the airplane from overstress but crashing it in the process. Advocates of fully integrated system control tell the old joke that describes the computer-controlled airplane of the future as having a seat in the cockpit for a pilot and a dog. The pilot's job is to the feed the dog, and the dog's job is to bite the pilot if he tries to touch anything.

Can technology save us from our own mistakes? Yes and no. Technology can improve the odds when we understand the range of possible actions of something like an aircraft or another technically controlled machine or system. But most businesses have many dimensions, and not all have accepted preprogrammed responses, so while technology may help, it is unlikely to stop business mistakes.

Debates about the appropriate use of technology are constant. In recent months, these have included issues such as whether the New York Stock Exchange should be replaced with an electronic exchange and whether the electric power grid in the United States can be improved with more technology. These and other examples involve complex systems of human, economic, and technical interaction with a range of

---

* Engineering bulletins issued by Airbus to operators indicated that certain aspects of the many interrelated inputs and controls were still being worked out at the time but apparently had not been applied to that specific airplane. Another A320 crashed in Bangalore, India, in 1990 and a third in France in 1992 fueled discussion about whether the new technology was ready for commercial service.

parameters under *normal* conditions. Yet all have the potential to spiral out of control when there are multiple mistakes or unusual situations that were not anticipated and built into operating parameters and designs.

This is the conundrum that surrounds multiple mistakes. We can anticipate many, but not all, mistakes that people or systems will induce in business or the operation of complex machines. If we can anticipate mistakes, should we train people to avoid the circumstances or build technology-based systems that prevent those things from happening? If we build programmed error-control systems, will we induce more mistakes or prevent recovery from mistakes we did not anticipate?

We can use technology to improve business processes like the supply chain, but computers cannot decide how you will identify and design new products that go into that supply chain or where and how they will be manufactured. This is where physical systems and businesses diverge. Business systems still require judgment, thus we need to continue to refine and improve the quality of judgment and decision-making abilities of individuals operating businesses.

Mental Preparation, Patterns, and Warning Signs

Many of the accidents or disasters described in this book and the mistake chains that caused them ended badly and were unusual because they had not been previously experienced in exactly the same form. Similar mistake chains may have occurred, but organizations and individuals failed to see the lesson if the learning was not internal and personal. Regardless of the history, though, some organizations and individuals clearly handle unexpected challenges better than others.

In successful cases, we will see that there was some combination of luck and skill, but the most important element in handling the unexpected in business is prior mental preparation. This preparation takes the form of training, orientation, expert consultation, and communication or cultural values for guidance, but it exists in some form. The converse is true with the multiple mistake scenarios that lead to severe damage or disaster. The success factors for others simply do not exist in the unsuccessful organizations, and thus the mistake chains are not broken.

Louis Pasteur reportedly said, "Half of scientific discovery is by chance, but chance favors the prepared mind." The power of multiple mistakes is strong, but it can be managed with preparation.

Insight #1: Mental preparation is critical because organizations and individuals are rarely good at learning by drawing parallels. They need to be taught to recognize types and patterns of mistakes and learn to extrapolate implications from other situations into their own.

In subsequent chapters, we will examine what constitutes a mistake and how in some circumstances, particularly around company strategy, it may take a long time to understand that a mistake chain is underway. We will see that managers and employees at all levels can have an impact on monitoring and understanding mistakes. Additionally, the initiative and bias for action of individuals who may not even have formal responsibility in an area is often the difference between success and failure in avoiding or minimizing damage. We will also contrast some of the most visible mistakes that companies and organizations have made with the often less visible efforts of excellent companies that never seem to find themselves in much difficulty.

Our exploration of mistakes, both in business and nonbusiness settings across industries, reveals patterns that are so repetitive that every manager should recognize them as potential red flags. All of these are behaviors or actions that each of us has encountered or observed at some point in our careers, but they continue to be catalysts for events that inflict serious damage in the form of reputation, money, management time, and other resources. Look for the following things as you read the examples we will describe, and begin to ask yourself if these catalysts are already at work in your organization:

- Failure to believe information that you do not like
- Failure to evaluate assumptions
- Success that breeds arrogance and adversely affects decision-making
- Frequent communications absence, failure, or misunderstanding (internal and external, including customers)
- Failure to have and/or follow standard procedures
- Cultures that suppress initiative, information, or action

- Lack of understanding and respect for the laws of economics
  and cycles
- Failure to evaluate past mistakes and learn from them

These patterns are more common that we might believe, but an instance or two of one or two items from this list is rarely fatal. The interesting thing is how these same things come together in ways that create damaging disasters for those who do not pay enough attention to "break the chain of mistakes."

There are warning signs that presage many of these typical mistake patterns. The following list of "red flags" will reveal themselves in the incidents we discuss throughout the book. In most cases, if the warnings had been observed and acted upon, there would have been significant economic value added in breaking or avoiding a mistake chain or sequence that led to significant economic and/or physical damage. As you read the stories in subsequent chapters, look for these warning signs as indicators and ask yourself if the same ones apply in your business:

- Situations you have not seen before
- Operating experience different than your competitors
- Unusual or rapidly changing data (about operations or customers)
- Results off plan
- Results on plan through luck
- Constant revision of plan/budget
- Failures of control systems
- Need to retrain significant numbers of personnel because they are not performing
- Frequent operational problems that are not addressed by standard procedures
- Problems caused by communications issues
- Problems where help was available but not utilized

The occurrence of an item from this list does not in itself mean that you are about to have a disaster. But these are warning signs that further investigation may be required to ensure that you are not already in the process of starting a series of mistakes that will create a disaster for your business.

2

Execution Mistakes

"Football is a mistake. It combines the two worst elements of American life. Violence and committee meetings."

—George F. Will

There are lots of things in the world that are hard to believe, but when it comes to managing multiple mistakes, we constantly find ourselves looking at news stories and saying, "How did they do that?" In most cases, it was easy to mess up very badly:

- An Eastern Airlines flight attendant led passengers in singing Christmas carols while standing in a Florida swamp on a dark December night after a crash caused by a burned out light bulb.

- In 1999, The Coca-Cola Company downplayed reports of sick kids in Belgium who blamed their condition on Coke, losing customer confidence in the process. As a result of a recall, a ban on the sale of its product in a number of countries, and an expensive marketing program to rebuild confidence and stimulate demand, the company wrote off over $100 million.

- American Express announced a write-off of $155 million, or 8 percent of the receivables on its four-year-old Optima card in 1991.

■ Air Florida flight 90 took off from Washington National Airport and immediately crashed into the Fourteenth Street Bridge and then into the icy waters of the Potomac River after a takeoff that never should have happened.

■ An Air Canada crew landed a 767 safely after running out of fuel in a remote area.

■ Webvan burned through more than $1 billion in capital and could not create a sustainable business, declaring bankruptcy in 2001 and laying off 2,000 employees.

These and other accidents illustrate how easy it is to fall into traps where we convince ourselves that we are doing just fine, only to be shocked into the recognition that we are "in extremis"* and have to do something immediately to avoid disaster. This chapter will discuss some execution-related accidents that were significant, although most of these did not bring down a whole business. In the case of one of our examples (Webvan), the mistake chain did bring down the business, but there were multiple chances to break the chain. We will use this example to learn the hard lesson of how much you risk by not recognizing that you are in extremis and making "breaking the chain" the highest priority.

As shown in Figure 2.1, some of the initiating events that drive disasters from minor incidents to full-blown crises are generated within the organization, and others come from outside. Regardless of the source, the process of recognizing that a mistake chain has started and needs to be managed is similar, although mistake chains initiated internally may actually be harder to stop for reasons we will discuss later. Mistakes can rapidly escalate from an operational issue to a level that has strategic implications and finally to those that threaten survival.

Note that most of the initiating sources of the crises for the situations in this chapter were internal—related to execution. Unfortunately, as we will see in other examples, that is the most common source of the mistakes that businesses make, the proverbial "shooting yourself in the foot." That is why M^3 is an important management function. In most

---

* Derived from Latin meaning in "extreme circumstances," commonly used in nautical terminology and admiralty law to indicate that such extreme danger exists that operators of ships are likely to depart from normal procedures, and will not always be held liable for doing so if they were not the cause of the "in extremis" condition.

cases, the future of the business depends as much or more on your ability to execute, without mistakes, than it does on making good strategic decisions.

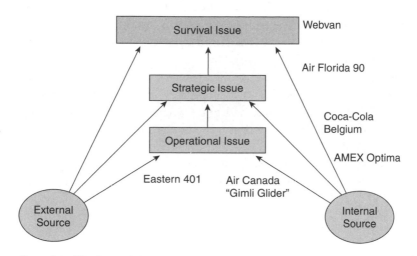

Figure 2.1 Mistake escalation.

"Fly the Airplane"–Christmas Carols in the Everglades

We will examine a few aircraft "accidents" that were not really accidents, but were human mistake chains that became very visible in the form of family anguish and twisted metal headlined in the news. Your first reaction might be to dismiss aviation accidents as unrelated, but the mistake chains that take place in cockpits turn out to be very similar to execution mistakes made by many businesses. These are situations that involve the operation of complex systems (physical or business) in environments that change (atmospheric or competitive) with people (pilots, managers of units, or CEOs) who are called upon to make difficult decisions (affecting lives or livelihoods).

Even if you are not particularly interested in aviation, you will find parallels that apply to many business situations, especially independent operations of almost any kind and especially to the successful operation of units within a larger business. There will be business examples mixed in and entire chapters with business examples, but some aviation examples provide a strong basis for understanding the principles of how mistake chains get started in any context.

Eastern Airlines flight 401 was one of the many sad incidents that showed us how a mundane technical problem can mushroom into tragedy as a result of an entire team (the flight crew in this case) zoning in on a detail while completely ignoring the big picture. The Lockheed L-1011 crashed into the Florida Everglades on December 29, 1972 with a very experienced captain who was 55 years old with 29,700 flying hours.

The flight from New York had gone without incident until the crew tried to lower the landing gear in preparation for landing in Miami and did not see a "gear down and locked" light for the nose gear. The crew received permission from the controller to proceed west to an isolated area over the Everglades and investigate the problem while maintaining 2,000 feet (a low altitude).

Six minutes before impact, the captain asked the first officer to engage the autopilot. The second officer (sometimes known as the flight engineer in the days of three-crew cockpits) entered the electronics bay below the cockpit to check the indication on a manual gear indicator located there. An Eastern maintenance specialist was aboard the flight as an observer in the cockpit. He also entered the electronics bay below.

The flight data recorder indicates that the airplane began a slow descent just after the captain asked the first officer to engage the autopilot. It is not known whether the altitude hold function on the autopilot was not engaged, failed to engage, or if a brush or bump against a disconnect switch on the yoke occurred while the crew was twisting in their seats to look around and speak with the individuals behind and below them in the electronics bay.

The controller noticed that the flight showed only 900 feet of altitude on his radar display and called the crew to see "how it was going." The crew must have confirmed that the gear was down, despite the malfunctioning light, because the reply came back to the controller, "Okay, we'd like to turn around and come, come back in," following which the controller said, "Eastern 401 turn left heading one eight zero." A few seconds later, with a left bank angle of 28 degrees in the turn, the crew discovered the lost altitude, but it was too late to recover. The airplane crashed into the Everglades, killing 101 passengers and crew

(99 in the accident and two that died subsequently). A total of 75 passengers and crew survived, and we later heard stories of how they stood in the swamp at midnight, on a dark night with no moon, singing Christmas carols led by one of the flight attendants.

What was the cause that managed to distract three experienced crewmembers and a maintenance expert so much that they crashed? A burned out light bulb* in the nose gear indicator light[6], leading to a complete failure of discipline on the part of the crew as they focused on something that was completely unimportant. The nose gear was fine, but even if it had not been extended, a landing with the nose gear up would have likely resulted in only minor damage and no deaths.

As multiple mistakes go, the Eastern crash was fairly simple—not so much a multitude of mistakes, but a couple of really serious ones, especially the first two listed below:

- **Focus on the wrong thing.** In this case, determining the exact position of the nose gear rather than flying the airplane.

- **Failure to coordinate and allocate important tasks** with specific assignments. If one of the crew had been specifically assigned to fly the plane and ignore the other activities, this crash would not have occurred.

- **Failures to cross-check important information** on the part of the crew. The controller gave an indirect alert when he asked the crew about their status, but the crew was already focused in the wrong direction, perhaps literally since the hatch to the compartment below was behind the cockpit center console, requiring the captain and first officer to turn around to see what was going on in the vicinity.

- **Failure to be specific** on the part of the controller. If he had said "Eastern 401 check altitude" instead of being polite and asking about the flight's status when he saw the altitude indication on his radar screen, perhaps he could have broken the chain of mistakes.

- **Failure to roll out of the turn,** which might have given the flight a few more feet of clearance while trying to recover, although the captain noticed the low altitude so late that he may have seen it literally just a second or two before impact.

---

* Many cockpit lights are in holders that are designed to easily screw out so that a pilot can check the bulb. A spare or even one from another indicator known to be working can be inserted. In this case, it is believed that the indicator bulb holder was jammed and could not be unscrewed.

A single airplane crash for an established airline is an operational problem, but it rarely threatens the survival of the whole airline unless they make it a habit. Eastern Airlines ceased operations in 1991 for a variety of reasons that were part of an even larger mistake chain like others discussed in Chapter 8, "Watching Entire Industries Lose It," when we look at problems with entire industries.

There is an old aviation adage—"fly the airplane." This has evolved from thousands of stories like this in which a simple, nonthreatening problem has led to deaths because pilots lose focus on what is important. In fact, one of my Navy ROTC classmates died in a military aircraft accident with a minor problem on board, within easy landing distance of a runway. The outcome would likely have been different if he had just focused on "flying the airplane" and completely ignored the problem.

For pilots, keeping the airplane under control should always be the highest priority because many crashes are survivable if the airplane is not wildly out of control. The same applies to many other disasters and business situations. Would Enron have been "survivable" if top management had focused on "flying the airplane" (the "real" business)? In this context, that would have meant paying more attention to what was going on in the "real" businesses, such as pipeline operations and even energy trading, instead of becoming distracted by trading bandwidth and financing power projects that should have been financed by foreign governments.

This "fly the airplane" concept also reminds me of a high school girlfriend who crashed her car into a post while trying to swat a bee that was inside the car. Luckily, she was not seriously injured. She avoided a possible bee sting but as a consequence received a broken arm and a car beyond repair. There are times when focus is needed, but we let our minds drift and focus on something that is not the highest priority.

> **Insight #2: "Fly the airplane."** It is easy to get distracted, and there are times when you need to have a stern talk with yourself and ask if you are spending your time on the most important things.

"Fly the airplane" is a useful adage for much of business life as well as operating airplanes or other machinery. Following its first quarterly loss ever, McDonald's recently decided to "fly the airplane" again by focusing on improving operations instead of continuing to add more outlets.

Coca-Cola—Don't Change the Formula, Change the CEO

The Coca-Cola Company started in Atlanta in 1886 and was doing business in Belgium by 1927, formally incorporating in 1930. Initially, deliveries were made via tricycle in and around Brussels. But all the market share, goodwill, profitability, and trust built up over 70 years was sorely tested in a few weeks in the summer of 1999.

The timing of the mistakes could not have been worse for Coca-Cola. Europe had suffered a number of food-safety scares in recent months. Public concern over food safety was so serious that it led to the toppling of the Belgian government in a June 12 election following revelations of large quantities of dioxin-contaminated pork and chicken produced in Belgium.

Only days after that election, there were reports of school children getting sick after drinking Coke in western Belgium. Coca-Cola management initially denied that it had anything to do with their products, even though customers were complaining of a "strange odor" associated with the product.

On the heels of other food scares, the Belgian government and the European Union (EU) responded quickly to first warn consumers not to consume Coca-Cola and a few days later banned all Coca-Cola products from stores in Belgium. It was not long before Coke was banned in the Netherlands and parts of Germany and France.

More than 200 cases of nausea, headache, and upset stomach were reported. Coca-Cola claimed it was unlikely that the problems were caused by its products but continued to investigate. In a short period of time, it became evident that all those who were ill had consumed product that was bottled at Coca-Cola plants in Antwerp and Dunkirk. The Antwerp plant had used some carbon dioxide (which produces the bubbles in carbonated drinks) that was not to specification, and wooden pallets at the Dunkirk plant had been contaminated with some fungicide that ended up on the exterior of some cans.

On the surface, these problems did not seem significant enough, in a technical sense, to cause the illnesses being attributed to them. It did turn out that bottling plant personnel had failed to complete required quality checks on the carbon dioxide and that the bad batch was responsible for a foul taste, but some local scientists even released a statement indicating that it was unlikely that this would cause illness.

The fungicide on the cans also produced a bad smell but did not contaminate the product, unless a consumer ingested it by getting it on his or her hands or lips through handling or drinking from a can. Once again, scientists came forward to say that the amounts involved were small and unlikely to cause illness.

This was a classic set of operational mistakes that, if they had happened individually, might not have caused a problem, but because they occurred in sequence and were emotionally enhanced, they created a mess for Coca-Cola:

- Incorrect manufacturing of carbon dioxide by a supplier
- Supplier quality control failure
- Coca-Cola bottler failure to conduct quality checks on carbon dioxide
- Supplier contamination of pallets (different plant) with fungicide
- Failure to acknowledge the serious nature of the problem as perceived by consumers and government
- Top management playing down the public's concern about the problem

This chain of mistakes was very serious as far as the public was concerned, and Chairman M. Douglas Ivester issued a statement indicating deep regret for the problems and later promised to buy everyone in Belgium a Coke when the crisis was past. But it was two weeks before Ivester felt the situation warranted his presence in Belgium, a decision that clearly angered local officials and consumers. The countries involved constituted less than 2 percent of Coke's worldwide volume, but the global coverage of the situation was damaging the brand, so Ivester decided it was time to go to Europe and be personally involved.

The Belgian government set conditions on cleanliness for plants and allowed Coca-Cola to resume production within a few weeks of the incident. Ivester delivered on his promise to buy everyone in Belgium a Coke by delivering coupons good for a 1.5 liter bottle of Coke.

Coca-Cola has recovered in Europe, but the result of this series of mistakes was a recall of over 17 million cases of Coke. Coca-Cola Enterprises (CCE), the bottling company that produces and distributes products in North America and parts of Europe and is still 38 percent owned by Coca-Cola, wrote off over $100 million in connection with this problem.

Once the products were back in full production, CCE started "Operation Restore" to try to rebuild confidence and volume in Belgium. It only lasted two months before the EU forced a shutdown of the program on the basis that giving away or discounting product to hotels and restaurants was a veiled attempt to increase market power, not simply to restore confidence.

This was not the first time Coca-Cola had come head-to-head in an unpleasant confrontation in Europe. In the two years prior to the Belgian crisis, Coca-Cola had attempted to acquire Orangina and had been rebuffed by France for fear of market concentration. They also attempted to acquire Cadbury Schweppes international brands and found no tolerance for the European part of the transaction.

In December 1999, the Coca-Cola board announced that it had "reluctantly accepted" Ivester's resignation as chairman and CEO. It is not clear what the real reasons behind the resignation were and whether it was voluntary or forced by the board. However, it is safe to assume that the mishandling of the situation in Belgium and failed European acquisitions, when combined with other economic problems, were part of the picture, regardless of who suggested his departure.

News headlines like "Coke Loses Some of Its Fizz"[7] suggested that the company had lost some of its magic, but it lost more. The substandard carbon dioxide and fungicide on the delivery pallets were not *substantive* problems, but the public did not know that was the case. The public relations mistakes made by Ivester and his team left the company looking arrogant and aloof and clearly angered public officials and consumers. This was a case of a minor operational problem that mushroomed into something larger before management realized what was happening, but this is typical of many similar situations in which companies, for many reasons, do not want to admit that a problem exists—a posture they usually regret.

Despite the delayed response, we could argue that Ivester actually did help break the mistake chain when he finally went to Belgium. It could have been worse. Coca-Cola and its local bottler could have taken longer to discover the cause. They could have argued harder that there was no scientific basis for any relationship between Coca-Cola and the sicknesses being reported. In fact, unbiased observers have pointed out that it is likely that much of what happened in Belgium was mass hysteria. The Coke incident occurred immediately after a significant unrelated food scare. The Belgians had been to the polls only a few days before to vote against a government they felt had not protected them from contaminated poultry and pork.

But rational or not, this was judged by nearly everyone as a public relations blunder. It also followed a classic pattern of mistakes:

- **Failure to follow established procedures.** The carbon dioxide was apparently accepted and used without the quality checks called for in standard operating procedures.

- **Difference between company and outside perception.** In fact, technically this was not a serious situation, but the difference between the company's technical understandings and consumer or government perceptions about the problem was significant.

- **Underestimating political issues.** Europeans in general seem more sensitive to food-related issues than we do in the United States. This, coupled with recent crises and political turmoil around the subject, meant that anything other than an instantaneous and effective response was doomed.

- **Cultural lapse in accepting responsibility.** In many cultures around the world, having the most senior executive appear publicly and personally accept responsibility for a problem is an important part of convincing the public that you are sorry about a mistake. This is most extreme in Japan, where it is quite common for a senior executive to retire in disgrace or even commit hara-kiri. In the United States, we have, until recently, seen few individual corporate scapegoats. No one of sufficient stature showed up to play this role for two weeks in this situation.

- **Unclear lines of responsibility.** While this story has been discussed many times, I have not seen anyone mention the fact that Coca-Cola Enterprises (the bottler) and The Coca-Cola Company are two separate entities. Coca-Cola owns 38 percent of CCE, and they clearly have a very tight relationship, but technically it is CCE who mixes Coke's concentrate with local ingredients, puts the drink in the container, and distributes it. Most of the public does not understand or see this distinction and sees only one big red sign that says "Coca-Cola." Since this was the largest recall in the company's history, it may be that there were not clear procedures for handling such situations between the entities, and that was worked out behind the scenes as the crisis unfolded.

Coca-Cola recovered in Europe, but the damage continues to be the manner in which a situation like this is remembered and used as an example of how not to handle a crisis. In the land of multiple mistakes, it might have looked different and not been remembered negatively in the same way if the response had been quicker and perceived as more sincere. If Ivester had taken more definitive action, admitted responsibility, and worked with the local government earlier, confidence might never have been lost. This approach could have even saved money, especially when one considers what had to be spent rebuilding a tarnished reputation in Europe.

Insight #3: You cannot afford even a whiff of an ethical lapse.
Issues of trust are serious and strategic in today's world, largely because there have been so many ethical lapses that consumers do not trust the actions of corporate executives. The slightest sense of uncertainty or lack of openness creates suspicion that mushrooms into a lack of confidence that can cost a great deal, as it did for Coca-Cola and in an Intel case discussed in Chapter 3, "Execution Mistakes and Successes as Catalysts for Change."

American Express Surprises the Market with Optima— Then Optima Surprises AmEx

I received my first American Express green card in 1965 when I graduated from college and was commissioned as a naval officer. I needed one because, at that time, credit cards were primarily local convenience cards issued by individual department stores or merchant's associations, and anyone who traveled a lot needed some other means of covering payments. The oil companies issued credit cards that were good around the country, but they were only good for purchases at their service stations. Forerunners of Visa (Bank of America) and MasterCard were getting started, but the most widely accepted national or international cards at the time were AmEx and Diners Club.

By the late 1970s, American Express Chairman and CEO, James D. Robinson III, began putting together a strategy to build the company from what was then known as a traveler's check and credit card company into a much broader financial powerhouse. Through the 1980s, this meant numerous acquisitions in insurance (Fireman's Fund), brokerage (Shearson and later Lehman Brothers and E.F. Hutton), travel, and banking (Trade Development Bank).

There were a number of lost merger opportunities and erratic performance of the various entities, but the one thing that never wavered was the traveler's check and charge card profitability. There was trouble brewing in the card business, however, in the form of a merchant rebellion over the fees American Express charged, especially compared to the rapidly growing Visa and MasterCard. Additionally, while profitable, AmEx's credit cards were travel and entertainment (T&E) cards designed for the convenience of those who traveled for business and paid their balance in full every month. There was no provision for carrying a balance, save some special extended payment programs AmEx started for airline tickets.

Culturally, AmEx really believed the "membership has it privileges" campaign they flogged for so long. They believed it so much that they looked down on the bankcard market and the customers who used the cards. Harvey Gulob, the chairman and CEO through most of the 1990s, admitted as much publicly and also admitted in retrospect that this attitude was a "big mistake" because their snobbishness caused them to ignore a much larger, profitable market even though it was less affluent.

As they saw the money being made by banks on credit card balances, American Express realized that they needed to be in the business of lending money to individuals through credit cards to keep up their growth and margins. The product was dubbed the Optima Card and was launched in 1987—AmEx's first card that allowed you to carry a balance and make monthly payments instead of paying your balance in full.

In late 1991, American Express announced that its Travel Related Services (TRS) division would take a $265 million charge consisting of a $110 million restructuring charge and $155 million related to a write-off of receivables for the Optima card. Things had come apart pretty quickly for Robinson and his strategy, and the reasons were simpler than you might imagine and were also another classic chain of operational and managerial mistakes that went unnoticed until it was too late:

- **Commitment to a niche market that would not meet their growth goals.** AmEx's growth objectives needed a market with growth greater than the narrow high-end T&E market could provide. Even though they were very successful in their chosen niche, this philosophy limited their potential.

- **Delayed entry into the market** where their biggest competitors were growing the most—the revolving balance card. AmEx eventually realized that they had to move into this market, but by 1987, they were very far behind Visa and MasterCard, which had a lock on virtually the entire bank-sponsored card market.

- **Invalid assumptions related to how their current customers would act** when extended credit—because they thought they had a "better" customer base:
  - That would have better credit experience
  - That would allow AmEx to offer a low annual card fee and lower interest rates
  - That would act the same as they did with the T&E card and pay their extended payments on time
  - Resulting in an overall lower delinquency rate and higher profitability than competitors

- **Delayed recognition that their experience was different than expected.** Reality began to set in when the 1990-91 recession hit, and AmEx found out that the customers it thought were so different acted like everyone else when they got in trouble—they didn't pay their bills on time. Optima's receivables over 180 days ballooned to over 8 percent, or twice the average rate that other bankcards experienced. To make matters worse, other companies with more experience started managing their potential bad debt accounts more rapidly than AmEx as the recession began and kept their rates under control as the recession unfolded. AmEx had no such program.

- **Inadequate personnel and systems for managing the business—** business that was different than the one they had been in for so long. In essence, they did not have staff and systems used to dealing with the problems of those who carry balances since they had never had those kinds of customers in their system.

- **Middle management cover up of actual results** in an effort to "hit the numbers" while trying to get things under control—as reported by American Express when they hired a law firm to investigate.

The net result for American Express was a write-off that was significant and that brought the stock to its lowest level in the 1990s.

The company was not doing well in a number of areas, and in early 1993, about 16 months after the Optima write-off, Robinson resigned as chairman and CEO. Optima did not threaten the survival of American Express, but it did once again indicate that successful executives and managers in very successful companies are just as capable of being out of touch with markets as anyone else, perhaps even more so if they have built a culture that goes beyond thinking they are good to thinking they are always right.

One of the most important lessons with AmEx is one that companies learn over and over again:

Insight #4: Execution mistakes can be generated through a lack of resources or knowledge. Even a good strategy will fail without adequate resources, training, and discipline around implementation.

Failing to Learn–Air Florida Flies North

At 3:59 PM on January 13, 1982, Air Florida flight 90 finally began to roll to the north on Runway 36* at Washington National Airport outside Washington, D.C. Two minutes later, it clipped Washington's Fourteenth Street Bridge, hitting rush hour traffic and killing four persons on the bridge, as it skimmed over the edge and crashed into the icy waters of the Potomac River. Local and national TV viewers watched live coverage of the unfolding events as Leonard Scutnick, a government employee who happened to be passing by on his way home from work, risked his life by diving into the river to help save a flight attendant who was one of only four survivors of the 79 souls on board.

For his heroism, Mr. Scutnick was introduced by President Ronald Regan during his State of the Union address to a standing ovation. We never would have heard of Mr. Scutnick were it not for his laudatory actions in the depths of winter in icy water, but those actions would not have been necessary had it not been for a serious chain of mistakes committed by the Air Florida crew.

---

* Runways are numbered according to their magnetic heading approximated to the nearest 10 degrees. Runway 36 is roughly aligned on a magnetic heading of 360 degrees, which is north. Going the opposite direction on the same runway, the runway is number 18 because 180 degrees, or south, is the exact opposite direction of 360 degrees.

The mistake chain for Air Florida 90 is one of the longest and most serious that I have seen chronicled anywhere.[8] The flight was scheduled to leave Washington at 2:15 PM bound for Tampa and on to Ft. Lauderdale. The aircraft had arrived late from Ft. Lauderdale as snow was falling. Snowfall was reported as "heavy." By 1:38 PM, airport operations were halted so that runway snow removal could take place.

At about 2:20 PM, the captain of the Air Florida flight had the ground crew begin to de-ice the Boeing 737 aircraft while still parked at the gate. The captain had an estimate that the airport would reopen at 2:30 PM and wanted to be de-iced and ready to get in line for departure as soon as the airport opened again. The crew observed about a half inch of wet snow covering the airplane. They de-iced only about 10 square feet of the left wing surface before the captain stopped the de-icing because he learned that runway plowing was not yet complete.

At 2:45 PM, the de-icing resumed on the aircraft while it was still parked at the gate. The operator recalled later that it was snowing heavily as he began de-icing again on the left side. He finished the left side, and another operator de-iced the right side of the aircraft, using a different procedure and mix of heated ethylene glycol and water.

A number of major mistakes occurred before the airplane left the gate. Some occurred because Air Florida was a small airline and thus did not have its own ground operations personnel in Washington. Services were provided under contract with American Airlines, which did not operate Boeing 737 aircraft at the time and thus did not have manuals for the airplane. They used de-icing techniques similar to those used on American's aircraft, increasing the ethylene glycol content as a safety measure.

The Boeing manual calls for any heavy snow to be removed with brooms before de-icing fluid is applied because of the danger of a refreeze. This was not done. Additionally, the Air Florida manual calls for engine inlet covers to be installed when the airplane is exposed to heavy snow or ice for even short periods. This was not done either.

Finally, investigation after the accident revealed that the de-icing nozzle had been changed to a nonstandard nozzle that was defective. The ethylene glycol concentrations the operators dialed in were not dispensed correctly. The nozzle actually delivered only about 60 percent of the ethylene glycol concentration that the operators thought they were getting. This airplane was sitting still with multiple mistakes frozen all over it before it ever left the gate, but it was made even worse by the cockpit crew.

With de-icing completed, the crew requested pushback clearance, but because of congestion, this did not come until 3:25 PM. There was difficulty getting the plane to move because of the slippery ramp, and the crew attempted, against company policy, to use engine reverse thrust to move the plane back. This did not help, but it did blow snow forward onto the wings. Another tug, with tire chains, finally pushed the plane back. An Air Florida staff member in the terminal noticed that the plane had a coating of light snow on the fuselage and left wing as it taxied away.

It was another 33 minutes before the crew received takeoff clearance. But this was enough time for an almost continuous chain of mistakes to become even worse, and the crew made it worse with almost every move from the gate through the takeoff, including:

- **The first officer questioned the captain** about a critical item, the engine anti-ice equipment. The captain replied "Off," and nothing more was said by either crewmember. In fact, under the conditions, the Boeing manual makes clear that this must be on to prevent erroneous EPR* indications, the primary method for setting engine power. The first officer questioned different EPR indications on the two engines while taxing, and it still did not prompt them to turn on the engine anti-ice system.

- **The captain pulled the aircraft close behind a waiting DC-9** and joked about using the DC-9's engine exhaust to try to de-ice their aircraft. The first officer commented, "All we need is the inside of the wing anyway." Performance of the 737 with snow or ice on the wing was known to be problematic, but apparently not to this crew.

- **The crew discussed the slush on the runway** and decided nothing special was needed. The Boeing manual describes an "improved climb" procedure that was not used.

- **As the airplane accelerated, the frozen Pt2 probe†** led the pilots to believe the engines were at full power, but they were really developing only about 70 percent power.

---

* EPR is Engine Pressure Ratio, a measure of differential pressure across the lowest and highest pressure compressor stages of a turbojet engine. This is one, and on this airplane the primary, measure of the power the engine is producing. Incorrect indications would make it hard to set proper power levels on the engines.

† One of two probes necessary to sense pressure to produce EPR.

- **The first officer sensed something was wrong,** and on four occasions during the takeoff roll made comments to the effect that "something's not right." All were dismissed by the captain. Many call this "groupthink" when some in a group or team fail to question authority or just go along because they are not sure their idea is right or will gain acceptance.

- **Barely airborne and climbing very slowly, the crew failed to push the power levers** forward until the last second when it was too late. Jet engines are set using EPR and other parameters to avoid engine damage*, almost always below the full capability of the engine. With a much slower than normal climb rate and the "stick-shaker"† indicating the airplane was near a stall, they should have pushed the power all the way up and worried about any engine damage later.

Clearly, weather was a major factor in this accident, but under the conditions, this crew did very little right. There is an old saying among pilots that it's "better to be down here wishing you were up there, than up there wishing you were down here."

This is a flight that never should have started down the runway and was doomed once the crew committed to the takeoff. They never debated whether takeoff was a good decision, just some small mechanical aspects of the process. With slush on the runway, the captain should have briefed his copilot on a possible rejected take off (RTO) ahead of time, but apparently he did not even consider it a possibility.

This crew was afflicted with one of the worst pilot mental states, "get there-itis." They had made the decision to go despite mounting warning signs that should have triggered extreme caution and reevaluation. They were going come hell or high water—or slushy snow.

Making a final decision on the basis of your biases before you have seen all the data obviously interferes with rational analysis of any subsequent information. Deciding you are going to takeoff, even as more data becomes available that screams "STOP," is a bias in decision-making caused by many past successful takeoffs, even if the conditions were different. Decision scientists call this the "representativeness heuristic." The pilots' past experience caused them to discount the

---

* Pressure, temperature, and overspeed are kept within tolerances that avoid engine damage.

† A device that pushes on the control yoke to make sure the pilot is aware that the airplane is about to stall.

serious nature of the situation. Successful past experience is a powerful force and is difficult to ignore. Failure to recognize that a situation requires actions not in your past experience is often fatal, in aviation or business.

The final, and simplest, thing that could have saved Air Florida 90 and the 74 persons who died would have been obeying a very simple legal regulation. Specifically, FAA regulations Part 121.69(b) states:

"No person may take off an aircraft when frost, ice, or snow is adhering to the wings, control surfaces, propellers, engine inlets, or other critical surfaces of the aircraft...."

Pilots know the regulations. They know why this regulation is written. Frost or ice adhering to a wing causes it to lose lift and possibly "stall." They must pass oral and written tests on regulations to initially be licensed to fly and during periodic recurrent training. Worse yet, the Boeing 737 was known, at that time, to have a serious "pitch up" flying characteristic when there was any frost or ice on the wings. This behavior is exactly what the pilots saw as Air Florida 90 lifted off, but by then it was too late.

The pilots certainly did not want to die and did not have any clue that the mistakes they were making were taking them and their passengers in that direction. The copilot clearly had some misgivings but consciously or subconsciously deferred to the captain. This accident is the epitome of why the commercial aviation at that time needed a focus on using crew resources more effectively.

The accident that initially brought this subject into perspective happened three years earlier (see Chapter 3) and resulted in a concept called "cockpit resource management" (CRM, later changed to mean crew resource management). Unfortunately, learning takes more time than we might like. The real question is whether we can teach operators, managers, and whole organizations, regardless of industry, to learn and draw parallels from the unusual experiences of others rather than having to see each and every deviation from normal procedure personally to gain the ability to function at peak performance.

It takes extraordinary time and diligence on the part of management to make an organization believe that safety is not a choice and that regulations and operating policies are not optional—regardless of the business. Air Florida did not learn this lesson in time. While we observed earlier that a single airline crash is rarely a survival issue for an established airline, Air Florida was not large or stable at the time. They were expanding and fighting fierce competition in the recently deregulated airline environment. This crash was not the single reason the airline went under a couple of years later (and sold its assets to Midway Express), but the loss of public confidence contributed to their increasing financial deterioration, just as it did 13 years later for ValuJet when it had a multiple-mistakes type of crash that should not have happened.

There are many things to learn from this accident, but the primary one has to do with following standard procedures that are known to work:

Insight #5: Establish and enforce standard operating procedures. Aviation knows how to do this (and did not follow them in this example), complex manufacturing operations know how to do this, but management teams do not like it because they believe not everything can be made routine. There is some truth to this, but you need to look for everything that can be standardized and make the procedures known, train for them, and hold those accountable who do not follow them.

Breaking the Chain with Skill and Extraordinary Luck— The "Gimli Glider"

Contrast the Air Florida failure to recognize a building set of warnings that led to disaster with the experience of the "Gimli Glider," an Air Canada 767 operating as flight AC-143 from Montreal to Ottawa to Edmonton on July 23, 1983. In the cockpit were Captain Robert Pearson and Copilot Maurice Quintal.

The airplane was a new Boeing 767 that had some intermittent fuel-gauging problems. For reasons that were not understood, all the fuel gauges would periodically go blank. The problem was not unique to this specific airplane. United had a problem with high indications on one of its airplanes (less fuel than indicated, a dangerous condition), and Boeing had warned the airlines to inspect and calibrate their systems to ensure that accurate fuel loads were on board. Honeywell, the fuel-gauging system supplier began a redesign, but operators were allowed to continue to fly the airplanes with certain precautions.*

The fuel gauges were acting up on July 23 and had gone blank and come back twice during the day. When Captain Pearson took over the airplane in Montreal, the gauges were blank, and no amount of coaxing could get them back on. He decided to measure the fuel in the tanks using "dipsticks" that were built into the tanks for manual confirmation of the fuel levels. By measuring the depth of fuel in the tanks and consulting a conversion table for temperature, the fuel weight could be determined.†

Measurements were taken. This was Air Canada's first airplane to use the metric system, so the dipsticks were calibrated in centimeters (cm). The resulting readings, converted to liters for the prevailing temperature, should have been multiplied by 0.8 to arrive at kilograms (kg), but instead were multiplied by 1.77 to convert to pounds, the measure in use at the time for all other Air Canada airplanes.[9] With the erroneous calculation for fuel in hand, Captain Pearson ordered a small amount of additional fuel added in one wing for balance. The flight departed with less than half the fuel they thought was on board and with fuel gauges that were not functioning.

While cruising at 41,000 feet, shortly after the captain looked down through the scattered clouds and commented that he could see the fish jumping in Red Lake, the crew suddenly heard an alarm and saw warnings of low fuel pressure on the #1 forward fuel pump.

Captain Pearson and his copilot initially had trouble diagnosing what was going on, but the captain made an immediate decision to head for Winnipeg, the closest major airport at 128 miles. Four minutes after the first alarm, the crew began descending from cruise altitude and then began to get more alarms for low pressure on other fuel pumps. Before long they realized that the probability of all the fuel pumps failing was very slim, and the crew realized that they did not have pump problems but a fuel problem.

At 8:18 PM the #1 (left) engine quit. At 8:21 PM the #2 engine also flamed out for lack of fuel, and the new 767 became at glider at 26,000

---

* This is not as unsafe as it sounds. If you have ever had a car with a malfunctioning gauge, you know that keeping track of miles traveled will help you estimate how much fuel is left, assuming you have past data on miles per gallon. Something analogous but more complex can be done in an airplane.

† Fuel weight is used instead of volume because of volume changes with temperature, especially the wide range of temperatures a jet encounters from ground level to high altitude.

feet and descending fast. With the loss of both engines, electrical power was limited to an emergency supply*, and the "glass cockpit"† went dark. Pearson radioed the Winnipeg air traffic control center and said, "This is a mayday, and we require a vector onto the closest available runway. We are down to 22,000 feet ... both engines have failed due to, looks like fuel starvation, and we are on emergency instruments...."[10]

The crew did not know the "best glide speed" without engines, so the captain estimated it to be about 220 knots for a balance between distance covered and altitude lost. The copilot calculated their descent rate manually (the vertical speed instrument was lost with the video screens) and found it to be about 5,000 feet for every 10 miles traveled. The controller continued to update the crew with the distance remaining to Winnipeg. While still 35 miles from Winnipeg and down to 9,500 feet, Quintel told Pearson they weren't going to make it. After hearing this, the controller suggested that a field called Gimli was on their right at 12 miles.

Luckily, Quintel had been based at Gimli while serving in the Canadian Air Force and knew the field had long runways. They had not seen the field because of clouds, but just as they had the conversation about the field, they cleared the clouds and saw the field. Pearson turned toward Gimli instantly.

The controller called the field at six miles, and the crew could see the glide path was good to make the field. The next problem was that they were now "hot and high"—too fast and too high for a straight-in glide to the runway. They discussed circling to lose altitude but rejected this idea because they were not sure how much altitude they would lose in the turn and they would also lose sight of the field in the turn.§ Instead, Pearson decided to "side-slip" the airplane to lose altitude and speed. This is not something that jet pilots do, but it is something that all pilots are trained to do in gliders and smaller airplanes, where Pearson had some experience.

---

* Emergency power is generated from a small air turbine that drops from the belly of the airplane in such a situation. It provides enough electrical power for radios, emergency instruments, and emergency hydraulics for control.

† "Glass cockpit" refers to eight separate video screens that show information for aircraft attitude, altitude, navigation, and status information for all important systems.

§ No one had ever trained for flying the 767 as a glider with both engines out, so they were gathering their own performance data as the event unfolded. Also, all pilots are taught to keep sight of the intended emergency landing point throughout emergency landing maneuvers so as not to misjudge altitude or alignment for landing.

The side-slip* is a safe maneuver, but it is disconcerting to those who do not understand what is going on. In this case, Pearson executed a left side-slip in which the left wing drops and the airplane seems to be falling toward the ground on a diagonal line between the nose and the left wing with the nose up slightly and to the right. To the passengers, it appeared as if the airplane was out of control, but the maneuver worked, and Pearson returned the attitude to normal when he judged that the excess altitude was lost.

At five miles, Quintel flipped the landing gear switch, but nothing happened. Realizing this was due to the lack of power, he then hit an emergency switch that allowed the gear to fall out of the wings by its own weight. The main (under wing) gear was down and locked, but the nose gear did not extend all the way. Quintel continued to try to find a way to get the nose gear down while Pearson was totally focused on the landing spot and any adjustments he could make for accuracy.

Both crewmembers saw their last major challenge at the last moment—there were cars and people on the runway where they were lined up to land. The plane touched down hard, and the crew stood on the brakes. The half-extended nose gear collapsed, and the nose scraping on the concrete acted as a brake. The jet stopped just short of the people and vehicles on the runway.

The runway crisis happened because the controller had advised them to land on the right runway of the two parallel runways. The runways were separated by some distance, and the crew did not see the right runway that was still used for aircraft, instead focusing on the first one they saw which was the left. The left runway had been converted for use as a drag strip and luckily had just enough empty space for the airplane to land and stop without injury to anyone or anything, except for relatively minor nose damage to the airplane as a result of the nose gear collapsing.

The airplane was given temporary repairs, flown out of Gimli, and eventually returned to service with Air Canada. Because of its landing spot, the airplane and the incident became known as the "Gimli Glider."

The mistake chain in this incident was significant and included categories we have seen in other accidents. These included an initial technology failure (that was itself two failures), a failure to spend more

---

* Those who do not like fly-by-wire technology point out that the computers on most fly-by-wire airplanes will not allow this maneuver because it involves "cross control" which can be dangerous in some situations.

time diagnosing an unusual situation, unjustified reliance on others for critical information in the unusual situation, and a desire to get on with the mission even with some discrepancies:

- **The fuel-gauging system had a loose wire** that failed to transmit data to a processing system, but the built-in redundant system failed to shift over to a second processor as it was designed to do because of a software problem.
- **The maintenance crew used the wrong conversion factor,** resulting in the belief that there was adequate fuel.
- **The crew failed to double-check the calculations** in enough detail to see the error.
- **The captain should not have departed with no fuel gauges working** since this was not allowed under the 767's approved "minimum equipment list." The captain claimed the ground crew convinced him that this was permissible because of the mechanical measurement, something the mechanics denied during the investigation.

What broke the chain and resulted in a safe outcome with minimum damage?

- **Extraordinary luck, especially good weather**. Had it been a drizzly, foggy day, the visual approach to the abandoned field would have been impossible, and the probability of a good outcome would have been significantly less.
  - **The time of year.** It was still daylight at 8:38 pm on a July evening.
  - **The copilot's past experience at Gimli.**
  - **The captain's past glider experience.**
  - **The location of the people and objects on the runway.**
- **Skill and great coordination.**
  - **An alert controller** who looked for all the options.
  - **Good crew resource management,** with the captain never forgetting to "fly the airplane." The first officer handled rate of descent and distance/time calculations with recommendations to the captain.

◆   Great "dead stick landing" on the part of the captain,
    including his judgment on "energy management" to use a
    side-slip to lose the excess altitude to be in a position to make
    the runway.

While this is a wonderful example of "breaking the chain," we cannot
use it as a model for how to stop accidents in airplanes or businesses
because luck was such a large part of the equation. Given luck, however,
this outcome was nearly perfect because the crew was effective,
organized, and used all their skills.

Unfortunately, even in the presence of good weather and an available
airfield, it is not clear that every crew would have been up to gliding a
767 to a dead stick landing. This was simply not something that was
part of the training syllabus at the time. We cannot always depend on
the luck portion of the equation, but we do have to make every effort to
anticipate and train for the unexpected.

In addition to some of the other points made with other accidents in
this chapter, one more important insight emerges here:

Insight #6: Make responsibilities clear. Whether it is Coca-Cola
Belgium or one of the airline crashes, mistakes are more likely to be
caught and stopped if you know who is responsible for what and
who should be providing additional oversight and advice. The
confusion over who had the authority to decide whether to even
dispatch the airplane with inoperative fuel gauges should have been
discussed in more detail, with someone stepping up to either state
the rule or find out what it was.

Webvan–Do You Want Someone to Deliver Your Groceries?

At the height of the dotcom boom, I was teaching some executive
classes on strategy and IT, which at the time translated as "e-commerce."
I got the worst teaching ratings of my life on and off during 1999
because I took to trashing a number of popular e-commerce plays, one of
which was Webvan. Like many things in life, you do not remember all
the things you have done well, but you remember the times things did
not go well. In this case, executives and managers in a number of classes

took the opportunity to write comments on evaluations suggesting that I was "a Neanderthal who doesn't get it" or "obviously too old to understand that the Web has changed everything."

Actually, I did understand that the Web had changed a lot of things, but it had not changed the fact that customers need to perceive value in a transaction in order to be willing to engage it repeatedly. I also understood that some laws of economics about industries apply regardless of how excited we were all getting about new channels. For some reason, I was able to see Webvan's coming mistake chain before most observers did, and I am sorry to say that it unfolded pretty much as I predicted.

The idea was simple. We all hate going to the grocery store. Why not have very efficient logistics, Internet ordering, and delivery systems that bring the groceries to your home? A number of small local services had operated with some success in Boston, Minneapolis, and other places, so why not roll out a national operation that would bring this convenience to everyone? At least that was the thinking during the heady days of dotcom everything.

Webvan's mistake chain was extraordinary. In a sense, it was a set of cultural mistakes because it was built on beliefs that were flawed but not questioned, but there were serious execution errors as well, which is why it is included here. There is merit to the online grocery business idea because grocery shopping is infrastructure support for our lives. Most of us see it as a chore that has to be done, but we have to give up something else to find the time.

Admitting that there is a need to be served for some portion of the time-starved population, here is the Webvan mistake chain:

- **The grocery business has massive inefficiencies.** This belief by Webvan led them to conclude that they could reorganize the grocery supply-and-distribution chain with highly automated central regional warehouses and make more money than anyone else through productivity improvements. The reality was they never got the warehouses operating properly (in their automated lines to move frozen foods, the conveyors moved too slowly due to the cold). The industry also might not have been as inefficient as they thought. While the complex web of growers, shippers, wholesalers, processors, distributors, and retailers looks inefficient from the outside, those who know the business point out that each serves a purpose that is difficult to combine in the supply chain because of the unique nature of food production. Additionally, an industry that is as competitive as this and still manages to eke out margins at all, albeit low, must be pretty good at operations.

- **Customer demand was lower than anticipated.** Average customer orders, by the time Webvan shut down, were running in the $70 range. Some estimated that Webvan's costs were about $130 per order. Worse, customers did not order on a regular basis. They were trying Webvan and not coming back for a number of weeks or were ordering only for special events. The flawed assumption was that, once acquired, customers would do all their business through Webvan and that the orders would be larger.

- **Expanded too rapidly.** Under pressure to grow big because they had gone public, Webvan rolled out plans to expand in a large number of cities before working out operational bugs in their launch markets in northern and southern California. Launching in Atlanta and Dallas burned up huge amounts of capital and perpetuated any operational mistakes in their model.

- **Wide selection is necessary.** With over 9,000 SKUs in their database, you could order lots of things from Webvan, but as any retailer will tell you, it costs a lot for variety. Smaller, successful online grocers have a much more limited selection of popular and easy-to-handle items in an effort to balance customer demand with logistics costs and complexity.

- **Delivery productivity.** Assumptions about the number of deliveries a driver could make an hour were seriously flawed. This happened because orders were smaller than they projected, requiring more small deliveries, and because their launch market was San Francisco. One satisfied Webvan customer who lived at the top of a hill with no driveway up the last 50 feet (vertically) told me how wonderful it was to have the driver carry all her groceries up for her. Good for this customer but not for the company. This is what an insurance company would call "adverse selection."

- **Customers know what they want and will order online.** This may have been the biggest mistake they made, which I have confirmed you can find out in a focus group in about five minutes. Most of us are not well enough organized to have an explicit list that includes everything we need, every time we shop, in advance of going to the grocery store. We know when we leave home, even if we do not like grocery shopping, that the process of being in the store and seeing items not on the list will help us remember that we are out of paper towels or some other item. This severely limits the potential for an online service unless you can get people to organize their lives.

When you add all these things together, Webvan was a business that started because a group of people wanted to start it, wanted to invest in it, and wanted to make it successful. The mistake chain had to do with:

- Faulty assumptions
- Incomplete investigation of the market
- Failure to believe some data on potential customers and competitors (which were traditional stores)
- Dismissal of their own poor operating data as not representative
- Failure to understand the strengths of the existing competitive systems
- Commitment to huge capital expenditures before proof-of-concept
- An executive team with no experience in the industry (which they saw as an advantage)

This brings us back to the cultural aspects that we will explore in more detail in subsequent chapters. The most telling indictment of Webvan was that none of the executive team had any experience in the grocery industry. The most serious mistake Webvan made was very likely one of their earliest decisions—they fundamentally decided that industry experience was irrelevant and they could do without it. If they had had some industry veterans as part of the team, they might not have made the subsequent mistakes.

Tesco, the United Kingdom grocery chain, has done well adding online grocery capability as one of the channels serviced from their physical stores and systems. They limit distribution to within a few miles of each store and charge a small delivery fee. In California, the Safeway chain has contracted with Tesco to roll out a limited online capability using their existing infrastructure.

Why Do We Fail to Learn?

Despite the significant lessons we see in both the positive and negative outcomes described in this chapter, we don't always learn when we see examples of accidents or near misses from the experiences of others. The issue of continuous learning and improvement is an issue that received much attention in the early 1990s in most industries. The quality movement swept the United States and other developed countries, partially as a result of Japan's reputation for the highest quality manufacturing operations in the world at the time. Quality improved in most businesses in this country as a result, but it took many years and highly visible national efforts such as the Malcolm Baldridge Award and mandated standards from buyers to suppliers.

The 1990s quality movement was focused on manufacturing but spilled over into service businesses as well. The problem with something as generic as "mistakes" is that they can occur in any industry, in any phase of work, in any location, and involving staff at any level in the organization. It is hard to get everyone focused on "mistakes" as the enemy, but there are a few organizations that have a reputation for doing this: Microsoft is very self-critical, and Walt Disney, especially their theme parks, is another example. But the biggest enemy of learning is that we do not realize that an event is or could be more than an isolated incident, that we should learn from it whether it is in our company or industry or not.

In business, there is no one source to look to at for a tally of mistakes from which we might learn. In some industries, associations or regulatory bodies collect information that is valuable to others. Training yourself and others in your organization to look at accidents, incidents, or disasters and the mistakes that led to them may be one of your most important management functions. Ask what you can learn that might be of value to change your mistake culture, just as the quality emphasis helped change attitudes about quality across our society.

Insights

The companies, situations, and mistake chains discussed in this chapter have added a number of important insights to our growing list, most of which apply to almost all business situations:

Insight #2: "Fly the airplane." It is easy to get distracted, and there are times when you need to have a stern talk with yourself and ask if you are spending your time on the most important things.

Insight #3: You cannot afford even a whiff of an ethical lapse. Issues of trust are serious and strategic in today's world, largely because there have been so many ethical lapses that consumers do not trust the actions of corporate executives. The slightest sense of uncertainty or lack of openness creates suspicion that mushrooms into a lack of confidence that can cost a great deal.

Insight #4: Execution mistakes can be generated through a lack of resources or knowledge. Even a good strategy will fail without adequate resources, training, and discipline around implementation.

Insight #5: Establish and enforce standard operating procedures. Aviation knows how to do this, complex manufacturing operations know how to do this, but management teams do not like it because they believe not everything can be made routine. There is some truth to this, but you need to look for everything that can be standardized and make the procedures known, train for them, and hold those accountable who do not follow them.

Insight #6: Make responsibilities clear. Whether it is Coca-Cola Belgium or one of the airline crashes, mistakes are more likely to be caught and stopped if you know who is responsible for what and who should be providing additional oversight and advice.

Insight #7 Seek advice and seek to understand assumptions. In a number of cases, we saw a disconnect between the views of customers and those of insiders or a lack of sensitivity to regional cultural and political views. In other cases, we saw outright disregard for data provided by others (Air Florida) or easily available data (Webvan or AmEx). Failure to seek and use advice and direct disregard for data on customer behavior is a significant cause of mistakes of all types.

And finally, with respect to Webvan, we see some significant mistakes that apply to many business situations:

Insight #8: If something does not make sense or feels confused, STOP and figure out what's going on. In most of the cases in this chapter, there was evidence of confusion or lack of information at some point that troubled those involved. Calling a "timeout" in one way or another to understand what is happening is a useful practice.

Insight #9: People are usually at the root of the problem. Looking at mishaps as system problems is the only way to move toward perfection. Multiple causes are far more likely than single causes, but multiple causes almost always mean some set of mistakes that was directly people related. An analysis that looks for simple answers, blaming only one cause or only a physical cause, will likely yield an inadequate understanding of the problem and will lead to repetition of the problems that caused the accident. It is critical to focus on people-related issues of process, training, and knowledge-building that will allow them to think their way through when technology or process fails.

3

Execution Mistakes and
Successes as Catalysts
for Change

"Never interrupt your enemy when he is making a mistake."

—Napoleon Bonaparte (1769–1821)

About ten years ago, I was teaching a short course on forecasting that was part of a broader "mini-MBA" executive education course for a group of middle managers in one of America's largest corporations. We ran this course every four to six weeks for over two years and thus saw many managers involved in operations for this company.

I started the day, almost by accident the first time, by asking how many in the room had to do formal forecasting as at least part of their job. Typically about 70 percent of the class would raise their hands. I then asked how many used quantitative methods such as modeling (even if simple) or regression analysis. No hands.

When I asked about the methods they used to forecast, the most common answer was something like "projections based on past experience." Because of the large number of courses we ran over a number of years, my sample eventually included hundreds of managers from every part of the company's operations. The answers were always

47

about the same, so it was either culture or training, but the company clearly used nothing more sophisticated than guesses for the future based on past experience.

Some might call this a SWAG (scientific wild-ass guess) or "Kentucky windage." The problem with the windage method is that sometimes the target zigs or zags or the wind changes. The SWAG method is essentially shooting with your eyes closed, aiming where the target was the last time you saw it. Either way, there is clearly a lack of understanding of the interrelationship of cause and effect. The "past as prologue for the future" model works for a while, but it will always fail miserably at some point.

The final question I would ask before moving into my planned material was, "Do you go back after the end of the year and formally evaluate why your forecast came out the way it did?" Without exaggeration, I can say that over two years and at least 500 managers in the courses, fewer than ten individuals said they had any process at all for reviewing the quality of past decisions.

This was one of America's best known corporations at the time, but it simply did not have a culture that encouraged understanding about what really caused success or failure. It has since gone from one strategic blunder to another, proving again the old saying, "If you don't know where you're going, any road will get you there."

The system that tolerated the lack of analysis was a cultural mistake, bred of many years of easy success. But even if "the system" did not hold each individual accountable, you would think that a larger number would actually be curious enough to investigate whether this key part of his or her job was succeeding or failing. They failed to take personal responsibility for anything other than *doing* their work and certainly not for the task of assessing its effectiveness. Further, I would guess that the lack of forecasting discipline might have precipitated even more mistakes than they realized in production and operations as things got out of synch in one way or another.

The first characteristic that an organization must cultivate if it is to succeed with M^3 is curiosity. The company in the preceding example did not have it. In fact, I have often said that this was the most uniformly mediocre and unimpressive group of middle managers that I have ever seen in one place in my entire career.

If you are not curious, individually or as an organization, how will you even know whether your performance can be improved? If your decisions are never analyzed, how do you know whether they were good decisions? Did you just get lucky or unlucky with a particular outcome? If you do not have standards by which you measure the results of your actions, what does success or failure look like? Finally, if there are no measurements, how do you evaluate people for retention, termination, or promotion?

> **Insight #10: A significant portion of execution-related mistakes occur because criteria for measuring progress and performance have not been identified and/or communicated explicitly.** This includes the need to understand not only what the measures are, but how frequently they should be checked and what the priorities and actions should be when an out-of-specification condition occurs.

While there is a difference between operating (business) and performance (personnel) metrics, they are clearly tightly coupled, especially in today's fast-paced, competitive world. In my experience, the businesses with the tightest operating metrics also have strong performance measurement metrics. Those that are loose are usually loose in both domains. The reason is simple—if you are not measuring the business results achieved in a way that relates actions and results, how can you evaluate people and the effectiveness of the things they do that make a difference? "Shows up, gets along, everyone likes him" is not what you want to have as the only measures about someone on your team. My involvement in executive education has given me insight into the management development and evaluation practices at companies all over the world. Those that are really good at what they do have added much more specific and quantifiable metrics for both operations and performance over the last decade.

Lack of enforcement of standards is only one of many reasons that multiple mistakes occur that lead to disasters for companies. Once mistakes are discovered, some organizations seem to do a better job of recovering, learning from mistakes, and using the experience as a catalyst for change, but this culture is by no means uniform.

This chapter will discuss some situations that, while serious and costly, did not ruin the responsible companies. These were limited threats to the businesses, sometimes only to a single product or line of business, but they had the potential to grow even larger. The mistake scenarios in this chapter, concerning Intel, "New Coke," and a United

Airlines crash, were each related to bad execution. (They were somewhat strategic as well, but the execution was what got them in trouble.) In the process, each of these companies learned valuable lessons that became catalysts for change. Each situation clearly illustrates multiple mistakes, but the chains were broken before sustained damage to the entire business occurred. In all of these examples, the companies involved realized that they had "dodged a bullet" and learned from the experience for future benefit. We will also examine the famous J&J/Tylenol case as an example of a company that has never found itself in a situation like the others examined here. J&J knows how to avoid mistakes, even when faced with something they have never seen before, because of their strong and historic focus on customer safety and their culture of acting on that as a priority.

Intel and the "Father Knows Best" Response

By 1994, Intel's newest chip was eating up the processor market, but then they made a mistake—Intel manufactured a chip with a flaw that became highly visible* and handled the situation very badly. With over five million Pentium computers in the market, the joke became, "It gives the wrong answer, but at least it's FAST!" The "Intel Inside" campaign was new and successful, and the success of the campaign made Intel an even bigger target for ridicule as their vulnerability was on display for the entire world.

The jokes, and later anger, about Intel's Pentium processor were the result of a combination of technical mistakes made worse with public relations blunders by the world's leader in microprocessors. The problem for Intel began when Dr. Thomas R. Nicely, professor of mathematics at Lynchburg College in Lynchburg, Virginia, began circulating a memo he wrote dated October 30, 1994 about a bug in the Pentium processor. Nicely was doing research on prime numbers and had been running a number of personal computers on the same problem for months. At some point in October 1994, he noticed a result on the only machine that had a Pentium processor (the others were older machines). This machine

---

* Many processor designs have flaws, but not all are detected before a product enters the market. Not all flaws turn out to be serious, and in some cases, software can be modified to accommodate hardware problems.

produced incorrect results because of errors in the answer beyond the eighth significant digit (to the right of the decimal place).*

Accuracy to the eighth decimal place is not a capability the average home computer user needs to be able to balance the checkbook or to send pictures to Grandma via e-mail. And therein was the problem for Intel—it did not affect everyone, so Intel took the position that, "You shouldn't be concerned unless you work with a lot of really long numbers." And "...this would only happen to the average person once every 27,000 years."[11]

Nicely first reported the flaw to Intel technical support by telephone on October 24 and was told by the technical representative that the flaw had not been reported previously. The reality, as later reported, was that Intel knew about the flaw and had already changed the chip so that newer chips would run correctly when they were produced. Intel's technical support staff did not provide any answers or guidance to Nicely, so he put together his now-famous memo and sent it to a number of friends and colleagues via e-mail. In 1994, the Internet was not as ubiquitous as it is today, but many people were using e-mail, and the memo was widely circulated fairly rapidly even though Nicely's initial personal distribution was to only about a dozen people.

Nicely became silent on the issue fairly rapidly under a nondisclosure agreement with Intel. Others took up the cause, however, and discovered that the flaw might affect more users than Intel claimed, though still not the mainstream. Yet Intel continued to deny that this problem was a significant threat and stonewalled demands by users for a fix.

Intel shifted from denying that there was a problem to explaining that the flaw only affected what is called "floating-point division," a capability they claimed most users do not often utilize. But many users needed this feature without realizing it since some underlying functions built into spreadsheets and other programs utilize this method of calculation without the user understanding what is going on behind the scenes.

Intel eventually admitted that the flaw existed and had been repaired in new versions of its chips. However, they made matters worse and showed their recalcitrance by announcing that, since the flaw was not serious, they would continue shipping the older, flawed chips until their

---

* If you would like to test your machine, the sample problem he used was (824633702441.0)* (1/824633702441.0). The answer should be precisely 1.0, but the Pentium machines at the time returned 0.999999996274709702.

supply was depleted. The publicity and Intel's continuing missteps caused the number of observers of Intel's actions to grow from a few techies to a ground swell of media and worried computer users.

On Thanksgiving Day 1994, the Intel senior management team was in an all-day meeting to try to figure out what to do about the growing public relations problem that they simply could not understand. As engineers, they understood the limited impact of the flaw and had trouble understanding why the public would not accept their technical explanation and position. But the heat was on—with class action lawsuits being organized and users going crazy, not over the flaw itself but over Intel's arrogance. Executives do not seem to learn well from other industries. We will see that communications and public relations fiascos are often part of the mistake sequence that increases damage in business disasters, but each company and industry seems to have to learn for itself that this is an area worth worrying about early.

A series of stories in the *Washington Post*[12] and other newspapers noted a half-hearted apology by Andy Grove, Intel's CEO, in which he stated that Intel would replace the chip for anyone who could prove that their applications required the high level of accuracy connected with the flaw. All you had to do was call Intel tech support and convince them why you needed to replace your processor that was known to be bad with a new one. This paternalistic "we know what is best for you" attitude cost Intel dearly in public opinion.

Grove made matters worse by fighting the battle with press releases and not holding any news conferences about the subject. Then, on December 12, an announcement from IBM stating that they were suspending shipments of computers using the Pentium processor pushed the situation further into crisis. Intel stock dropped precipitously and trading in it was temporarily halted.

Competitors were licking their chops, lawyers were counting what they would win in class-action suits, and computer manufacturers were afraid the problem would hurt sales. The Pentium flaw was the subject of numerous talk shows, techie message boards, and daily newspaper articles.

On December 20, 1994, Intel reluctantly caved in with a decision that involved the board of directors. They announced that anyone who owned a machine with the bad processor could receive, upon request, a new Pentium processor. I never replaced the one in the machine I had with that chip, but maybe I should have—that machine never ran smoothly.

Was it the Intel processor or something else? I'll never know, but the fact that I, and many others, still remember the incident a decade later is exactly the reason that Intel should have handled this differently.

In January 1995, Intel announced that, in the future, when it finds a flaw in its chips, it "...will make a full disclosure immediately to its software and hardware partners and then to the general public." Why should a company have to announce that they will disclose faulty products in the future? Obviously, they began to realize that brand equity goes beyond technology and that customer confidence is part of their ability to generate profits.

The opportunity was not lost on competitor AMD which, like most aggressive competitors in any industry, was trying to figure out a way to gain an advantage when their normally gorilla-size rival was down. AMD approached PC makers trying to get them to use the "more reliable" AMD chips, but Intel recovered too quickly for this event to make much difference for AMD.

This incident did not hurt Intel in the long run. Their best days were ahead of them, and their innovation, production, profits, and stock price went through the roof with the 1995–2000 technology boom. But their inept handling of this incident—the flaw itself, the denial, the limited recall, and especially their failure to understand the consumer's point of view—was a classic failure to manage multiple mistakes. It clearly illustrates how damage rises exponentially with each additional blunder.

Intel took a $475 million charge to account for losses as a result of the replacements, associated costs, and possible legal claims. This was about 25 percent of their net income that year—a pretty expensive mistake. What would it have cost if they had admitted the problem earlier, with the technical explanation, but had offered to exchange processors, no questions asked, for all who wanted them? It probably would have cost a lot less because fewer customers would have known enough to request the exchange, and the costs they eventually put into advertising and PR would have been avoided.

Once you have made mistakes or bad decisions, stopping the chain sooner rather than later will reduce physical, financial, and/or reputation damage. If we think back to our M^3 impact diagram, this was a self-inflicted set of mistakes that was of strategic importance to Intel, but the chain was broken before it became life threatening to the company.

A review of the Intel sequence of business mistakes looks a lot like some other cases we will discuss in later chapters for physical disasters such as the *Titanic*, Three Mile Island, and a number of air crashes. The specifics are different, but you will find the patterns are the same:

- **Ignoring data or assuming it was unimportant.** Intel knew about the flaw and worked to fix it, but they probably thought the flaw would not be discovered and so decided not to reveal its existence. (Denial of the factual situation as will be seen in TMI.)

- **Assuming a technical stance rather than a customer-focused position.** Some would excuse this and say that engineers just react with technology rather than empathy for customers, but a company that was already the world leader in its field should have known better. (They didn't "fly the airplane.")

- **Dismissing opinions of customers as "uninformed."** This serious mistake backfired when they grudgingly offered to replace processors only for those who could prove they needed them.

- **Failure to have market-based criteria** for acceptable levels/types of customer satisfaction and processes for dealing with problems. The clear assumption was, "We know best and will let you know when that changes."

- **Failure to communicate.** The use of press releases rather than direct personal contact through press conferences or other means created a perception, probably correctly, that Intel management did not want to talk to the customers. We would assume that a company this large would have had better and more persuasive public relations advice. The problem with personal communication is that, if you choose to do it, you must come across as credible and caring or it will make the situation worse.

- **Offering a limited solution.** The offer to replace the defective product, but only for those that could "show cause," clearly made everyone angry. Even those eligible to have their processor replaced believed the company was dodging its responsibility to customers.

- **Misjudging the time available for action and failing to get advice.** It was two months from the time of Nicely's memo until Intel capitulated and did what they should have done on day one. They clearly underestimated the ground swell of opposition and then actively fought against it even as they realized it was growing, hoping to avoid the cost of a recall. It is likely that IBM's decision to stop shipping product finally made them realize they had to stop the fight, but it should not have taken a drastic action of one of their key customers to bring them to reality. Did Intel utilize any outside PR/marketing talent to deal with this crisis, or did they develop their position and continue to rationalize it over and over again to themselves?

All of these mistakes were important in keeping the mistake sequence accelerating, but if you had to pick only one as the most serious mistake that could have changed everything, which one would it be? Catching the flaw and stopping it early is surely a candidate, but even that was survivable. Being too technical is excusable for a technology company if communications are decent. The top candidate for most important mistake, in my mind, has to do with ignoring or dismissing customer data. This is an axiom of business: If you take time to understand what is bothering your customers and act on it, you are usually well served. We will see a number of examples where companies ignoring such information put them in peril.

Intel is an extraordinary company that helped create an industry and has redefined itself a number of times with often-brilliant strategic decisions. They had the foresight to leave the commodity memory business and focus on higher-value-added processors when they realized that was the only way to achieve high profitability going forward. They have increasingly integrated external functions into their products (to the dismay of some other suppliers), adding better performance and value in the process. They have moved away from the idea that more speed in a single processor design will solve all problems and have begun to make more specialized processors that are optimized for specific applications, most recently mobile devices and laptop computers.

I have said for years that if you don't make some mistakes, you're not trying hard enough. If you wait to make every move until it is completely safe with success assured, you will by definition be a follower with little to distinguish you in a market. Taking risks will involve making some mistakes, but you would like those mistakes to be made early, cheap, and as invisible as possible because they are less expensive that way. This incident is a stark reminder that even companies that make world-class strategic moves sometimes blunder. It is also a reminder that, in business as in physical situations, breaking the chain before one is "in extremis" is possible, with subsequent recovery and even greater success based on the lessons learned.

Tylenol Relieves a Headache

Contrast the Intel response to a consumer "problem" of their own making with the famous response of Johnson & Johnson in the Tylenol case in October 1982. Mysterious deaths in the Chicago area became linked to Tylenol Extra Strength capsules, manufactured and sold by J&J's McNeil subsidiary. Within a few days, seven people died from cyanide poisoning.

J&J instituted an immediate national recall of over 31 million packages of Tylenol at a cost of over $125 million. There was no evidence that the tampering extended beyond Chicago, but J&J believed that safety was paramount and wanted to leave no doubt as to their commitment to their customers' interests.

J&J cooperated with law enforcement officials in an immediate investigation that confirmed the product lots involved were produced in different plants. Following plant inspections and a review of procedures, this rapidly led to the conclusion that this was external tampering rather than an internal J&J production problem.

While the swift recall was an impressive commitment to the customer, J&J's next move stunned everyone and benefited the shareholders. Within a month, J&J announced the return of Tylenol to the market in tamper-resistant packaging. With smart and sensitive advertising, product promotion, and discount coupons Tylenol more than regained its dominant market share in the pain relief category within a year.

J&J's history of commitment to the customer's interests dates back to the 1930s when General Robert Wood Johnson began trying to convince other business leaders that their interests would be best served by putting customers first and worrying about shareholders later. By the early 1940s, this was codified as the one-page Johnson & Johnson credo that states in part:

"We believe our first responsibility is to the doctors, nurses, and patients, to mothers and fathers and all others who use our products and services. In meeting their needs, everything we do must be of high quality."

Following this is a discussion of responsibilities to employees and community and then the credo concludes with responsibilities to stockholders:

"Our final responsibility is to our stockholders.
Business must make a sound profit....

When we operate according to these principles, the stockholders should realize a fair return."[13]

Over the years, many other companies have said that they believe the customer comes first and have claimed to act on that belief, but few have walked the talk as much as J&J did with the Tylenol case. Management probably had not thought about product tampering prior to this incident. But once the crisis began, the fact that they did not have an explicit plan made the management team realize they had to look to fundamental beliefs and principles for guidance.

J&J's credo worked. Even in the absence of specific procedures, it guided management to act quickly, decisively, and effectively to serve customers in a way that eventually rewarded shareholders as well. Would you rather spend $250 million (including estimates of costs of new packaging and relaunch) admitting a problem and fixing it instantly as J&J did, or would you rather deny the problem exists and be forced by the market to fix it at a cost of $475 million (or worse) as Intel did?

Some will say this is not an apples-to-apples comparison, but even if the numbers are off a bit, the choice is obvious. M^3 is cost effective. J&J instantly broke the chain that someone else started for them and 20 years later continues to benefit from the goodwill created by their actions. Intel denied the problem they created for themselves, probably spent more money in the process, and although they have changed, they're still remembered as a company that makes great products but was arrogant and tried to abuse its customers.

What J&J did is almost the mirror image of Intel's response to their crisis:

- **Believed data and considered it important.** J&J did not like what they saw but took it at face value and worked with authorities to determine the source.
- **Assumed a customer-focused position.** With an immediate recall, J&J made a dramatic statement about where their priorities lay.

- **Believed opinions of customers that Tylenol was involved.** The opposite of Intel's response to criticism of their chip.

- **Had cultural principles and norms that made decisions easy.** This meant that, even without experience or specific procedures, there was conceptual guidance understood by all.

- **Used communications as a tool.** J&J enlisted the support of the press and government to get the word out as rapidly as possible that product was not to be used under any circumstances. There was no ambivalence or embarrassment about the situation. There was focus on the objective and priorities.

- **Developed a permanent fix rapidly and reentered the market aggressively.** The development of tamper-resistant packaging in a matter of weeks and aggressive return to market strategies worked to their permanent advantage.

In summary, J&J used the incident that was thrust upon them not only as an opportunity to remedy the situation for their customers, but as a catalyst for improving safety in their packaging. The indirect effect of this incident and J&J's decision to bring tamper-resistant packaging to market was of benefit to the entire society. Their response began to change attitudes of business and society about the need for safe packaging and consumer protection from tampering.

"We're Not Going to Make the Airport"– The Case for CRM

Pilots operating an airplane are similar to middle managers operating businesses in a larger corporation. Rules, procedures, and structures govern operations, but for some period of time, pilots are carrying out their duties in a broadly defined fashion without immediate oversight. They encounter situations they have trained for and others they have not seen before. Sometimes they have time to consult with others, and sometimes they have to make decisions without the benefit of discussion. Teamwork may not exist or may be used effectively. The similarities present some lessons that will become clear as we look an accident that changed the way airlines look at the need for teamwork. The procedures that have evolved are now used in operations in healthcare delivery, manufacturing, and other settings.

The airline industry has focused, since its inception, on improving technology to help reduce risk. Long ago the industry began to realize that the ultimate risk-reduction improvement involves reducing pilot error and judgment mistakes. However, it was only in the late 1970s that the industry began to recognize the systemic nature of this type of error, and it was during the 1980s and 1990s that the organized discipline and processes evolved to combat these problems.

A major advance in understanding the role of human error and improved performance through communication and allocation of duties in aviation came as a result of a flight that included the communication sequence below. "Radio" indicates communication from the aircraft, "Approach" is air traffic control, and "Internal" is inside the cockpit:

Radio: "How far you show us from the field?"

Approach: "Ah ... call it 18 flying miles."

Radio: "All right."

Internal: "Boy, the fuel sure went to hell all of a sudden. I told you we had four."

Internal: "There's, ah, kind of an interstate highway type thing along the bank on the river in case we're short."

Internal: "Okay."

Internal: "That's Troutdale* over there, about six of one half dozen of the other."

Internal: "Let's take the shortest route to the airport."

Radio: "What's our distance now?"

Approach: "Twelve flying miles"

Internal: "Well, * *"

Internal: "About three minutes."

Internal: "Four."

Internal: "We've lost two engines guys."

Internal: "Sir?"

Internal: "We just lost two engines, one and two."

---

* A small airport that was closer than Portland from their position at the time.

Internal: "You got all the pumps on and everything?"

Approach: "United one seventy three heavy contact Portland tower one one eight point seven. You're about eight or niner flying miles from the airport."

Internal: "Yep."

Radio: "Okay, eighteen seven."

Approach: "Have a good one."

Internal: "They're all going."

Internal: "We can't make Troutdale."

Internal: "We can't make anything."

Internal: "Okay, declare a mayday."

Radio: "Portland tower United one seventy three heavy mayday ... we're ... the engines are flaming out, we're going down, we're not going to be able to make the airport."[14]

This rather casual sounding conversation took place on December 28, 1978 among the three cockpit crewmembers of United Airlines flight 173 and the Portland, Oregon approach and tower controllers. Five seconds after the mayday* declaration, the DC-8 crashed into a wooded suburban area six miles southeast of the runway at Portland International Airport.

The final report from the National Transportation Safety Board (NTSB)[3] indicates that the probable cause was as follows:

"The failure of the captain to monitor properly the aircraft's fuel state and to properly respond to the low fuel state and the crewmember's advisories regarding fuel state. This resulted in fuel exhaustion to all engines. His inattention resulted from preoccupation with a landing gear malfunction and preparations for a possible landing emergency. Contributing to the accident was the failure of the other two flight crewmembers either to fully

---

* Mayday is the international radio signal for the declaration of an emergency. In the aviation context, declaring an emergency causes controllers to provide priority for the aircraft in trouble.

comprehend the criticality of the fuel state or to successfully communicate their concern to the captain."

This accident clearly involved multiple mistakes. The crew originally had the required fuel for the flight* but became distracted by a landing gear problem that occurred when the gear was lowered while in the descent for landing. They loitered in a holding pattern to determine if the problem was real and to plan for an emergency landing that they thought might include the possible collapse of the gear under the right wing. During this time, they lost track of their fuel state and crashed short of the airport. They ran out of gas. The mistake chain included:

- **Failure to repair a known design problem** that had been identified on other aircraft a number of years earlier. The manufacturer had advised the repair, but the FAA did not mandate it. The problem resulted in damaging corrosion on a connecting rod in the landing gear retract mechanism that could lead to its failure, which is what happened on UA-173. The problem was being monitored to try to detect progression to a serious state that would force modification, but if it had been modified earlier instead of being monitored, the mistake chain would have been stopped.

- **Failure to land the aircraft** after determining that the gear was in fact down and locked based on a visual inspection of the mechanical indicator. Continued preparation for a possible gear collapse during landing seemed prudent, but the crew had information that should have given them confidence to proceed to land instead of delaying so long that the fuel was exhausted.

- **Excessive concern over not wanting to rush the cabin crew** in their preparation of the passengers, based on the faulty assumption that there was plenty of fuel. At some point, getting the airplane on the ground, under control, should have become the primary focus.

- **Failure to estimate accurately when they needed to start the landing sequence** to stay within their available fuel parameters. Even if the gear had collapsed, which it would not have done based

---

* By regulation, the aircraft must carry enough fuel to fly to the intended destination, conduct an approach, fly to an alternate airport reported to have weather that meets certain requirements, and fly for 45 minutes after that.

on postaccident investigation, a landing at the airport would have
been preferable to a crash in a wooded area.

■ **Failure to communicate effectively** among the three flight
crewmembers regarding the fuel situation. The DC-8 flew with a
three-person cockpit crew. At one point, as the captain discussed a
further delay, the flight engineer said that an additional "15
minutes is really going to run us low on fuel here." While the flight
engineer clearly knew the situation was critical, he made no further
effort to make sure the captain understood the exact time they
might run out of fuel.

Ten people were killed in the crash and 179 survived. The high
survival rate was partially due to the fact that there was no postcrash fire
because there was no fuel to ignite.

There were multiple opportunities to break the chain and land safely,
even after the initial mechanical problem occurred. The airplane was
between five and twenty miles from the airport for the whole hour
preceding the crash, but the crew's distraction and lack of focus caused
the loss of ten lives that likely would not have occurred if they had
simply been more disciplined in their problem solving and preparation
for landing, allowing them to make a timely approach to land.

In the accident report, the NTSB talks about the lack of effective
communication among the crew and makes an important statement that
was obvious to many in the industry but had rarely been a focus of safety
studies:

> "...the stature and management style of a captain may exert subtle
> pressure on his crew to conform to his way of thinking. It may
> hinder interaction and adequate monitoring..."

This was formal recognition of something that many knew was a
problem but had never thought was serious enough to attack in an
organized fashion. Thus was born the idea that a new category of mistake
needed attention—lack of effective management of cockpit and crew
resources. This is a problem area more difficult than fixing a technical
problem because creating more effective coordination among
crewmembers cannot be easily fixed with a design change and simply
installed on every airplane. It is something that must be "fixed" on a

continuous basis as long as people are involved. Thus, along with technical recommendations to prevent a recurrence of the UA-173 type of accident, the NTSB also recommended that the Federal Aviation Administration:

"Issue an operations bulletin to all air carrier operations inspectors, directing them to urge their assigned operators to ensure that their flight crews are indoctrinated in principles of flight deck resource management, with particular emphasis on the merits of participative management for captains and assertiveness training for other cockpit crewmembers."

This issue had been recognized previously and was addressed in United's Flight Operations manual well before this accident with paragraph 6.2, which stated:

"16. Except as otherwise specifically directed by the captain, all crew members noting a departure from prescribed procedures and safe practices should immediately advise the captain so that he is aware of and understands the particular situation and may take appropriate action."[15]

Of course, advising "...the captain so that he is aware and understands..." is very different than "... participative management for captains and assertiveness training for other cockpit crewmembers." This distinction and the NTSB's recognition of the role that a lack of assertiveness plays in safety were important. As a result, this accident and the attendant findings and recommendations became one catalyst for what became known as **cockpit resource management** and is now called **crew resource management (CRM)**, to reflect the need for broader involvement of effective coordination and use of resources beyond the flight crew itself.

Various agencies have investigated aircraft accidents, beginning when the first American, an Army officer, was killed while flying with Orville Wright in 1908. It was many years, however, before the emphasis shifted from investigation of accidents toward a serious focus on prevention. By the time of the UA-173 accident in 1978, the FAA, NTSB, all branches of the military, and NASA had become interested in driving the accident rate down through better understanding of causes.

NASA held a conference in 1979 and again in 1986 to focus on cockpit resource management. During the 1980s, all the major airlines and the military branches began programs focused on improving crew performance through better management, coordination, and communication. The problem of lack of focus and coordination of duties was not new, but it finally began to get some traction as a concept when a number of agencies and organizations developed an interest in doing something about the number of accidents that resulted from blatant ineptitude at a team level.

While the CRM concept in the civilian world was pioneered in aviation, it is now used heavily in a number of other areas where human coordination is important to safety, such as fire fighting, shipboard operations, most manufacturing environments, and in recent years, the medical field.

The FAA publishes guidelines for CRM training[16], and most airlines have required programs for their personnel, but the impact of the training has taken two decades to have the desired effect. In the last 20 years, as the concept has been refined and deployed, there have been fewer accidents involving a failure of effective coordination, but there continue to be enough to show the need for not only teaching CRM but practicing it on a daily basis.

New Coke–Understanding Customers and Capabilities

Between April 23 and July 11, 1985, The Coca-Cola Company found itself in the middle of a customer revolt and controversy that had the press and consumers puzzled and stunned saying, "Why in the world did they do that?"

They did not hurt anyone, endanger anyone (except shareholders), threaten anyone, or violate any laws. They changed the formulation of their core product for the first time in 99 years. They changed the "formula" to make it taste more like Pepsi because Pepsi was gaining in the head-to-head battle where consumers had a choice of product.

Customers were saying, "How dare they change the formula that we all grew up with?" My mother even laughingly admits that she put it in our baby bottles from time to time as a treat.

The problem was the blind taste tests. The consumers lied. They, according to the company, showed a strong preference for the new formula in over 200,000 tests and then rebelled when the product hit the market. The chorus was loud and persistent, and on July 11 the company announced that it would market two varieties of Coca-Cola: "Classic Coke" and Coca-Cola ("New Coke"). This was news that made newspaper and evening news headlines. The angry calls and letters subsided, the protests quieted down, and the company found itself selling more product than ever, although New Coke eventually died of its own taste.

It turned out that consumers that wanted Coke wanted it as it was, and changing it to be more like Pepsi was not going to convert Pepsi drinkers but would clearly alienate previously loyal Coke drinkers. What was the mistake chain here? Since this is not an accident that was investigated by a blue-ribbon committee, we will have to postulate some of the mistakes, but most are obvious:

- **A focus on a single competitor rather than the noncustomers.** This is a classic blunder in any business—the obsession with a competitor that causes you to look and act more like them than what the customers who use neither product might like. In fact, it was in this time frame that the noncola drinks market was accelerating, and the majors were not playing in the game as they would later. This obsession likely set up a flawed decision mindset.

- **Believing it was all or nothing,** probably because of bottling efficiencies. Efficiency is rarely a good strategy if you have any other way to differentiate your product, yet it would appear that became the priority because Coca-Cola shifted production over all at once. They had decided this was the new taste, and it would be a lot less costly to bottle and sell only one sugared cola product.

- **Skipping regional introduction.** I always thought you tested new pudding in Rochester or Peoria before launching it nationwide. Why didn't they do a test market rollout in a middle-size city before making an irreversible commitment? Probably because they perceived they would lose the marketing buzz surrounding a national introduction if word slipped out ahead of time. This mistake was likely related to the single competitor obsession.

- **Underestimating the cultural attachment to the product** and missing the real market—Coke customers liked their product the way it was.

Coca-Cola recovered from the New Coke incident and even celebrated the 10-year anniversary of the mistake to point out they had learned from the incident. The soft-drink wars continue today, but it is no longer about carbonated soft drinks (CSD) alone. Around the world, a range of juices, waters, sports drinks, coffees, teas, health drinks, and other specialty drinks compete with CSDs for the consumer's share of stomach.

Coca-Cola's transformation following New Coke was the recognition that, whether they liked it or not, they were entering the land of multiple consumer preferences, segments, and more SKUs*. The simple segments of the past were disappearing, just as they were in many other consumer-focused industries including autos, clothing, and personal-care products. Today the company has high growth in non-CSD areas and introduces dozens of new products each year to meet differing local needs and preferences around the globe.

For Coca-Cola, the mistake chain in 1985 was serious and threatening, but it was broken in 79 days. Some would say it should have been avoided altogether, but it was broken and transformational learning about customers and messing with the brand took place as a result.

Insights: Different Products and Services with Similar Lessons for Transformation

The Intel Pentium incident, the Tylenol tampering, the United 173 crash, and the New Coke launch exhibited similarities in the lessons about the damage that multiple mistakes can inflict and the damage that can be avoided by breaking the chain early. More importantly, each of these particular incidents went beyond insights around the narrow management of multiple mistakes because they occurred in a time and place where those involved realized the potential for more generalized learning.

Intel has a different respect for customers and the handling of processor errors. Tylenol set new standards for society in packaging. UA-173 led United and other airlines to get serious about CRM, and other industries have picked up the principles pioneered in aviation. New Coke helped Coca-Cola broaden their horizons to realize that ongoing product development and variety is an important reality of consumer life because you cannot protect your core product forever as consumer preferences change.

* Retail talk for unique numbers or "stock keeping units" assigned to each product and variant.

Some of the insights from these incidents that can be added to those in Chapters 1 and 2 include:

Insight #10: A significant portion of execution-related mistakes occur because criteria for measuring progress and performance have not been identified and/or communicated explicitly. This includes the need to understand not only what the measures are, but how frequently they should be checked and what the priorities and actions should be when an out of specification condition occurs.

Insight #11: Failure to analyze data points and ask what they mean is a major source of mistakes. This seems obvious, but we block our interest and ability to be analytic with time pressures, distractions, and cultures that are not curious. The question, "I see it, but what does it mean?" may be the most important thing you can ask to begin to break a mistake chain. The answer will not always be obvious, but starting the inquiry process is a necessity.

Insight #12: Ignoring data is dangerous; ignoring or misinterpreting customer data can be catastrophic. Intel initially ignored customer concerns, while in the Tylenol case, J&J never lost sight of their responsibility to their customer. Coca-Cola did not adequately test the depth of their data with hard-core users of their product.

Insight #13: Across industries and situations, ineffective communications can accelerate deterioration of a mistake chain. Conversely, effective communication is one of the keys to breaking a mistake chain.

Insight #14: Spending time and money to build a culture that takes mistakes seriously may have the highest ROI of anything you can do as a manager. This is something that paid off for the airline industry in improving safety and for Intel, J&J, and Coca-Cola.

Insight #15: Look for the opportunity for an accident or even a major success to be a rallying cry for change and transformation. This is a unique opportunity that should not be ignored. This is the silver lining in an accident—your ability to identify some greater benefit that comes from the learning.

In the Introduction, we laid out some common patterns in crises that have adverse outcomes. Note that, in the undesirable situations described in this chapter, we have seen patterns very similar to the original list. These are things managers need to learn to recognize, look for, and act on to minimize the potential for mistakes and damage:

- An initial problem, often minor in isolation, that goes uncorrected
- A subsequent problem that compounds the effect of the initial problem
- An inept corrective effect
- Disbelief at the accelerating seriousness of the situation
- Generally, an attempt to hide the truth about what is going on while an attempt is made at remediation
- Sudden recognition that the situation is out of control, or "in extremis"
- Finally, the ultimate disaster scenario involving significant loss of life, financial resources, or both, and ultimately the recriminations

Remember the diagram in Figure 3.1 and watch for the patterns— they are real.

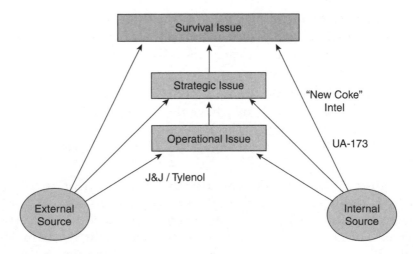

Figure 3.1   Mistake escalation.

4

Strategy—How Do You Know It's a Mistake?

"It ain't over till it's over."

−Yogi Berra

Examples of mistakes and mistake chains in previous chapters have been easy to recognize. Individuals involved in creating the mistakes may not have recognized them immediately, but recognition was obvious, sometimes brutally so, in a relatively short timeframe. But what if recognition of mistakes takes months, years, or even a decade? Can we speed up the recognition process and break a chain of strategic mistakes early enough to avoid permanent damage?

Some companies seem to do everything right and still end up in trouble. The difficulty, of course, is that business decisions, especially strategy-related decisions, cannot always be judged "right" or "wrong" on the basis of immediate results. The old adage "time will tell" is heard frequently in discussions about whether recent business decisions are right or wrong. Decision theorists point out that decision-making "quality" should be judged on the information available at the time, but strategy decisions involve bets and assumptions about the future and thus must be judged retrospectively.

However, when there are extant competitors in a market or technology sector, the time frame and criteria by which to judge such decisions are more rigorous. If you are early and fail, you are seen as visionary. If you are late and fail, you are seen as dumb. Bill Lear's 8-track tape system, while superior in some respects, ultimately lost in a standardization battle. Chrysler's attempt to put a phonograph in vehicles in 1956 playing special 16 rpm records was a decent idea, but the technology was not really ready until CDs came along in the 1990s. Ford actually tried a 4-track tape system about the same time and found few takers. Everyone knew that audio would be important in the automobile in the future, but early experiments beyond the basic radio were not successes.

Companies and technologies come to market early or late, and the market rather brutally decides whether or not it is ready for the offering. Experimenting with new technologies is one thing, but diversifying into someone else's space takes real courage and is very tough to do well. It does not matter if it is good; it is a question of whether or not the widget or service racks up sales because customers perceive that it adds value now, especially against an entrenched competitor. Mistimed market strategies are not limited to startups. Does anyone remember McDonald Douglas Automation, an attempt by one of many aerospace companies to get into the data-processing business in the 1980s? How about Lockheed trying to compete with HP in the printer business and getting wiped out?

There are famous cases of bad timing and/or bad judgment where what is thought to be the "right" decision at the time looks very wrong in retrospect. Some would consider it a huge mistake that Kodak, GE, and others turned down the opportunity to commercialize the technology that would later become Xerox when it was offered to them. I have seen the first machine the inventor showed to potential large company partners. It is a crude-looking device that operated in a cumbersome fashion. Somehow, even in retrospect, it is hard to imagine that a wooden box with a tin hat top with a light bulb at the apex could launch a $15 billion company, and those who saw it in the late 1930s and 1940s obviously thought the same thing.

Was it a mistake, a "bad" decision, for those companies to turn away the man with the cumbersome copy box that had to "bake" every copy for a couple of minutes? Many believe that focus in your areas of competence is necessary for success. Even if a large company of the day had not turned him away, would it have been able to develop the business when it had other businesses to worry about? But what if you are the one to develop a whole new set of technologies, not just adapt them to a new use? And what if you do not recognize the potential? That brings us to Xerox, Motorola, and Kodak—successful technology leaders who invented and reinvented themselves more than once and then missed the boat strategically and technically in a later cycle.

Xerox–No Walk in the PARC

Chester Carlson, a patent attorney who observed that there were never enough carbon copies of documents in his office, realized the need for a quick and inexpensive way to obtain copies. He began a quest to build a copying device, and on October 22, 1938, Carlson and his assistant proved that with a straightforward (but messy) electrostatic and chemical process they could duplicate an ink image on one surface to another.

Carlson sought a corporate partner to help him develop the business, but his proposals were spurned by virtually every major corporation of the day that would have been a suitable partner. It took Carlson 10 years to transform his technology into his first viable product with the help of Battelle Memorial Institute and finally the Haloid Corporation, a small photographic paper manufacturer that became Xerox.

Growth was slow at first, but the technology and machines were refined and improved, and when Xerox introduced the first plain paper copier in 1959, machines began popping up in offices all over the world. The company became one of the most profitable in the United States, its stock was admired as a growth stock, and few saw any impediment to Xerox's growth.

Xerox's increasing presence in offices gave the company a unique understanding of the challenges and opportunities for productivity improvement. Its corporate managers saw a bright future in providing products and services to offices, and in 1968, the company entered the computer industry by purchasing a time share and data services company renamed as Xerox Data Systems. In 1970, Xerox established the Palo Alto Research Center (PARC) to explore computing architecture and potential implications for offices. Xerox PARC was one of the most important sources in the world for inventions and innovations in the evolution of personal computing, networking, and printing. By 1973, Xerox PARC scientists and engineers had developed the following:

- The world's first laser printer
- Client/server architecture
- The concept of distributed personal computing
- Ethernet, the protocol that allows most of the world's computers to connect with one another
- The Alto, the first personal computer that evolved to include the mouse, local hard drive, and graphical user interface (GUI), all of which we know as components of today's personal computers and operating systems

Xerox PARC continued its unbelievable development pace through the 1970s and, by 1979, had a corporate network with over 1,000 of its personal workstations connected by Ethernet and using word processors designed by PARC. Xerox staffers were using technology most of us would not see for another 10 to 15 years. They were using computers when the rest of us were evaluating the potential for shifting from IBM Selectric typewriters to the new expensive "memory typewriters" offered by many companies including IBM, Xerox, and even Exxon.*

Xerox, as the copier company that now calls itself the "document company," did everything right up through the mid-1970s. Whole books have been written about what happened next[17]. Xerox management's missteps in commercializing PARC's work in the emerging small and networked environments are legendary. The company was in a position to become the leader in the evolving office, personal, and distributed computing industries but did not realize the potential. Mistakes and contributing circumstances to the failure to commercialize PARC technologies include:

- **Focused their efforts on the copier business.** As competition intensified, especially when the Japanese entered the market, Xerox focused on producing, selling, and protecting their copier business.
- **Exited the computer business** by selling the acquired time share computers to Honeywell.

---

* This is a good example of diversification that was so unrelated it was bound to be killed by the oil culture, even though the product was decent.

- **Failed to notice the brain drain** as those working on computer-related projects left to found computer-related companies including Silicon Graphics (Jim Clark), Adobe (John Warnock), 3Com (Robert Metcalfe), and others.

- **PARC's focus on interesting research and not product development.** This was a great strength from a research standpoint, but it also relieved PARC of worrying about turning anything they developed into a revenue stream.

- **Failure to believe the trends** as office markets changed dramatically with personal computers and as new software gained in popularity.

These were considered by most to be fundamental mistakes. There were many more mistakes in the details, which takes us back to Drucker's admonition about "sacrificing tomorrow's opportunities on the altar of yesterday."

> **Insight #16: A very successful business can blind you to opportunity.** This is because you will make comparative judgments on the basis of current business criteria that may not last while underestimating the potential of new businesses that have not yet grown far enough to show their full potential. Being successful also raises, often inappropriately, your confidence in your own decision-making.

> **Insight #17: Your competitors are not who you think they are.** Until recently, Xerox did not realize that the biggest threat to the copier business in smaller market segments was not Canon or Minolta but Hewlett-Packard and the laser printer that Xerox invented.

Xerox's core business became very competitive in the 1990s, not just with the number of players but also with the continuing shift toward fully digital technology. They pushed the sales force harder and also pushed the accounting envelope with aggressive revenue recognition policies. In 2000, the SEC began an investigation into the company's accounting policies. A fraud charge came in 2002, with the company eventually settling with a fine of $10 million, at the time the largest ever paid by a company to the SEC.

When the financial restatements were done, more than $6.4 billion in revenue and $1.4 billion in profits were restated for the years 1997 through 2001. Xerox is recovering under new leadership and is focusing on markets where they believe they have a competitive advantage. They recently exited the small office/home office segment and are focusing on larger enterprises.

Xerox clearly made a number of decisions that left it as an insignificant player in the computer industry, despite inventing world-class technologies. The company continued to focus on the traditional copier business and, too slowly, shifted its strategy to document management. Xerox has continued to change as the market has changed, but it has lost much of its leadership to a range of other companies that were not seen as their competitors a decade ago.

The accounting problems were clearly a mistake that exacerbated Xerox's attempts to change. This was not the precipitating event of the fall from grace; it merely accelerated the loss of respect in the financial and investor community.

Finally, was it a really a mistake for Xerox to fail to commercialize PARC's computer-related technologies? Or was it just a clumsy way of carrying out a decision the company made to not be in the computer industry?

If it was Xerox's intent to not be involved in the computer industry, should they have sold off products and/or licenses rather than letting the concepts leak out into the market as Apple's standard-setting menus, graphical user interface, and WYSIWYG (what you see is what you get) displays did? If they intended to be a significant player, then this was a mistake chain.

But the biggest mistake of all may have been that they were not sure what they wanted to do, made no conscious decisions, and just "went with the flow" until the market made them a nonplayer. Whenever I have been involved in strategy work, I have always advised that the biggest and most dangerous decision that executives make is to not make a decision. As we said in Chapter 1, "There is no partial credit in the Fleet."

Opinions on whether this was a mistake chain for Xerox would likely vary between two extremes, depending on who you asked and when. By the early 1990s, most would have considered this mistake chain a serious failure for Xerox. But by the first half of 1999, Xerox stock was at an all-time high, and some would have said, "Are you crazy? Xerox is doing just fine in their core business. Why would they want to be in the computer business where the prices are dropping and the competition is getting worse?"

Others might have responded, "Of course they made a mistake with PARC. They would be one of the top computer companies in the world now if they had just paid attention to commercializing what they came up with instead of focusing on the original business."

While many of Xerox PARC's technologies are legendary, the companies that commercialized them, such as Apple, Adobe, and 3Com, have not had continuous smooth sailing. Apple is a great company but a niche player. Adobe is well known but has not lived up to expectations, and 3Com has lost the market it invented to Cisco. As for personal computers, all the value has gone to the consumer in the form of lower prices and higher performance, while Dell calls the shots with their extraordinary ability to manage manufacturing, logistics, and customer service.

Xerox's current focus is on the high end of their markets—production operations and offices, excluding small and home offices. Where are the bottlenecks in production and offices today? Not with computing or networking.

Problems with powerful computing, standard office applications, and networking have been solved and will see only incremental improvements going forward. The real bottleneck is with integration of data in separate databases, document integration, and knowledge management—all areas where Xerox has been working hard and where PARC and other Xerox assets have made significant contributions.

Perhaps this was not a mistake chain. Perhaps this was an apparent mistake chain that, once started and evaluated, was allowed to run its course because the company realized it did not want to be in the industries it helped seed. Perhaps this has left Xerox focused on the "next big thing," with unique assets that will give it a competitive advantage. Xerox's new competitors may well be Microsoft, EDS, IBM, SAP, and others that seek to integrate offices and business processes. Xerox has invested significantly in technologies and service capabilities to serve these markets and has even acquired or seeded a number of entrepreneurial operations to commercialize technologies important to the new vision.

It took a long time, but perhaps what we have witnessed at Xerox is "breaking the chain" of mistakes that many thought had already been fatal. But the market is evolving rapidly. Did they learn enough? The next few years will be interesting, and not making further mistakes, strategically or operationally, will be critical to Xerox.

There is some irony in the fact that Xerox became successful independently because many of the large companies of the 1940s and 1950s did not want to own them. It will be interesting to see if they can become a leader once again or will fall victim to their own mentality that turned down serious entry into the computer business, just as Chester Carlson's innovation was rejected a half century ago.

> **Insight #18: Sometimes a mistake is not a mistake.** If a mistake is a wrong action, then we have to make some judgment about whether a strategic business decision is "right" or "wrong," and that may not be obvious as quickly as we think. This reinforces the importance of continuing analysis of decisions after the fact and potential future scenarios, which we will discuss subsequently.

Motorola's Reinventions—Does a Cat Have Nine Lives?

My dad worked for a company that was a wholesale distributor for products from Motorola and a few other (noncompetitive) manufacturers. I have never forgotten an incident that occurred sometime in the early 1950s when I was seven or eight years old. He returned from a business trip to Chicago and at dinnertime pulled a small device out of his pocket, dropped it on the table, and said, "This is going to make it possible to hang a TV on the wall in a picture frame someday."

We were all suitably impressed, especially as we glanced into the living room and looked at the huge piece of mahogany furniture wrapped around the Motorola TV. What dad had in his hand was a single transistor. I do not know what happened to it, but I remember it vividly. It was a rectangular volume about the size of an eraser assembly on the end of a wooden pencil, encased in black plastic with three wires coming out of the bottom for connections to a circuit board. Dad predicted that Motorola would have the "picture frame TV" within 10 to 12 years.

Motorola started in 1928 when brothers Paul and Joseph Galvin purchased a battery eliminator* company and incorporated as Galvin

---

* In the early days of radio, batteries powered all radios. As more homes became electrified, consumers sought devices that would allow them to eliminate the batteries—usually messy lead-acid types.

Manufacturing Corporation. By 1930, the Galvins had developed the world's first practical car radio, introduced with the "Motorola" brand, followed in 1936 by a police radio. In the years leading up to World War II, Galvin Manufacturing introduced a variety of Motorola radio and phonograph products for the home market. In 1943, the famous "walkie-talkie" was developed under contract with the Army Signal Corps.

Following the war, the company developed a gasoline-powered heater for automobiles, but this ended up as their first significant failure. When the product was dropped, Paul Galvin indicated that "Galvin Manufacturing Corporation will now stick to electronics."[18]

In 1947, Galvin Manufacturing, under the Motorola brand, brought out the first TV priced under $200 (a fair amount of money then) and sold 100,000 in the first year. The Motorola brand became so well known that Galvin Manufacturing Corporation changed its name to Motorola, Inc.

One of my first memories is of my dad bringing a "portable" Motorola TV* to the hospital ward where I was a patient in 1948. Every person in the hospital who could walk showed up in the ward where I was at 4 PM to see TV for the first time in his or her life, and it was *Howdy Doody*— the only show other than the news on television that day.

Motorola grew rapidly in the consumer market, along with other manufacturers, as the technology improved, the networks began to produce programs, sponsors lined up, and the public became addicted to the boob tube, hi-fi phonographs, and portable radios. Motorola also continued to innovate in communications and semiconductor design and manufacturing, having had the foresight to establish a research and development (R&D) facility in Phoenix in 1949.

While other consumer electronics manufacturers such as RCA, Philco, Zenith, and Magnavox followed a strategy that took them into a land of undifferentiated commodities, Motorola was thinking about where their competencies could best be utilized for the future. By the 1970s, Motorola began to believe they could get a better return on their assets if they were deployed in communications and high-tech electronics, including semiconductors.

Motorola created the Quasar TV in 1967, the first all-transistor color TV, with the "works in a drawer"† for easy servicing. By 1974, Motorola

---

* If my memory serves me, it wasn't really "portable," just a table model that one or two able-bodied men could carry.

† Their marketing slogan for the new product.

sold its entire television business to Japan's Matsushita Electric, which continued marketing under the Quasar brand. Motorola redeployed its assets to focus on communications and semiconductor technologies and products, becoming one of the world leaders in its chosen fields.

Motorola's first 16-bit microprocessor in 1977 was soon followed by the world's first portable cell phone in 1984. (It weighed 1.7 pounds.) They became dominant in the cell phone business and, by the early 1990s, were in an alliance with Apple and IBM to produce what would become, and still are, some of the most powerful microprocessors in the world.

Innovation and reinvention happened so regularly at Motorola that we could call them core competencies. During its first 65 years, Motorola:

- Shifted from the battery eliminator business into radios
- Moved from fixed to mobile communications
- Was an early pioneer in television
- Successfully exited the television business while it still had value
- Developed specialized integrated circuits for use in many industries
- Became a world leader in cellular technologies and products
- Became a significant player in semiconductor manufacturing
- Developed some of the world's most powerful microprocessors

Motorola successfully reinvented itself a number of times as technologies changed, competitors changed, and industrial and consumer markets and preferences changed. The mistakes they made were few, their R&D was effective, market decisions were excellent, and they globalized successfully. Significant in this continuing reinvention was a commitment to the development of people and processes as they built one of the world's most respected training organizations.

Motorola received a signal that they had a quality problem when Matsushita was immediately able to improve quality in the Quasar line they purchased from Motorola. By the early 1980s, Motorola had begun a relentless effort to improve quality that became known as "Six Sigma™," a term now familiar to most business people and a rallying cry for business improvement around the world.

But the last few years have not been kind to Motorola. Revenues peaked in 2000 at nearly $38 billion and have since declined by nearly

30 percent. Net income went from $1.8 billion in 2000 to a loss of $2.4 billion in 2002, with improvement in 2003 to a $900 million profit on no revenue growth. Returns on capital and shareholder equity are each down by 75 percent since they peaked in 1994.

With such a significant history of innovation and reinvention, how did Motorola manage to stumble so badly in recent years? The mistakes can be found in both strategy and execution:

- **Motorola was the world leader in cell phone sales until Nokia came along** and made cell phones even smaller and, perhaps more importantly, stylish. Motorola went from being a leader to a follower as cell phones took on fashion characteristics.

- **Motorola was slow to engage the shift from analog to digital cell phone technology** and was again competitively disadvantaged by the upstarts like Nokia. Motorola's global market share has dropped from over 30 percent to 15 to 16 percent. Telecom companies like the newer digital technology because it uses bandwidth more efficiently and makes new services possible. Customers like it because the phones are smaller and use less power, meaning batteries last longer. Motorola somehow did not see this coming, even though they supply other equipment to make the systems work for the telecom companies.

- **The semiconductor business has lost money for a number of years** as product cycles have shortened, specialized application needs have multiplied, and new players around the world have commoditized the segment. Late in 2003, Motorola announced that their semiconductor business would be spun out as a separate company.

- **Parts shortage for new generation phones.** In 2002, the company did not anticipate demand for color-screen phones and had problems meeting demand. In 2003, they had a similar problem but with lenses for cameras built into phones.

- **Iridium, one of the most colossal failures in business history,** was a technologist's approach to solving the "ultimate problem" for wireless communications—covering virtually every part of the earth with satellite reception. This was a major strategic mistake that had its own mistake chain:

- ◆ **A complex system involving satellites and new types of phones meant development time was too long** for a market where technology changes rapidly. The system was conceived in the late 1980s, publicly announced in 1990, but did not begin to operate until late 1998.
- ◆ **Potential customer estimates were exaggerated.** Much less expensive terrestrial wireless systems evolved quickly, making great coverage possible nearly all the time for nearly all the populations of developed countries.
- ◆ **Pricing was extraordinary.** At $2 to $7 per minute plus, with a $2,500 phone and monthly fees, only the most desperate customers were likely to sign up and use such a service. Prices were later reduced but to little avail.
- ◆ **Capital requirements were huge,** requiring complex financing from Motorola guaranteed debt, equity raised in an IPO, and investments from Hewlett-Packard, Lockheed Martin, Raytheon, Sprint, and Siemens.

This left Iridium with a small market, a phone the size and weight of a brick that would not receive inside a building, and very high rates. A maximum of 50,000 customers signed up in the first year, less than 10 percent of those needed to achieve breakeven. Bankruptcy was inevitable before it began operations. More than $5.5 billion was spent on Iridium by the group of partners, investors, and suppliers. Motorola wrote off over $1 billion as their portion of the investment, loans, and loan guarantees.

Ironically, Iridium is still operating under an agreement with an entrepreneur who essentially received rights to operate the system without the burden of the capital costs, allowing for more competitive pricing. Technology has made possible a phone that is smaller and lighter than the original, and government contracts have provided a base business. There is a market for wireless service to remote locations, but it may never be large enough as a viable business without subsidy or special arrangements.

- ■ **Leadership instability during the 1990s** is a serious issue that has recently come to a head for Motorola. The Galvin brothers founded the company with an insight into a very specific market need and did an amazing job evolving the company with the times and new technologies. Paul Galvin ran the company until 1956, and his son Robert W. Galvin ran Motorola for 30 years, turning the reins over to George Fisher, a Motorola insider who ran the company until he left in 1993 to run Kodak (unsuccessfully). Gary Tooker, another insider, followed Fisher, and Robert Galvin's son Christopher became CEO in 1996. Chris Galvin was fired in late 2003 by the board and was replaced with Edward J. Zander, the first outsider to run Motorola in its 75-year history. Some effective stability at the top would be useful internally and for external confidence for Motorola.

Motorola's history of reinventing itself, shifting products and product lines as customers' preferences and market conditions change, has been world-class. Its push into quality and productivity through Six Sigma and employee education has had dramatic results for the company and indirect results for the U.S. economy as these principles have been emulated and adopted by others. Process improvement is only part of the picture in a successful company, however.

The challenge faced by Motorola, and other companies that are so successful that they become large and complex, is that growth opportunities become harder to find, and it becomes more difficult to articulate a single unified strategy that is viable. This is when companies realize that *capabilities* are more important than specific products, and the quest becomes finding profitable applications for those capabilities or asking whether it is time to develop or acquire new capabilities.

Just as with Xerox, Motorola's recent subpar performance is not due to a chain of related mistakes that will ruin the entire company, but the unfortunate confluence of strategic and execution mistakes in different parts of a multisegment business. The mistakes are of similar types, however, that, if systemic and not corrected, have the potential to ruin the business. Note that fixing these mistakes has more to do with refining or developing competencies rather than fixing processes:

- **Design philosophy.** Consumer electronic products today sell with sizzle because the feature set of most products is similar, with any new innovation copied rapidly. Motorola has not had a history of having the "hip" products, but this is likely to be a necessary competence if they intend to continue as leaders in consumer segments.

- **Design speed.** Product life cycles are shorter in all arenas, and speed to market is needed in every segment. The digital conversion in cell phones and the addition of cameras to cell phones both left Motorola playing catch up. I do not personally want or need a camera phone, but millions of consumers do, and Motorola needs to learn to play the product extension game more effectively, as they have in the past. Some ask why Motorola, the inventor of pagers, did not develop the BlackBerry™ or why they have not been players in satellite radio. Did they consider these extensions and not pursue them, or did they not even look at the possibilities?

- **Supply chain execution.** The recent parts shortages may be isolated incidents, but they are not a good sign for a company with such an outstanding reputation in quality manufacturing.

- **More focus on technology commercialization cycles.** The Iridium business case was an indication of an organization seriously out of touch with reality. The red flags began to wave long before the project was launched in the market. There was a failure to understand customers, costs, and alternatives. The phrase "sunk costs are irrelevant" comes to mind. Realizing that a project is in trouble, what often distracts managers and executives is what has been spent and will have to written off rather than the likely business case for the project under changed conditions. A good idea in 1986 turned into a questionable idea by the early 1990s and a bad idea by the mid-1990s, but the plan to go to market with a very expensive service went forward. Others were involved, but Motorola, as the founder of Iridium, should have cut their losses and pulled the plug much earlier.

Motorola's capabilities are in electronics, and most would argue that any company with great strengths should continue to focus in areas they know. Even the areas where they have had great success are changing, however, and other traditional hardware manufacturers are getting into services. Apple is selling music online, and IBM derives more than 60 percent of its revenue from software and services. Is Motorola going to need to develop new competencies and approaches for the future to avoid further mistakes?

Insight #19: Even companies that have successfully reinvented themselves have to work hard, perhaps even harder, to understand when it is time to do so again. Motorola reinvented itself when it was early to the new TV market and when it sold Quasar and committed everything to communications and semiconductors. It made a huge leap from older communications products based on single sideband technologies to cellular communications. A number of strategic blunders that no one expected from a company with that history caused it to stumble as the twentieth century closed.

Kodak–Doing Everything "Right" for 100 Years

Kodak almost never made a mistake. They did everything right in the film-based photography industry for over 100 years. You cannot say they failed to innovate; Kodak scientists and engineers were granted 19,576 U.S. patents during the twentieth century[19]. You cannot say they failed to market; one of the best known brands around the world is Kodak, and virtually everyone in the United States has owned a Kodak camera, used film packaged in a yellow box, or had photographs processed at an outlet using Kodak paper and chemicals.

They did everything "right," but they are in trouble. Kodak's year-over-year film sales declined* in 2002[20], and in 2003[21], for the first time, the board decreased the dividend on the stock. At the same time, Kodak announced they were focusing their energies and resources on the digital market going forward, in essence using film-based profits and the dividend reduction to fund the investments needed for their new strategy.

Kodak's problem is a simple one. They make too much money. Other than Coca-Cola syrup, there is probably no product on the face of the earth that has been so highly profitable, so consistently, for so long as chemical-based imaging and processing. This is not to say that Kodak has not worked hard, been very productive in R&D, had great foresight in creating markets, and touched all of us with products and capabilities that provided value for which we willingly parted with money.

---

* Decline in volume of consumer film products for 2001 to 2002 was 2 percent globally and 7 percent for the United States, but when price and mix changes were included, the declines were 6 percent and 12 percent, respectively.

There are two problems: digital photography and Fujifilm. The last decade has been a difficult, competitive environment for filmmakers. Fujifilm and Kodak have been engaged in a bitter rivalry that in 1997 went beyond a quality war and into an ugly price war. The net result is that you can buy top-quality consumer-type film for less than you could a decade ago. Price wars rarely help any competitor in the long run, but Fujifilm is good enough that Kodak was forced to play along or lose even more market share.

It has been clear for a decade or more to those of us who follow emerging technologies that Kodak was a company in trouble, for reasons beyond the competition from Fujifilm. It was not a question of "if" the new digital technologies would be disruptive for Kodak; it was a question of "when."

Disruptive technologies changed many industries over the last couple of centuries. The concept was studied and described in some detail by Clayton Christensen in his book, *The Innovator's Dilemma*[22], where he points out that nearly all technology-based companies, even good ones, do the "right" thing by evolving their capabilities and then fail because they cannot see a disruption coming. The very act of being the best and knowing more than anyone else about your technologies makes you blind to the changes that are coming.

The origins of digital photography actually go back to the 1950s when Bing Crosby studios developed, with Ampex, the first video tape recorder where an electrical impulse was recorded on magnetic tape to store movies. By the 1960s and 1970s, NASA began shifting to filmless cameras to be able to transmit pictures back from space, with Kodak providing some of the technology. Sony brought out a digital camera in 1981, but it produced still photographs by freeze-framing a movie.

But Kodak did see the new technology coming and was right in the middle of its evolution. In 1986, their scientists created the world's first 1.4 megapixel sensor that could record enough data to produce a 5×7 print that looked something like a photograph. It was crude and the resolution was poor, but it was the beginning of digital photography—and Kodak was an innovator. By 1987, Kodak was introducing digital products into the market and, by the early 1990s, brought out a high-end professional digital camera along with their Photo CD system targeted toward consumers.

The Photo CD system was high priced and ahead of its time. One of the problems with new technologies, from airplanes to medical science, is the issue of converging technologies. The convergence was not there when Kodak brought out Photo CD because most people did not have computers at home and the Internet did not exist in the easy-to-use form we have today. But worst of all, Kodak decided they would use their own proprietary format for the CDs and sell you a special player ($400 but it also played audio CDs) to view the pictures with a TV or computer monitor. I have been an amateur photographer all my life, but I looked at this and said, "You must be kidding. I'll stick with my slides and slide trays." Most consumers said the same thing, and the product flopped.

Insight #20: With disruptive technology, prices usually drop and value shifts to customers—ignore this at your peril.

During the 1980s, Kodak saw a need to diversify and use the wide range of technological capabilities they had developed. They entered many markets including batteries, storage mediums (floppy disk and others), clinical laboratory machines, and pharmaceuticals. When George Fisher arrived as CEO (from Motorola) in 1993, they began to reverse the diversification by selling or shutting down these operations.

Kodak brought out a line of digital cameras for consumers and professionals, but so did every company who had any relationship to the photography, computer, or printing business. In 2001, Kodak purchased Ofoto, an online digital-processing company, when they began to realize customers would want to print some pictures, compose albums for sharing, and have a repository for images. Joint ventures were abundant for technology development and marketing, including Phogenix, to develop mini-labs for retail photofinishing with Hewlett-Packard. Continued evaluation showed that decent returns were unlikely, and the venture was shut down in 2003. By 2002, Kodak had over 39,000 kiosks in place around the world for printing pictures using thermal imaging technologies.

By early 2004, Kodak announced it had plans to reduce headcount by 15,000, about 20 percent of its workforce at the time, by 2006. The company pointed out that this was part of the effort that would be required to get costs down in a world where, even if they are a leader, their revenues and profitability are likely to shrink for some time.

Kodak will be in business for many years to come, but they will not be the money machine they were for nearly a century. While their largest business segment, traditional photography, will continue to decline in developed markets, they have shown dramatic growth in developing markets, especially China. Despite the rapid growth of digital photography, it will not replace chemical-based imaging immediately or completely. This is analogous to the transistor replacing vacuum tubes— it happened over a number of years. In fact, there are still some vacuum tubes sold today for specialized purposes such as high-end audio amplifiers, which some audiophiles believe produce sound with more "character" than solid state models.

Second, film-based photography may grow for years in developing countries because there is little capital cost and no infrastructure required in the home. Even in more affluent areas, there are many consumers who are not likely to switch to digital technology. Some amateur and professional photographers will always believe they can do more with film, especially under certain conditions, and there are those who are not comfortable with technology, especially computers, who will never see a good reason to switch.

Kodak's next largest segment, medical imaging, has done well and is not beset with the same problems, but it is not immune either from competition or technology changes. In other areas, Kodak's scientists continue to develop technologies that have significant potential, especially things like organic light emitting diodes (OLED). This technology, pioneered and patented by Kodak, has immense potential to replace traditional LEDs because it requires less power, is more compact, and produces more vibrant colors.

Kodak has an amazing past and a promising future, but it may never again be the dominant player in a segment as it was in the past. Having said this, what mistakes did Kodak managers and executives make?

- **Loss of focus** when they deployed their capabilities in a number of other industries during the 1980s, although some would say that they needed to do this given the potential for disruptive technology. In either case, it was a loss of focus. They either lost focus on the core business or lost focus on the goal of diversification, but either way, the diversification did little to advance Kodak.

- **Failure to aggressively commercialize digital technologies.** Although they tried to begin this, their initial efforts were not guided by good product development and marketing principles because their financial expectations were probably too high, using their traditional business as a guide.

- **Too much focus on physical products in the traditional business.** The last stage of most maturing technologies is a flurry of incremental products. Kodak launched hundreds in the last decade, including the weakly received Advantix film system based on a common industry standard (APS) that Kodak developed in collaboration with others in the industry.

- **Too little focus on services in the traditional business.** As it became clear that the business was changing, Kodak missed opportunities to help consumers, even those with film-based pictures. Our wedding pictures were lost in a move some years ago. Would a segment of the population pay a small fee annually to have Kodak safely store their negatives (or digital files)? Kodak has recently entered the image and information management sector, but businesses could have been interested in innovative products in this arena much earlier. Kodak only thought of continuing revenue on the basis of developing another roll of film, not around extension of services that could have been easily provided.

Insight #21: Some changes happen without your permission. Learn to recognize the signs and get on board early.

Insight #22: Many more industries and companies will see the value continue to shift from hardware to software and services. Even companies like Motorola and Kodak, which at one time thought they were primarily manufacturers, are likely to move more deeply into services for growth.

Recognizing Strategy Mistakes and Competitive Changes

As you read this chapter, has it occurred to you that perhaps Xerox, Motorola, and Kodak are the primary competitors in a new "info-image-document management" (IIDM) sector and just don't know it yet? The origin and history of these companies is around physical products with services mixed in, but technology and customer needs are pushing them into many of the same customer segments. There are major differences, of course, but the truth is that in many industries (such as electronics, financial services, pharmaceuticals, consumer products, utilities) the traditional clear boundaries that separated companies and their businesses and customers have become blurred.

How then does management recognize a strategic mistake chain? It is neither easy nor exact, particularly because of the time dimension discussed earlier. But there are some clues that should set off some alarms for further investigation.

The Dirty Dozen Strategy Deficiency Clues

- **Employees don't understand the strategy.** Most organizations endure some sort of internal grousing about the direction of the business. Some of this is a failure to communicate on management's part, but do not dismiss these comments capriciously. They are often early indicators, from those on the front lines who are in a position to know, that things are not going as well as you might believe.

  A colleague tells the story about a marketing executive who arrived for work at Kodak in the mid-1990s, and the first meeting he went to was a shouting match about the future of digital photography. The hard-liners said digital cameras were never going to be in Kodak's future, while the new hires all battled for a digital vision of the future. The new executive said he knew within two weeks of being at Kodak that he had made a huge career mistake. Everyone was in denial of digital imaging. He was gone in exactly one year.

- **"Surprise" competitive products,** usually characterized by a sick feeling in the gut when you pickup a newspaper or trade journal and see that a competitor has announced a breakthrough product or service that you thought was beyond their competence. If Motorola owned the pager business at some point, why did RIM bring the BlackBerry to market? Did Motorola think there was no opportunity there, or did they ignore it because it was too small? For all of its history in radio, why doesn't Motorola have a position in satellite radio? Motorola did announce a chipset to improve sound quality in radios that receive existing AM and FM signals, but the press release sounds like a defense as to why they are not in the satellite radio market.[23]

- **"Surprise" competitors.** This is similar to the surprise product problem, but it makes you feel even worse when you realize that a company you have never heard of or thought was insignificant is in your space stealing your customers. Is Kodak surprised to find Dell selling cameras? Probably not at this stage because everyone is moving into their space.

- **Missed opportunities**—another way to look at surprise products, pre-emptive market entry by others, technical breakthroughs you had on the shelf, and other forms of business humiliation.
- **Looking outside for growth or technology** because organic growth has become difficult if not impossible.
- **Difficulty finding opportunities.** Is it the people, the technology, or the market?
- **Early to market, early to lose.** Kodak was too early with Photo CD and too late with more broadly applicable products.
- **Loss of pricing power on flat or declining volume**—the first stage of commoditization.
- **Indirect loss of pricing power** (for example, more free add-ins), an indication of increased competitive pressure.
- **No returns on R&D.** Xerox might have said this about PARC at some point, but the answer depends on the time frame for evaluation.
- **Feeling your competencies are undifferentiated.** If you are really honest, are you competitors as good as you are in most respects?
- **Declining price/earnings (P/E) and financials.** Unfortunately this is a look in the rearview mirror, not an early warning indicator. By the time you see this, you usually have very serious problems.

You will examine some ways to deal with these signals when you see them in a subsequent chapter, but the first step is to create a culture that is willing to ask questions about the preceding items and be honest about the answers.

Xerox, Motorola, and Kodak are amazing companies that have contributed mightily with technological accomplishments, growth, and profitability for decades. But success and size make it tougher to keep being that good for 50 to 100 years. Each faces unique challenges, but they have similarities. The associated insights from their stories are worth reviewing again:

Insight #16: A very successful business can blind you to opportunity. This is because you will make comparative judgments on the basis of current business criteria that may not last while underestimating the potential of new businesses that have not yet grown far enough to show their full potential. Being successful also raises, often inappropriately, your confidence in your own decision-making.

Insight #17: Your competitors are not who you think they are. Until recently, Xerox did not realize that the biggest threat to the copier business in smaller market segments was not Canon or Minolta but Hewlett-Packard and the laser printer that Xerox invented.

Insight #18: Sometimes a mistake is not a mistake. If a mistake is a wrong action, then we have to make some judgment about whether a strategic business decision is "right" or "wrong," and that may not be obvious as quickly as we think. This reinforces the importance of continuing analysis of decisions after the fact and potential future scenarios, which we will discuss subsequently.

Insight #19: Even companies that have successfully reinvented themselves have to work hard, perhaps even harder, to understand when it is time to do so again. Motorola reinvented itself when it was early to the new TV market and when it sold Quasar and committed everything to communications and semiconductors. It made a huge leap from older communications products based on single sideband technologies to cellular communications. A number of strategic blunders that no one expected from a company with that history caused it to stumble as the twentieth century closed.

Insight #20: With disruptive technology, prices usually drop and value shifts to customers—ignore this at your peril.

Insight #21: Some changes happen without your permission. Learn to recognize the signs and get on board early.

Insight #22: Many more industries and companies will see the value continue to shift from hardware to software and services. Even companies like Motorola and Kodak, which at one time thought they were primarily manufacturers, are likely to move more deeply into services for growth.

5

Physical Disasters with Cultural Foundations and Business Implications

"The last line of defense against errors is usually a safety system."

—Columbia Accident Investigation Board 2003[24]

We have seen a number of business mistake chains related to execution, strategy, or both. We have hinted that some of these, such as Xerox, Intel, and Kodak, also involved strong cultural underpinnings that made it easier for a mistake chain to start and/or continue, whereas cultural forces helped save a company like J&J from what could have been a disaster. In this and two subsequent chapters, we will examine the cultural context for mistakes because this turns out to be one of the strongest forces driving multiple-mistake scenarios, regardless of industry.

Titanic, Three Mile Island, and NASA's space shuttles *Challenger* and *Columbia* were worlds apart in time and technology, but each created front-page headlines for months. Your initial thought might be that the 70- to 90-year time span would yield few similarities across these disasters. Yet if it were not for multiple mistakes of the most severe variety, the instant worldwide recognition of names like *Titanic,* Three Mile Island (TMI), *Challenger,* and *Columbia* would not exist.

Both *Titanic* and TMI involved systems whose designers understood that the benefits of new, advanced technologies also require a measure of caution to ensure safe operation. In both cases, very specific design decisions were made that were oriented toward improving performance and safety with minimal operator intervention, but in both cases, humans interfered with the safety designs in one way or another. The result was designs that appeared safe but turned out to be far more dangerous than imagined. In NASA's case, the technologies were in an earlier stage of evolution and were less robust that previously believed. The real issue for NASA, however, was not the technology but human decision-making that was at the heart of the mistake chain.

Mistakes made by humans is a common theme throughout the incidents described in this book, but *Titanic*, TMI, and NASA are special cases because they are such extreme examples of assumptions that were incorrect, systems that were misunderstood, and actions that exhibited extraordinary lack of preparation and insight. In short, these were disasters that were completely preventable, but incorrect human actions either created or failed to stop a dangerous sequence of events that led to disaster.

No, these are not business disasters, but they have much to teach you. You could be only a few employees away from a disaster of this magnitude because in some of the largest, best-known, and most damaging business and physical disasters in history, it took surprisingly few people, with the power to make decisions or execute, to do the damage. In these examples, the combination of cultural arrogance and poor execution was truly stunning.

Titanic

When the movie *Titanic* came out, my wife was eager to see it. I, of course, joked that I didn't need to see a mushy love story, especially one where I knew the ending. We all know the ending because the 1912 saga of the *Titanic* is one of the saddest, most publicized disasters of the twentieth century. It was made popular for another couple of generations by the 1985 discovery of the wreckage and recovery of artifacts, along with the 1997 Academy Award–winning movie.

Walter Lord tells the stories[25] of two great ships, the *Titanic* and *Great Eastern*, each of which suffered hull damage below the waterline. *Great Eastern* was constructed in 1858 and was a monster for her time, at 680 feet in length with a double hull and enough bulkheads to provide 50 watertight compartments to improve survivability in the event of damage. While not her originally intended mission, she plied the North Atlantic for a few years and then struck an uncharted rock in 1862 in Long Island Sound, resulting in an 83-foot-long, 9-foot-wide gash in the outer hull. The reason you may not have heard of the *Great Eastern* is that her first line of defense, the double hull, worked and her inner hull held, allowing her to steam into New York Harbor.

Although this technical design saved the *Great Eastern*, she was a victim of multiple mistakes as a business venture. She was a massive and innovative ship for her day, with steam-driven twin paddle wheels and a center screw along with six masts for sails. She was designed to compete effectively with fast clipper ships on the England-to-Far East route around the Cape of Good Hope. She was large enough to carry 4,000 passengers and cargo but was also large enough to carry enough coal for a round-trip voyage since coal was not available everywhere along her intended routes.

The complexity resulting from her size and safety enhancements was compounded by the use of a new material—iron—for her hull. At this early stage, the weight and lack of experience with iron as a shipbuilding material resulted in a tedious process of riveting plates (strips) of iron together to form the hull*. This meant an expensive learning process for shipbuilders and a very slow construction process. The project was so large and expensive that it attracted great notoriety, and it is reported that 10,000 people showed up to witness the launching, which actually failed because the ship was so large that the builders could not get it to move off the shipway until hydraulic jacks were used a year later.

By the time she was completed the Suez Canal had opened, but *Great Eastern* was too big for passage, so even the slower, less capable ships she was designed to pass on the voyage around the Cape of Good Hope could now complete the shorter route much faster, making *Great Eastern* a technical marvel that was instantly obsolete.[26] She began transatlantic passenger service and had very limited success. Her greatest success,

---

* Later, steel was used with rivets, and eventually welding advanced the design and construction process. The shift from iron to steel, which continued to improve quality, and from rivets to welding improved strength and reduced weight.

after bankrupting a few owners, came after conversion to the world's first cable laying ship, laying the first transatlantic cable in 1866. She finished her life from 1885 to 1888 ignominiously as a floating amusement park. It is reported that even when she was finally sold for scrap in 1888, she was built with such strength that it took 200 men two years to dismantle her.

Great Eastern was a ship that avoided the physical disaster that later struck *Titanic*, but it was a business disaster for a whole series of owners, perhaps with the exception of the salvage yard that took her apart for scrap; it may have made the largest profit anyone did from owning *Great Eastern*. From a business perspective, the mistakes included:

- Being socially responsible regarding safety at a time when the technology was still too cumbersome to make it affordable, which resulted in overengineering for safety and size at the expense of cost and flexibility of operation
- Assuming that people would want to travel on a ship carrying 4,000 passengers
- Assuming that there would be no impact of the Suez Canal on the operating assumptions

This mistake chain is fairly benign as multiple mistakes go, and while this disaster hurt investors and owners, it did not hurt passengers. In fact, the ship was so massive and complex to build that the jobs created probably benefited the local economy in England. But this was a business disaster nonetheless. Unfortunately, the safety lessons learned here from innovative advanced design features did not carry over to the *Titanic*.

Within a few years, other ships began using advanced safety features, and Brander discusses the case of the liner *Arizona*[27] that hit an iceberg while doing 15 knots in dense fog. *Arizona*'s bow telescoped (collapsed) 25 feet, but because she had transverse bulkheads that went all the way to the top deck, she survived and made port in Halifax. This and other incidents helped increase public perception that iron and steel ships were safe. We could even argue that the advanced safety features incorporated into *Great Eastern* and later ships worked so well that the public, especially operators and naval architects, became overconfident about the safety of the "modern" ships of the day. As competitive pressures increased, tradeoffs and compromises were made.

We can assume that when *Titanic* was launched 53 years after *Great Eastern*, marine architects knew of the success of the safety aspect of designs like *Great Eastern* and *Arizona*. They probably also knew that *Great Eastern* was a commercial failure and from all accounts made commercial versus safety tradeoffs. *Titanic* and her sister ships, *Olympic* and *Britannic*, were designed as the largest ships of their day at nearly 900 feet in length and had double hulls and *supposedly* watertight compartments.

The White Star Line set out to build the ships with an emphasis on speed and world-class comfort, but they clearly did not want to repeat the business folly of the *Great Eastern*. While safety was apparently a concern, there clearly was not enough learning from the well-engineered design of the *Great Eastern* that included 15 transverse bulkheads and one longitudinal bulkhead along with watertight lower decks. Significantly, *Great Eastern*'s bulkheads were built up to 30 feet above the waterline.

Titanic's designers divided her into 16 separate compartments using 15 transverse bulkheads but no longitudinal bulkhead. Additionally, the bulkheads were only 10 feet above the waterline versus *Great Eastern*'s 30 feet. As Lord put it:

> "Passengers demanded attention; stewards could serve them more easily if doors were cut in the watertight bulkheads. A grand staircase required a spacious opening at every level, making a watertight deck impossible. ... A double hull ate up valuable passenger and cargo space; a double bottom would be enough."[28]

The result was a design that was hailed as both an engineering marvel and the most lavish ship to ever sail. *Titanic* offered every modern luxury and convenience, and J. Bruce Ismay, managing director of the White Star Line, believed this would allow his company to compete with the Cunard Line's already faster ships[29]. Often referred to as a "floating palace," *Titanic* also included windows forward on the A deck to shield passengers from spray, and the Café Parisian was designed to give the air of a Paris sidewalk restaurant.

But the lack of true watertight compartments was a design mistake made to accommodate fashion and convenience that was perhaps the mostly deadly mistake in the long chain. Truly watertight compartments* require the ability to fully isolate all sources of entry or exit of water. It is possible to put isolation valves in piping and ventilation systems, but for a door to be watertight it must be capable of being "dogged," or secured with multiple strong mechanisms all the way around. This is the reason why watertight doors (as in warships) have an oval opening, including a lower section that provides watertight integrity at the bottom. You must step over this lower portion of the bulkhead to get through each door. While desirable aboard warships, the thought of well-dressed ladies tripping as they stepped up and over the lips of watertight doors was obviously thought to be undesirable aboard the most fashionable luxury liner in the world. The designers considered this safety enhancement unnecessary above a certain height above the waterline, in this case 10 feet, a judgment that would prove to be disastrous.

In fact, this mistake was so serious that one could argue that there was almost no way to prevent a serious catastrophe with this design once a collision of any significance occurred. However, there were many other human mistakes that contributed to the collision itself and significantly increased the needless loss of life. The public's perception was that *Titanic* was unsinkable, something that was the result of press coverage that discussed the claim that she could stay afloat with 2 of her 16 compartments flooded, thus labeling the ship as "practically unsinkable."

Those who were superstitious might have been worried about certain events as *Titanic's* departure time approached. It had been four years from the conception of plans for the sister ships *Olympic*, *Britannic*, and *Titanic* until the sailing of *Titanic* in 1912, and her owners were eager to have her begin to generate revenue. Sea trials were abbreviated to one day following a weather delay. Immediately upon completion of sea trials, she made the voyage from Belfast to Southampton for final work, provisioning, and to pick up passengers. A near collision with the moored liner *New York* was not a good sign as *Titanic* left port in Southampton en route to Cherbourg to pick up additional passengers. During the early days of the voyage, the crew had to cope with a coalbunker fire, a wireless that did not work, and other new-vessel-related items.

---

* To understand a truly watertight compartment, remember the case of the battleship *USS Oklahoma* (BB-37) that capsized when Japan attacked Pearl Harbor on December 7, 1941. In the next few days, 32 men were cut out of the hull of *Oklahoma*. They survived because true watertight compartments kept the water out and provided an air pocket that allowed them to survive until rescued.

Provisions boarded at Southampton included all the necessary linens, china, food, and drink befitting the finest luxury liner of the time. Among the items on the list of provisions were 40 tons of potatoes, 6,000 pounds of butter, 12,000 dinner plates, and 7,500 bath towels. Drinks reflected the mix of three classes of passengers and their preferences for 20,000 bottles of beer, 1,200 bottles of wine, 850 bottles of spirits, and 15,000 bottles of mineral water.[30]

Workmen were still finishing final touches on paint and carpet as passengers arrived. *Titanic* departed Southampton on April 10 with a fuel load of 4,400 tons of coal that her owners managed to acquire only because other liners' trips were cancelled because of a coal strike.

One of the modern conveniences aboard *Titanic* was a wireless telegraph set with two operators provided by Marconi's under agreement with the White Star Line. Known as Cable & Wireless today, The Wireless Telegraph and Signal Company was founded in 1897 and in 1900 changed its name to Marconi's Wireless Telegraph Company[31]. Transatlantic wireless service began in 1909 and was thus only three years old when *Titanic* sailed. *Titanic* and other passenger ships later involved in the rescue of *Titanic*'s passengers, such as *Carpathia* and *California*, had the latest wireless technology, but operators were still learning how to use it effectively. The technology was understood to have significant potential but was in an early stage of adoption. Even though state-of-the-art for the time, this fledgling technology played a critical role in the loss of life aboard *Titanic* as a result of the limited technological capability and lack of standard operating procedures.

The initial impetus for the adoption of the wireless technology that played such a crucial role in the mistake chain of *Titanic* was not safety but revenue generation. Passengers wanted to use the new technology to stay in touch and to get business news and stock quotes[32].

Does this sound like today's desire to stay connected with BlackBerry™, WiFi, and airline Internet links via satellite? The issues are no different—customer convenience in return for revenue—and *Titanic* carried the most powerful transmitter then at sea. This revenue focus meant that, on *Titanic* and other passenger ships, the incoming and outgoing passenger messages had priority. In fact, cargo ships did not immediately adopt the wireless technology at the same rate as passenger ships because it appeared to increase cost for little practical use.

After departing Southampton, it took *Titanic* another day to pick up passengers in Cherbourg, France and Queenstown (now Cobh) near Cork,

Ireland before she started her much anticipated Atlantic crossing in the early afternoon on April 11, 1912 with over 2,200 passengers and crew. The seas were smooth and Captain E.J. Smith was in command, expecting that *Titanic*'s Atlantic crossing would be his last before retiring after spending 40 years at sea. When asked about his experience, he remarked that his career had been rather uneventful, never having even been near a disaster or in a threatening situation.[33]

This comfort with the sea on the part of Captain Smith, the result of a long accident-free career, when combined with the perception held by the public that his ship was unsinkable, certainly set a dangerous context for decision making. Smith's confidence, and exceptionally good weather, led him to continue to increase speed, with some speculating that one of the objectives on the first voyage was to beat sister ship *Olympic*'s first voyage crossing time. Whether he was trying to set a company record or not, he clearly exercised extremely poor judgment when he proceeded at full speed, even as he received reports of icebergs in the area.

Following the third warning of ice, J. Bruce Ismay, chairman of White Star, suggested to a passenger that *Titanic* might speed up to get clear of the ice field.[34] Captain Smith was aware of a number of ice warnings from other ships as he attended a dinner party until approximately 9:oo PM on April 14. Following the dinner party, he went to the bridge to check on the status of his ship. It was a clear, starlit night with no moon and a calm sea. He instructed the officer on watch to inform him if visibility decreased and retired to his cabin about 9:30 PM.

This combination of Captain Smith's past experience, his chairman's clear interest in speed, the calm weather, and perceived minimal risk was leading the Captain to ignore numerous warnings of potential danger. The fact that he had ignored warnings all afternoon was known to his crew because the wireless operators had been delivering the messages to the bridge and the captain, and there had been no change in operations and standing orders that you would expect from a confident captain in good conditions—"Full steam ahead, let me know if the visibility changes."

This is one of the most powerful mistakes made in accidents, the setting of a tone by a senior authority figure that subordinates then interpret for themselves as empowerment to continue in the same manner regardless of new facts. And at sea, the captain is *the* authority figure. His judgment is rarely questioned, especially at that time in the world, with a new ship and a 40-year officer with an unblemished record in charge. This was not a technical question—it was judgment, and who was strong enough to question the captain on such a matter?

Titanic was making good progress. The lookouts were in the crow's nest*, and the machinery was working smoothly. There were three ice warnings that evening. The captain did not receive the first because he was at dinner. A later one arrived after he retired, and the wireless operator was busy with wireless traffic for passengers and did not see fit to send the warning to the bridge or bother the captain.

The pattern of mistakes was set and building further at this point, and while not recognized by the captain or his crew, the only thing that would have saved *Titanic* would have been an exceptional effort by someone in the crew to take personal responsibility to break the chain. This did not happen, just as it does not happen in a variety of situations, business or otherwise, with an imperious leader. The crew trusted his judgment, knew his experience, and while some may have experienced trepidation, they were likely calmed by his lack of concern. The scene was set to test how the crew would react to the total shock of an unexpected event.

What would it have taken to break the chain that, as each of us now knows, was about to unfold? While the magnitude of the final disaster can be partially blamed on technology-related design decisions, it was human factors that really caused this accident, and right up until the moment of impact, humans could have intervened to prevent the accident. Some "normal" actions that might have avoided the accident include:

- **Making information sharing and analysis a priority.**
  - ◆ The many warnings of ice in the area were ignored, often arrogantly, as indicated by Ismay's comment. Many reports gave general positions with their ice warnings, but there were at least two reports on April 14 that gave specific position reports of the iceberg that *Titanic* ultimately hit, at exactly the position where it had been reported by *Amerika* at 11:00 AM that day and by *Mesnaba* at 9:40 PM, just two hours before the collision.[35] The message from *Mesnaba* never reached the bridge, but all the others had reached various officers, including the captain, and

* A lookout platform mounted high on a mast to provide longer-range visibility in good weather. Such lookouts are not used on commercial ships at sea in today's radar-equipped world.

had been posted on the bridge and in the chart room. The extent of the warnings that Captain Smith and his crew ignored from ships that were stopped in or moving slowly through the ice field was significant:

- Six warnings from other ships on April 11
- Five warnings on April 12
- Three warnings on April 13
- Seven warnings on April 14, the day of the collision[36]

Information was trying to save them, and they ignored it. What would have happened if:

- One officer or wireless operator who had seen some or all of the traffic had suggested caution? Would the captain have rebuked this person as overly cautious? Would the captain have consulted Ismay (chairman of White Star), who would likely have pushed to continue the speed? Or would the captain, faced with a mounting volume of warnings, have seen the potential danger and broken the chain by stopping until daybreak, slowing down, or changing course away from the location of the specific warnings about an ice field?

- The captain had changed the routine because of the warnings and had a more formal meeting of his top officers to discuss the warnings and the possible scenarios? Would concern have emerged in a group discussion, or would the captain's inclination and vast experience simply have overwhelmed any concern expressed by others?

- **Changing the mental mindset.**
  - What if J. Bruce Ismay had been concerned and had interfered with his captain's authority for the ship at sea and suggested that he be more cautious? This would have at least implied that safety was more important than a speed-related public relations win for the voyage.
  - What if someone in the officer corps of the ship had realized that *Titanic*'s design would fail in certain kinds of collisions? Could an energetic discussion have changed the outcome if someone had successfully argued that the ship was being pushed to or past a safety limit with the speed and conditions that existed?

- **Seeking information.**

   - *Titanic* received many incoming messages warning of ice, but
     there is no mention of her inquiring of others for updates or more
     information. What if someone was curious enough to ask for
     more information from the ships in the area? Would a discussion
     have ensued that would have created alarm? In fact, to the
     contrary, the infamous action of the wireless operator, Jack
     Phillips, showed complete disregard for the stream of very
     important but unsolicited information*, as evidenced by Phillips
     telling a wireless operator who sent another ice warning from the
     nearby *Californian* to "Shut up" because he was busy with
     passenger traffic. Phillips' now infamous snub highlighted that
     generating revenue (from messages) and passenger service was
     more important than ice warnings.[37]

Any of these actions could have broken the chain of mistakes or
limited damage, but no action was taken. *Titanic* was set up for the
exponential damage associated with unconstrained multiple mistake
chains brought about through a combination of external circumstances
and serious mistakes of internal origin, as shown in Figure 5.1.

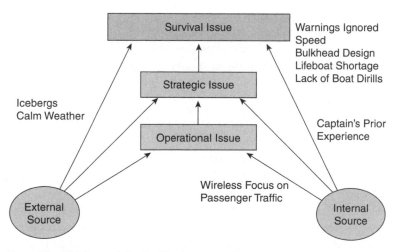

Figure 5.1   Mistake escalation for *Titanic*.

---

* The technology of the day was limited. All ships were using the same frequency, thus there was "limited
bandwidth" to use today's term. All ships and the shore stations within range were sharing a common
frequency and thus traffic by one ship was done at the expense of others ability to use the frequency.
Titanic's focus on the passenger traffic clearly interfered with more important operational matters.

At 11:40 PM on April 14, 1912, lookout Frederick Fleet saw a mass in the dark, immediately signaled the bridge, and picked up a handset in the crow's nest to report that he saw an iceberg ahead. Sixth Officer James Moody, who was on watch, immediately ordered a hard turn to port, shut the automatic watertight doors below decks, and attempted to reverse the propellers. The ship did turn slightly to port, avoiding a head-on collision with the iceberg but with a resulting scrape down the starboard side that opened a gash estimated to be 300 feet long. The dangerous aspect of this type of collision was that a number of the transverse watertight bulkheads were breached in the process, perhaps a result that was worse than a head-on collision might have been.

Once the collision occurred, the race was on to see whether the damage could be mitigated or if even more mistakes would lead to substantial loss of life. Unfortunately, the latter was the case as a result of a series of preordained mistakes compounded by more human error. These included:

- Delayed recognition of being "in extremis" because of the general perception that the ship was "almost unsinkable." The crew seemed to go about a routine damage assessment following the collision. But Thomas Andrews, one of the ship's designers, was on board, and he immediately made a tour below decks to assess damage. By the time he reported to Captain Smith, the news was not good. He told the captain directly that the ship would sink in two hours or less. It was at this point that the captain gave the order to prepare the lifeboats, but strangely he did not give the order to load them for another 30 minutes.

- Andrews knew that *Titanic* could sustain four flooded compartments, but he found out rather quickly that at least five had been breached. Since all were forward, the ship would sink lower by the bow, and once she did, water would spill over the top of the bulkheads that were built only ten feet above the waterline, flooding other compartments until the ship sank. The fact that Andrews apparently sensed this without equivocation from the start must have been an instant and horrible realization to him of the weakness of the design, something that had been decided three to four years earlier as *Titanic's* sister ships were designed and built.

- Passengers reportedly wandered about for a time, inquiring about what was going on. The initial lack of concern on the part of the crew probably reassured them that the event was not serious.

- Titanic carried 20 lifeboats, an economy move decided on by White Star, even though the builders offered a new, more expensive davits that could have carried 48 boats in essentially the same space. The capacity of the boats amounted to about half of the passengers and crew embarked, but this was within the very outdated law in force at the time. The boats included 16 wooden boats, each 30 feet in length and designed to carry 65 persons, and 4 collapsible side canvas lifeboats with a capacity of 47 persons each.

- No lifeboat drills had been conducted since the passengers had boarded. Thus, when it came time to board lifeboats, the passengers were confused. The resulting confusion meant that most of the lifeboats departed with less than a full load of passengers. Those that were designed for 65 passengers departed with as few as 12 aboard. Toward the end, as all realized the severity of the situation, the last few boats were fully loaded, with one boat designed for 65 passengers carrying 70. Brander points out[38] that, during World War I, ships of similar size (such as *Arabic*) that conducted life boat drills were sunk by German submarines with as many as 90 percent of those on board saved from a ship that sank in only nine minutes.

- Occupants of lifeboats with space available after launch "voted," with few exceptions, to not return to pick up more survivors, fearful that too many would swamp the boat, endangering all.

- The Leyland Liner *Californian,* originally designed to carry cotton but modified with some staterooms to carry passengers, was 5 to 10 miles away but stopped for the night due to heavy ice in the area. In a conversation between her captain and the third mate, the captain speculated about a light that was seen nearby. A few minutes later, the captain asked the radio operator if there were any other ships nearby, and he replied that only *Titanic* was in the area. Captain Lord ordered his radio operator to warn *Titanic* about the ice, which he did. As late as 11:30 PM, just 10 minutes prior to *Titanic*'s collision, Captain Lord could see her starboard (green) running light and ordered his crew to try to make contact by signal lamp, but there was no reply.

■ Between midnight and 2:00 AM, various members of the crew of
  Californian saw lights in the distance, but each time were convinced
  they were seeing shooting stars. The watch officer even awoke the
  captain at one point to report more lights, but when the captain
  asked if there were any colors in them, which would be the case for
  a distress signal, the reply was that they were white, further
  reinforcing the view that they were seeing stars.

■ By about 12:30 AM *Californian*'s wireless operator secured his set and
  retired for the evening, neglecting to set a device that would have
  awakened him for incoming traffic. When he came on duty a few
  hours later, the captain asked him to inquire of a ship they had
  sighted visually (*Frankfurt*), and they were stunned to hear that the
  Titanic had sunk during the night. *Californian* had been the closest
  ship, but because her crew did not follow up the signals they saw
  more aggressively, they played no role in the rescue other than
  continuing to search for survivors after *Carpathia* left. Their mindset
  was that there were no problems present and that the lights they
  saw had to be natural occurrences.

To the extent that the mistake chain was broken at all, it was by
Captain Arthur Rostran, who was in command of the *RMS Carpathia*, a
Cunard passenger liner that was 58 miles away from *Titanic* at the time
she transmitted her SOS*. Captain Rostran steamed at full speed to
Titanic's reported position and made full preparations for receiving and
caring for survivors while in route. Even though Captain Rostran had
never participated in an actual sea rescue, his actions were subsequently
lauded as exemplary. These included preparing lifeboats, setting up first
aid stations, preparing extra food and beverages, rigging electric lights,
collecting blankets and clothing, briefing his crew, and a variety of other
actions that he and his crew anticipated would be required.

When *Carpathia* arrived at the reported position, she saw little and
slowed almost to a stop to look more carefully for another half-hour.
Finally, a lifeboat was spotted, and she maneuvered to begin picking up
survivors. It would be over four hours until the last of the 705 survivors
was aboard *Carpathia*. She stayed in the area another five or six hours,
continuing to look for survivors, but there were no more.

---

* Initially transmitted as "CQD" for "come quick danger," which had been the standard distress signal as
  wireless began to be used. SOS had just been adopted as the standard, and Jack Phillips, the wireless
  operator, shifted to this and became one of the first to use the new signal.

Despite increasingly bad weather, *Carpathia* finished the crossing to New York uneventfully and delivered her passengers and the grateful *Titanic* survivors. Ironically, a German U boat sank *Carpathia* off the coast of Ireland in 1918, but most of her crew and passengers were rescued.

The numerous mistakes that contributed significantly to this accident or made it worse fall into a number of categories. Looking at the categories and not just the individual mistakes is instructive because the category patterns repeat over and over again in other business as well as physical contexts, while the specific mistakes might be unique to the situation. These categories of mistakes are eerily similar to those we see in major business mistake chains as well:

- **Faulty assumptions and mindsets.** The "watertight" compartment design that was not really watertight because of bulkhead height and lack of a longitudinal bulkhead was likely the most serious faulty assumption made in the design stage. It was made on the basis of an assumption about the worst-case scenario that was not broad enough. Further, these faulty assumptions created the illusion of safety and thus affected decisions about the number of lifeboats. If the ship is "nearly unsinkable," why spend more money on lifeboats that will not be needed?

  Californian had a number of clues that there was a problem but did not investigate beyond a cursory effort. Their wireless was secured, assuming that if they were not underway there was no use for it. The use of the device for safety was not yet seen as the primary mission for the technology, and thus the service was not staffed to allow around-the-clock operation.

  Captain Smith's assumption that his ship was the finest technology afloat clearly left him unconcerned about the danger of transiting a known ice field at night.

- **Disregarding or not believing valid information.** Disregard for information that one does not expect to hear is a powerful factor in many accidents. In some circumstances, one can argue that this comes directly from the faulty assumptions and mindsets just described. But in cases such as *Titanic* and others, the volume of information and direct warnings that could have alerted *Titanic*'s captain and officers to danger and was ignored is hard to believe.

This is an area where we can all improve—training ourselves to at least investigate the unbelievable before disregarding it. Investigation in this case might have been at least a reduction in speed in the specific area where icebergs were reported by more than one source. We saw this pattern of disregarding bad news in business situations like Intel, AmEx, and Kodak as well.

- **Inadequate training and preparation.** The lack of lifeboat drills for the passengers and crew clearly contributed to confusion and incompetence in loading and assignment of trained crew to operate and supervise the boats. This is the reason that most boats left with less than a full load of passengers. Reportedly, there were also initial attempts to segregate passengers by attempting to keep third-class passengers below decks. The officer of the deck apparently took the appropriate actions once "in extremis" (collision imminent) by turning, reversing engines, and shutting watertight doors, but this was a mere formality that did little to reduce damage given the ship's speed.

- **Poor decision-making conditioned by previous experience.** Clearly Captain Smith and Bruce Ismay perceived little risk in the speed *Titanic* maintained. This decision was not one based on a rational analysis of the risks, but one made on the basis of past experience of always missing icebergs. Some have suggested that Smith's past experience with many successful passages without incident conditioned him to believe in what pilots call the "big sky theory." The belief is that it is a big ocean (or sky) with relatively few ships in it and thus the probability of a collision is very small. Of course, this ignores the fact that those operating ships between nearby ports make similar choices about their routes. Extension of this idea to icebergs might yield the thought that an iceberg is very small and it is a very big ocean. What is the probability that we will end up in the same place at the same time? Obviously, the probability was finite. Experience can have a perverse effect on decision-making. In some cases, those who have taken risks in the past without adverse effect perceive the risk to be smaller going forward and take ever-bigger risks.

The investigations following the *Titanic* disaster were front page news in both the United States and the United Kingdom. In the United States, a Senate committee held hearings for more than a month beginning four days after the sinking. In Britain Lord Mersey, the Wreck Commission headed the inquiry and conducted hearings through May and June 1912, resulting in recommendations for:

- Enough lifeboats to accommodate all on board
- Improved watertight compartments
- Wireless capability for all passenger ships with a 24-hour watch
- Staffing and training of boat crews with drills
- Prudent navigation in the vicinity of ice during night hours
- Regulation of lookouts
- Making failure to go to the aid of a vessel in distress a misdemeanor
- An international conference on standardizing these and other regulations
- Other branches of government that were criticized in the report for failing to keep regulations up-to-date with changing technology in the maritime industry

Interestingly, as in most disasters until recently, the inquiries focused on mechanical *things* and regulations that might fix problems. Other than the admonition for reducing speed and changing course in the presence of ice at night, there was little attention to judgment. It is, of course, impossible to legislate or regulate judgment. Requiring 24-hour manning of the wireless and making it a crime to fail to go to the aid of a ship in distress was a move to eliminate any need for judgment.

Even unmitigated disasters such as the *Titanic* can have small silver linings. There were numerous accounts of selfless acts of kindness and sacrifice toward others from strangers aboard *Titanic*, in the lifeboats, and aboard *Carpathia* after rescue.

One story that has endured is how the leadership of one Margaret "Molly" Brown of Denver in a lifeboat apparently earned her the famous nickname "The Unsinkable Molly Brown." Molly Brown was the wife of a very successful gold mine owner in Colorado and was traveling in the first-class section of *Titanic* at a cost of $4,350 for the one-way passage, about the cost of today's first-class airfare on the London-to-New York route (but obviously a great deal more in 1912 dollars). She reportedly helped other passengers to lifeboats before she was told to get into lifeboat #6, the first to be launched from the port side of the ship. It departed with only 24 persons on board a 65-person-capacity boat.

Once in the boat, with the ship's quartermaster in charge, Molly Brown began to row with other women. An argument broke out, led by Molly Brown, about going back to seek other survivors. The quartermaster ultimately prevailed, and *Carpathia* rescued the group with the others later that morning. Once aboard *Carpathia*, Molly helped organize services to comfort others and, because of her language skills, provided interpretation services for some of the passengers. Additionally, "She compiled lists of survivors and arranged for information to be radioed to their families at her expense.... She rallied the first-class passengers to donate money to help less fortunate passengers. Before the *Carpathia* reached New York, $10,000 had been raised."[39]

Our final note on the *Titanic* comes from Lawrence Beesley, a survivor who was encouraged to write a book about the accident within a few months of returning, while his memory was still fresh. While his description of the events is at times personal and touching, his final summary of the event and its causes is rather cold in its belief of the inevitability of such incidents. It is eerily applicable to a number of other situations nearly a century later:

> "It is a blot on our civilization that these things are necessary from time to time, to arouse those responsible for the safety of human life from the lethargic selfishness which has governed them. The *Titanic's* two thousand–odd passengers went aboard thinking they were on an absolutely safe ship, and all the time there were many people—designers, builders, experts, government officials—who knew there were insufficient boats on board, that the *Titanic* had no right to go fast in iceberg regions, who knew these things and took no steps and enacted no laws to prevent their happening. Not that they omitted to do these things deliberately, but were lulled into a state of selfish inaction from which it needed such a tragedy as this to arouse them."[40]

Three Mile Island

It is hard to believe that it has been over 25 years—a quarter of a century—since Three Mile Island and "TMI" became well known parts of the lexicon. Airline flights into Philadelphia from the west descend over the area, and the Pennsylvania Turnpike runs nearby. Whether flying over or driving across the Susquehanna River, you cannot miss seeing four very large concrete stacks that are the natural draft cooling towers for Units 1 and 2 at the Three Mile Island nuclear power plant. Unit 1 still operates, so unless it is shut down for maintenance, you will see water vapor rising like smoke from a chimney from one or two of the cooling towers. But the other two towers are cold and have been for 25 years since the accident at Unit 2 made it America's worst nuclear accident, resulting in a partial core meltdown and effectively stopping any consideration of expansion of the industry in the United States until recently.

The summary of the TMI disaster is straightforward and is one of the worst multiple-mistake scenarios ever seen. TMI Unit 2 was a new plant that had been on line producing electricity commercially for only about 90 days at the time of the accident. A malfunction in the non-nuclear part of the plant led to a chain of mechanical and human mistakes, some unnoticed and others initiated deliberately in fits of incompetence almost unparalleled in engineering history. There was significant physical disaster to the plant that was contained because of the ultimate safety measure—the design of the containment structure was sound.

The details are more complex but provide an extreme but enlightening example of the failure to manage multiple mistakes. Fortunately, one person finally broke the chain of mistakes by catching and stopping a serious ongoing mistake. Unfortunately, the plant was already "in extremis," and while stopping the mistake at that point was crucial, the only result was to limit further damage. It was too late to stop the disaster from occurring.

"Turbine Trip—Reactor Trip" is a term that is familiar to nuclear plant operators and is the title of Chapter 1 of Volume 1 of the report[41] produced in 1980 for the public to understand what happened at Three Mile Island. As an engineering officer of the watch overseeing the operation of a nuclear power plant, as I did as an officer in the U.S. Navy submarine force, hearing these or similar words* from one of the operators tells you instantly that you have a problem and that you are likely to be a while getting things straightened out. Even when training, with an instructor watching, you are nervous.

---

* Another common term used is "scram" to indicate a condition where the reactor control rods have been dropped on an emergency basis to shut down the reactor.

But hearing "turbine trip—reactor scram" unexpectedly in a real operating situation sends a quick chill through you. It starts adrenalin pumping, you start looking for status indicators, you start spouting memorized immediate responses, and you pull out the manual for verification. Your mind should go from trained reaction, for stabilization purposes, into problem analysis mode to understand what is really happening and to ensure appropriate continuing responses.

I am sure that the operators at TMI felt that chill up their spines when at 36 seconds past 4:00 AM on March 28, 1979, one of the feedwater pumps tripped (disconnected electrically). This stopped the supply of fresh water to the steam generators that produce the steam to drive the turbines to generate electricity. The turbine tripped as steam pressure decreased and eight seconds later the reactor automatically scrammed as the emergency systems worked, as designed, to prevent reactor damage. All of this was normal operation, with the exception of knowing why the feedwater pump tripped in the first place.

The type of reactor system at TMI is known as a pressurized water reactor (PWR). These systems were among the earliest commercial designs for nuclear reactors and are the type most widely used in the United States, although other types exist*. The U.S. Navy used PWRs exclusively in submarines (with the exception of one short-lived experiment) for a number of reasons related to safety and adaptability to their environment. The horrible accident at Chernobyl in 1986 was a reactor with an inherently less stable, less safe design that is not used elsewhere, other than the former Soviet Union and a few of her former allies in Eastern Europe.

The PWR, as shown here simplistically in Figure 5.2, is a complex design based on the fairly simple principle of heating water with nuclear fission in one loop (the primary loop) and transferring the heat to a secondary system (the secondary loop) that uses the heat to generate steam. Heat is transferred between the two loops, but the two fluids (reactor cooling water and steam generator feedwater) never physically come in contact with each other.

---

* There are 103 operating nuclear reactors generating electricity commercially in the United States today. Of those, 69 are of the PWR type and 34 are what are called boiling water reactors (BWR). The BWR design is less complex but does not have the isolation of the primary and secondary systems that the PWR provides. There are ongoing debates about which design is most effective when considering safety, cost, and reliability.

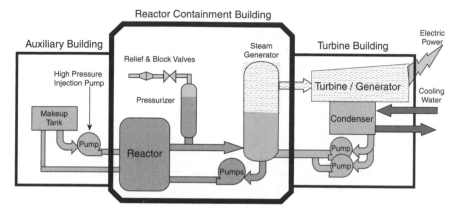

Figure 5.2 Simplified schematic of pressurized water reactor plant.

The primary loop in a PWR operates at a very high pressure (2,155psi* at TMI) to keep the hot water from boiling. This makes it easy to pump as a liquid to transfer heat to the steam generator where the steam is generated to drive the turbines.

The size of a large commercial plant like those at TMI is staggering. At 850MW† (megawatts), each of these plants is many times the output of those used to power nuclear submarines when I was in the navy in the 1960s. The pipes in the primary loop are 36 inches in diameter and utilize four pumps driven by 3,600HP electric motors to circulate the hot water from the reactor core to the steam generators and back again.

At TMI, the reactor vessel that holds the specially manufactured uranium fuel and the control rods was a cylindrical steel tank 40 feet high with 8 1/2-inch diameter walls. The control rods are made of materials that absorb (stop) the free flow of neutrons. When the rods are withdrawn from the reactor core‡, neutrons flow freely and strike enriched uranium atoms, causing them to split into other elements, releasing significant amounts of heat and more neutrons. The water carries the heat away for heating the secondary loop for steam generation.

---

* Atmospheric pressure on earth is 14.7psi (pounds per square inch), thus 2,155psi is 146 times atmospheric pressure. This is very high pressure and requires specially engineered systems to operate properly.

† One megawatt (MW) is the ability to continuously generate heat that is the equivalent of a million watts. The two plants at TMI were together capable of providing enough power to supply 300,000 homes.

‡ The rods are not completely withdrawn. They are withdrawn enough to allow the required neutron flow to take place for a self-sustaining chain reaction. Rod positions will change as a function of fuel hours used.

Using the steam to turn the turbines extracts energy from the steam and it begins to cool. It leaves the turbine and passes through a very large condenser, where it is cooled*. Once cooled back into water, the water is recirculated in the secondary loop and enters the steam generator to be turned into steam again.

Following the feedwater pump trip just after 4:00 AM, the main steam turbine tripped, and in turn, the safety systems built into Unit 2 caused the reactor scram. The system worked as designed.

Since the heat being generated in the core was no longer being used to produce steam, the primary coolant (water) began to heat up†, causing the pressure in the loop to increase, which compressed the bubble in the pressurizer‡, increasing its pressure. When the pressure reached 2,250psi, or 100psi over the normal operating pressure, the PORV§ on the pressurizer opened, discharging steam into a drain tank located inside the containment building where it condensed into water (radioactive).

The PORV should have shut again as the pressure decreased, but it did not. The operators did not notice this problem for over two hours. During this time, steam that was the equivalent of 300 gallons per minute of water escaped. In the first 100 minutes of the accident, about 32,000 gallons of water, the equivalent of one third of the primary coolant system capacity, was lost and no one realized it.

Have you ever tried to have a conversation in your kitchen with your spouse or a friend while the TV on the kitchen counter blared the evening news, the TV in the nearby family room blasted a chorus from

---

* The condenser is cooled by water from an external source that does not come in direct contact with either the secondary or primary loop water. This coolant water is sprayed into the cooling towers, condensing and falling to a tank below to be recirculated through the condenser. Some waste is vaporized in the process, producing the characteristic white plume above the cooling towers. This water needs to be replenished in the system, which is why nuclear plants are usually located near a source of water like a river or ocean.

† Even after being shut down, a reactor has residual heat from its large mass plus new heat generated from decaying radioactive elements, which is initially equivalent to about 6 percent power. It takes a few days to reach a point where there is so little heat generation that it can be safely removed by a small set of pumps and a heat exchanger called the "decay heat removal system." This system must continue to run indefinitely for large reactors.

‡ The pressurizer is a surge tank designed to keep pressure in the primary loop stable as temperature in the system changes. It operates with a steam bubble at the top to manage slight changes in volume of the water in the system. The pressurizer at TMI is large. Its 1,500 cubic feet are similar in volume to a 12'×15'×8' bedroom.

§ PORV is the pilot-operated relief valve that opens to relieve pressure in the primary loop if it gets too high.

Sesame Street, the teenager in the room above was listening to music that vibrated the walls, the grandfather clock in the hall chimed seven times, the phone was ringing, and you failed to notice the pasta boiling over on the stove? Multiply that confusion by 100 times or more to imagine what the operators on watch in the control room at TMI saw and heard a little after 4:00 AM on March 28, 1979.

About 100 alarms were going off all over the control panels, with flashing lights, sirens, and horns all competing for the attention of Edward Frederick and Craig Faust, the two operators on duty in the TMI-2 control room. Available to assist them were Fred Scheimann, the TMI-2 shift foreman, and William Zewe, shift supervisor for both TMI-1 and 2.

Faust would later recall in testimony before the Nuclear Regulatory Commission (NRC), "I would have liked to have thrown away the alarm panel. It wasn't giving us any useful information."[42] It was in this environment that the operators tried to figure out what was going on with the plant.

One thing was certain—things were not stable. Within 12 seconds, there had been a loss of feedwater, a turbine trip, the reactor scram, an expected rise in system pressure, and the PORV stuck open (unknown to the operators). Within the next two minutes, the primary system pressure had dropped nearly 25 percent from 2,155psi to 1,640psi.

The sequence was actually started by Scheimann and a crew who were working on the #7 condensate polisher* and using compressed air and water to try to break up a clog in the device. It is now believed that this process interfered with the automatic valve control system, causing the polisher valves to close, which shut off the flow of condensate that in turn caused the feedwater pumps to shut down when they received no flow.

Later investigation would show that cleaning the polishers had been a persistent problem, compounded by the fact that the design did not allow for bypassing the system. This is a serious design flaw that was rectified with a full bypass system in other plants. While the polisher is needed, it was not urgent that it be in the loop 100 percent of the time. The designers obviously thought that if there were no bypass, this would ensure that the steam generator feedwater never had an undesirable level

---

* A device similar to, but more sophisticated than, a home water softener. It cleans the water in the secondary loop of chemicals and ions that might damage various system components. The polisher has to be cleaned periodically.

of impurities. This was the opposite of the *Titanic* designers building the watertight bulkheads to only 10 feet above the waterline to improve function but not safety. In this case, a design that had more to do with maintenance than safety ended up affecting safety adversely because it was too rigid.

In the control room, the plant initially responded as expected. After the scram, the pressure rose, the PORV opened briefly and then closed, or so the operators thought. In fact, the valve had stuck open, but the indicator light showed "closed." This occurred because the indicator triggered the presence of electric power at the valve actuator, not whether or not the valve actually moved—another serious design flaw.

The operators got many signals that something was wrong, but unfortunately they became hopelessly confused and took dangerously incorrect actions that they thought would stabilize the situation. Their real impact was to prevent the system from saving itself.

Even with the dangerous series of mechanical and human-related mistakes that occurred, TMI-2 would have safely tolerated at least the first three mistakes without serious damage. The TMI multiple-mistakes diagram would have looked like Figure 5.3, a minor incident that you would have never heard about. But it got worse for reasons that are both understandable and inexcusable. Not just inexcusable for the operators but for the designers, the operators, General Public Utilities (the owner), and the NRC.

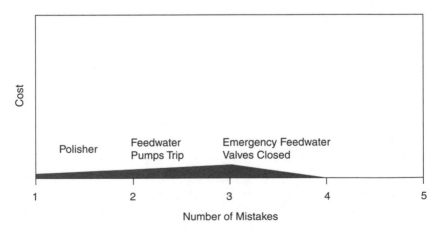

Figure 5.3 What TMI should have been.

The alarms continued to sound, and there only two telephone lines in the control room to try to get help and advice. The supervisors in the plant came to the control room to help, and others were called in. The operators were adding water to the primary loop, as was expected when the reactor shut down and the coolant began to cool. The pressurized level was rising (apparently), but plant pressure was dropping faster. As the pressure dropped, the HPI* pumps came on, and the pressurizer level continued rising, even though plant pressure was lower than it should have been.

It was at this point that the operators began to worry about another potential problem that all of us were scrupulously taught to avoid: "going solid." This meant that the pressurizer bubble was collapsed, and every piece of pipe and attached devices was filled with water. The potential danger is that extreme pressure can be generated quickly if the plant is "solid." This fear of accidentally taking the plant solid overrode any other thoughts the operators might have had about what was really going on, and they failed to focus on what other indicators were telling them.

In fact, the pressure had dropped while the pressurizer level (apparently) rose. Temperature had been rising but then leveled off. This is probably where the situation really became dangerous. The operators reduced the water injection and eventually shut it down completely because of their fear of going solid. About the same time, roughly five and a half minutes into the accident, the real damage began. The leveling of temperature probably indicated that the saturation† point had been reached, and the reactor was now a bubbling kettle producing steam bubbles inside that, if expanded, would uncover the core and damage the reactor.

The reality is that TMI-2 was still losing coolant, but no one recognized it because it was happening through the open relief valve (PORV) that was still unnoticed. Shutting down the water injection system that was trying to automatically save the plant was a horrible mistake, brought on by the fear of another condition that could not have possibly existed under the circumstances. The sad irony is that if they had tried to purposely "go solid," it might have saved the plant.

---

* High pressure injection pumps are designed to add large amounts of water to the primary coolant loop rapidly in an emergency.

† The temperature, for a given pressure, at which water will begin to boil, creating steam.

The symptoms were there though, and the fundamental issue that day was that the operators forgot that water boils if you reduce the pressure. The pressure in the plant dropped, and the water began to flash to steam, creating bubbles in the core, which prevented proper cooling and ultimately caused the damage that made the plant a physical memorial to the accident that we will see for a very long time.

The steam generators were also part of the emergency core cooling system (ECCS). In an emergency, a separate set of pumps called emergency feedwater pumps fed water to the steam generators to take the heat away from the primary coolant loop. The operators believed that the ECCS was working. At eight minutes into the accident, Ken Bryan, who had been asked to come over from Unit 1 to have the opportunity to see what went on following a reactor scram, walked into the control room. With a fresh set of eyes and a mind unencumbered by conflicting signals, he looked at the control panel and yelled out "The 12s are closed*."[43] Supervisor Zewe ordered the valves opened immediately.

The emergency cooling system had not had an opportunity to cool the primary loop because the inlet valves for the steam generator were closed. It is still not clear how or why the valves were closed, but it is known that they were closed two days before the accident as part of a routine maintenance procedure. It is likely they were never reopened, a mistake that probably related to failing to use a checklist at the completion of the procedure and a failure by operators on a number of subsequent shifts to verify the status of the plant.

Only 20 minutes into the accident, a coolant drain tank was full and its rupture disk broke, a signal that the PORV was leaking. Radioactive water spilled to the floor of the containment vessel, and temperature and pressure in the building continued to increase for some time, another indication that the PORV was open and dumping into the containment building through the now open drain tank.

Throughout the accident, Zewe and others missed a continuous and consistent warning that could have stopped the whole scenario if it had been analyzed correctly in the first five minutes. Because of past problems with the PORV, the plant designers (Babcock & Wilcox [B&W]) had placed a remote controlled block valve in the line between the pressurizer and the PORV. This has to be used with care—no engineer ever wants to manually shut off a safety valve that is designed as the last resort to keep you from "going solid," but it was there.

---

* This refers to a set of valves in the emergency cooling system.

Additionally, a temperature sensor had been added downstream of the PORV in the pipe that carried the steam/water to the drain tank. If the temperature sensor was higher than the ambient temperature in the containment building, then it was likely that hot water from the pressurizer was passing through the pipe. It was a very strong signal about the status of the PORV. High temperature in this line was reported and known by Zewe and other operators over the entire course of the accident, but it was discounted because of the history of unreliability of the PORV itself.

Once again, the mind was conditioned by prior experience to not believe the indications of what was going on in the plant. This was no different than the captain of the *Titanic* ignoring multiple warnings of ice in the area. It is no different, other than in time frame, than Kodak ignoring signals that photography would shift toward digital. It began to leak out slowly and was ignored until it was too late.

By 6:00 AM, Brian Mehler arrived at work to relieve Bill Zewe as shift supervisor. After he had been there about 20 minutes, he looked at temperatures in different parts of the primary coolant system, noticed differences, and decided that there had to be a bubble in the system somewhere other than the pressurizer; otherwise, the temperatures would be more uniform. He also realized that the PORV must be leaking and ordered the blocking valve closed.

Finally! After more than two hours, someone had diagnosed the fundamental problem of inconsistent data that was telling the story all along. Significantly, it was someone who had been outside the operation at the onset of the incident who was able to take a fresh look and diagnose the problem.

Interestingly, the problem was diagnosed over the telephone at about the same time. Leland Rogers, the B&W site manager, had just learned about the accident and was being briefed on the accident over the phone at his home. One of the questions he asked was if the pressurized blocking valve was closed. Mehler had just walked in and ordered it closed, and when the operators checked, they told Rogers that it was closed.

The action of closing the PORV blocking valve was the most significant thing the team had done to stop the progress of the accident, but the challenge was not yet over. It is important to note that outside advice from other operators and technical advisors quickly zeroed in on the true problem. This is a dilemma that any of us could face. In the heat of straightening out a confusing situation, when is the right time to seek other advice and counsel? Will it be helpful or distracting?

There were so many ignored signals in the case of TMI-2 that listing them in one place illustrates the massive escalation of events from a straightforward operating anomaly to a serious case of failure to manage multiple mistakes:

- Failure to note the "12 valves" closed for a number of days, causing the steam generators to boil dry when the emergency occurred
- Failure to understand the PORV discharge pipe temperature indications
- Reducing and then shutting down the HPI (water injection system)
- Failure to understand that temperature leveling as pressure dropped was the saturation point
- Failure to see rising pressurizer levels with dropping pressure as inconsistent and requiring further analysis
- Ignoring the drain tank disk rupture as related to PORV status and coolant loss
- Shutting down the main coolant pumps that were cavitating*, fearing damage to the pumps or piping and not realizing steam was present
- Ignoring readings of unexplained increased neutron density in the core, an indication that water was not present[†]

The impact of the accident got worse. There were increasing radiation levels in the containment building caused by significant core damage and dumping radioactive water onto the floor through the open PORV.

The estimated radiation level inside the dome was 800 REM/hr[‡], an extraordinary level and a definite sign that there was a loss of coolant and that the core was damaged. There were small airborne radiation releases

---

* Cavitate means the creation of bubbles in a fluid, usually because of reduced pressure.

† Water is a natural "moderator," slowing down neutrons. With the reactor shut down, water and the control rods prevent the reactor from starting.

‡ REM is/was a standard measure of radiation received. For comparison, a standard chest x-ray might expose you to 750mrem (at that time; technology has since improved) or less than 1REM. As monitored by film badges, I received less than 800mrem of radiation in my entire five years in the Navy submarine force—less than I would have received from natural radiation if living in a brick house.

outside the plant that were a result of the flow of overflow water between the containment building and an adjacent auxiliary building. This building was eventually isolated. The radiation release, while minimal, raised concern and unrest outside TMI about whether there would be a *China Syndrome** meltdown.

A hydrogen bubble did form in the reactor, and some of the hydrogen escaped into the containment building through the PORV, causing a small explosion that was contained. The "thud," as it was called, was not diagnosed as an explosion until the next day, despite a rise in pressure in the containment building—another ignored signal. Debate went on for some time about whether the hydrogen bubble would collapse safely or explode.

The operators turned on and shut off the HPI pumps twice during the morning, finally leaving them on for a lengthy period between 8:26 AM and 10:30 AM. The core was probably partially uncovered from 5:15 AM until 10:30 AM. Later the operators decided to try to depressurize the plant in an attempt to start natural circulation cooling†, but in the process they uncovered the core again. The depressurization attempt went on until after 3:00 PM, but how long the core was uncovered is not known.

There were many more blunders in public relations, government and regulatory processes, and emergency management. We will not pursue these further except to say they were a direct result of confusing, conflicting, and misunderstood information combined with a serious lack of preparedness and policies on the part of a variety of entities and agencies.

The pool of resources to deal with the aftermath was expanded in an effort to make sure that early mistakes of inexperience and lack of thought were not extended. In addition to the NRC and state and local governments, TMI became a learning and advisory experience for the nuclear industry. By Friday, March 30, two days after the accident, the president of the utility had worked with the industry to form an advisory committee to advise on the completion of the stabilization of the plant and ultimately the cleanup.

The bottom line on TMI was a damning report on the ability of humans to mess up a physical system that was designed to operate safely.

---

* A movie about a reactor meltdown that was, ironically, in theatres at the time of the accident.

† A process that causes coolant water to circulate without pumps due to temperature differences.

However, the designers and regulators also came under sharp criticism for their lack of action on known problems in other plants and at TMI specifically.

Somewhere along the way, the industry that designed and delivered the systems, the operators who managed and ran them everyday, and the regulators who oversaw the situation all came to believe that things were going smoothly. Full speed ahead—don't worry about icebergs, leaking PORVs, polishers that can't be bypassed—the design is great and we've never had an accident, so everything must be OK.

The culture that tolerated small mistakes because the big picture had always worked out lost its curiosity, and operators who were able to do things by rote lost their ability to think and be analytic. How does this happen? Does it creep in because everything is going well and no one pushes the envelope? Is it from lack of rigor because real "worst-case" scenarios were never conceived or considered? Was it because operating nuclear plants is fundamentally different than operating other types of power-generating plants, and perhaps they should have been clustered with larger companies with more focused expertise?

It was a little of each of these, but it was fundamentally cultural. The lack of rigor in training, preparation, disaster preparedness, and even communications was significant. Multiple mistakes, not an accident, caused the TMI disaster, and the signs, signals, and lack of discipline were all there to be discovered for some time before it came apart. Learning seems to be very difficult here as in other situations we will explore.

The interesting thing about the Three Mile Island nuclear accident is that, although it occurred nearly 70 years after the *Titanic* and with unrelated technologies (with the exception that steam was being generated in both cases), the patterns and categories of mistakes are quite similar (see Figure 5.4). Of course, this reinforces the fact that a common element in most disaster scenarios, whether business or physical, is human intervention that is incompetent or inattentive. While systems can be improved with better design and more reliable components, man must continue to hone his analytic decision-making skills. Not only must we continue to learn, but until we develop "plug-compatible" brain dumps, each new generation must start learning from scratch but at a higher level. This makes understanding M^3 in both substance and process more important than ever to accelerate learning about avoiding disasters. But most importantly, it is an organization's culture that encourages, discourages, or is indifferent about rigorous learning and execution. Unless continuous learning is made part of the culture of an organization, from top to bottom, mediocrity will reign, and the probability of a disaster increases with time.

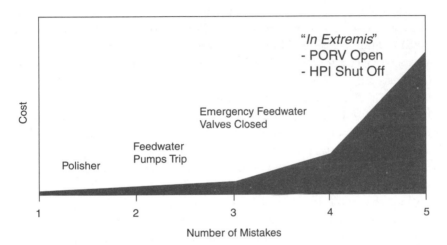

Figure 5.4 Multiple mistakes: The TMI result.

TMI-2 is owned by GPU (formerly General Public Utilities), which in the 1990s exited the generation business by selling off its plants to focus on transmission and delivery of power. In 2001, GPU merged with First Energy, which is the Ohio utility generally thought to be responsible for triggering the massive northeast blackout of August 2003. Some people in central Pennsylvania talk about the First Energy/GPU merger as a merger of equals because they can't figure out which company had the worst culture around quality. GPU sold TMI-1, which still operates, to another utility but retains ownership of TMI-2 while it continues to be decontaminated and decommissioned.

NASA–Launch Unless Proven Unsafe

"NASA cannot afford financially or politically to lose another orbiter."

–Elisabeth Paté-Cornell and Paul Fishbeck 1994[44]

Anyone with access to news knows that the space shuttle *Columbia*, also known as STS-107, burned up on reentry into the atmosphere, scattering charred debris across north Texas and Louisiana, on February 1, 2003. This happened almost 41 years after the first manned venture into space by the Soviet Union's Yuri Gagarin; his April 12, 1961 orbital flight lasted all of 108 minutes.

Mechanically, this disaster was due to a series of errors that caused a failure of the thermal protection system (TPS) on the space shuttle. TPS—the mechanism for safely dissipating the heat generated during high-velocity reentry into the Earth's atmosphere from space without burning up—has been one of many serious scientific and engineering challenges that all space programs have faced.

When the reusable space shuttle was developed, NASA shifted away from the ablative heat shield used on earlier capsule-style vehicles. The older capsule shield was designed to burn up during reentry to protect the capsule and its occupants, and it was the reason for the fiery, but normal, reentry we were used to seeing. Instead a high-tech "tile" was developed as one of the elements of the TPS for the space shuttle. These tiles weigh only 10 percent as much as the older ablative material that would be required, are composed of approximately 10 percent silica and 90 percent air, are very effective insulators that resist heat transmission instead of being consumed by the heat, and are reusable. The individual tiles require very careful installation and inspection and, if damaged, must be replaced to maintain the integrity of the heat shield.

It turns out that the risk associated with a heat shield failure is extreme but not uniform over the entire vehicle. A 1990 study conducted at Stanford University by Elisabeth Paté-Cornell and Paul Fishbeck, published publicly in 1994 by NASA and paid for partially with NASA funds, estimated that 15 percent of the tiles are responsible for 85 percent of the tile-related risk on the space shuttle.[45] This probabilistic risk assessment also looked, for the first time, at the role that management decisions and activities played in risk, albeit only for the tile subsystem. The analysis discussed operational management details that affected the quality of work, such as lack of enforcement of standard procedures for installation, lower pay of the important tile technicians as compared to other labor specialties, and a lack of priorities when it came to installation and maintenance of the tile subsystem.

This 1990 study was eerily prescient of *Columbia*'s 2003 experience, discussing all the dangers and risks of mismanagement of the tile subsystem but especially faulting higher-level management decision-making at NASA. The authors point out that there was such pressure to produce results after the introduction of the space shuttles that NASA shifted from a "launch if proven safe" attitude to a clearly communicated "launch unless proven unsafe" mindset.

This was a very significant shift in priorities that became interpreted over time as, "We've got to find a way to launch." When that begins to happen—in any business or organization, not just NASA—subtle signals ripple through an organization that change priorities, practices, and mindsets in ways that may not have been intended and are likely to be dangerous. This sounds strangely similar to the mindset that pervaded operations for the White Star Line and *Titanic*.

NASA actually forbade overall probabilistic risk assessment of flights dating back before the space shuttle program began. This resulted from an assessment prior to the *Apollo* manned moon mission that showed a relatively low probability of success. NASA's fear of scaring the public about the mission led them to simply ban such total assessments. Instead they focused on analysis of individual subsystems and projections of mean time between failure (MTBF) for components that, while individually and directionally correct, do not adequately look at total risk for the overall system.

The National Aeronautics and Space Administration (NASA) was formed in 1958. The 1961 "We can go to the moon" challenge by President Kennedy resulted in massive funding, growth, and success for NASA. The first serious accident was in 1967; during a launch pad test, three astronauts were killed in a fire aboard the *Apollo-1* capsule. The success of manned space flight programs, the moon landings, and the praiseworthy management and outcome of the *Apollo 13* crisis created a "can do" culture at NASA—until *Challenger* in 1986.

The public began to believe, as NASA hoped they would, that spaceflight was safe and almost routine. The shuttle missions were being opened up to persons from all walks of life, and a schoolteacher, Christa McAuliffe, was onboard as the world saw *Challenger* explode due to the failure of O-rings used as seals in a solid rocket motor joint. The reason for the technical failure was soon clear, but the analysis and decision to launch under cold-weather conditions known to increase risk for the O-rings was fundamentally a chain of managerial and cultural mistakes:

- The O-rings were known to be vulnerable to failure at low temperatures.

- The launch team and engineers knew the temperatures were below limits.

- The team, in consultation with contractors, debated the problem but decided to launch.

- NASA senior management was unaware of the debate.

- In general, NASA was found to be an organization that had become more willing to accept higher risks and afforded the safety organization (within NASA) little clout.

This was clearly a chain of mistakes that was driven by a culture that wanted to prove that "everything is nominal," "all systems are go," and "it's as safe as getting on an airplane." With the most complex system ever built by man, NASA, its contractors, and the public had become complacent, and the *Challenger* disaster in 1986 was the price paid for cultural complacency.

Many changes were made as a result of the Rogers Commission that investigated the *Challenger* disaster, including the establishment of a more powerful safety office reporting directly to the NASA administrator. A variety of other changes were recommended, including some technical issues, launch review procedures, and importantly, recommendations for changes in the management culture at NASA. Many of these changes were implemented, and in a little less than three years space shuttles were being launched again.

Unfortunately, the changes in attitudes and safety systems did not last. *Columbia* was not lost to a failed O-ring as *Challenger* was, but it was lost to something far worse—a recurrence of a flawed cultural attitude toward risk that had been previously discovered, supposedly corrected, and reoccurred with a vengeance. The *Columbia* Accident Investigation Board said in its August 2003 report:

"By the eve of the *Columbia* accident, institutional practices that were in effect at the time of the *Challenger* accident—such as inadequate concern over deviations from expected performance, a silent safety program, and schedule pressure—had returned to NASA."[46]

The loss of *Columbia* is well known and fresh in the minds of millions who followed it on live television or through the endless replays following the disaster. The series of mistakes that led to this stomach-turning disaster unfolded over the entire 17-day mission but really began much earlier with the culture that allowed an analysis of the importance of the tiles to be largely ignored for over 10 years. The short-term, mission-specific mistake chain evolved as follows:[47]

- The day after *Columbia*'s liftoff, a routine analysis by the Intercenter Photo Working Group* of higher-resolution images that had been developed overnight following the launch showed a debris strike to the orbiter at 81.9 seconds into the flight. A large object (suspected to be foam insulation from the external fuel tank) struck the orbiter on the underside of the left wing.

- Concern about possible damage led personnel in the Photo Group to request that their superiors in NASA ask the Department of Defense (DOD) to obtain very high-resolution images of the shuttle while on-orbit (NASA terminology). This was the first of three such specific requests over a period of days; NASA management denied all of the requests.

- The Photo Group assembled a report and video clips that it sent to various groups within NASA and contractors with major shuttle responsibility. NASA engineers and contractors formed a "Debris Assessment Team" to conduct a formal review and met for the first time on day five (January 21) of the mission. This group also requested (through a number of layers of bureaucracy) that NASA request DOD assistance with imaging. This became the second denied request.

* An internal NASA organization that reviewed images.

- Without images, the engineering team went to mathematical modeling as a tool for assessing potential damage and risk. They concluded over a six-day period that some localized heating damage was likely but could not state with certainty that this would lead to structural damage.

- Results and impressions from the Debris Assessment Team were passed along to the Mission Evaluation Room and then to the Mission Management Team as a verbal summary without data. This group decided the issue was a "turnaround" issue, meaning that it was classified as a small problem that should be checked after the shuttle landed and before its next flight. Note that on day eight of the mission, mission control e-mailed the shuttle crew that the foam strike situation had been reviewed and there was, "...absolutely no concern for entry."[48]

- Engineers across NASA and mission control continued to exchange numerous e-mails expressing concern and speculating on possible events even after the decision had been made that this was a turnaround issue.

- Mission control, including specialist teams such as the Entry Flight Control Team, exhibited no concern about "de-orbit," and by 8:10 AM on February 1, the Mission Control Center Entry Flight Director had polled all in mission control for a GO/NOGO decision and informed the *Columbia* crew they were "GO for de-orbit burn."

The mistakes had all been made; a chain that started culturally a decade or more before could no longer be broken. It culminated as a group of engineers, who had doubts about the decisions their superiors had made, watched with the rest of us as *Columbia* burned up on reentry. As civilian, military, and police personnel began to find pieces of the wreckage across the countryside of northeast Texas and northwest Louisiana, people across the world showed deep respect for the astronauts on the most multinational and multicultural mission in history.

Respect for the bravery and sacrifice of the crew was countered with questions about the cause. Questions about the strike damage, the tiles, and NASA's decision-making were on the table quickly. In terms of making progress against stamping out mistakes, it is unfortunate that the investigation could not have been completed in a week. Over time, the public emotion about a tragedy like this subsides, and we revert back to Perrow's "normal accident" hypothesis and just accept that bad things sometimes happen when engaged in risky endeavors.

We should not kid ourselves. NASA has proven repeatedly that it cannot fix itself. Neither *Challenger* nor *Columbia* was an "accident;" they were the predictable outcome of management complacency and incompetence. In fact, it turns out that foam loss occurred on 80 percent of the 79 flights where imagery was available to determine if this occurred. This was once again a case of, "We've never hit an iceberg before—full speed ahead," only this time it was foam icebergs coming off the fuel tank in a space launch. Complacency created by a lack of damage from similar occurrences in the past led NASA management to believe that this was an innocuous deficiency that should be tolerated and ignored. Once the organization saw the anomaly as "normal," it led not only to disregarding information, but to blatant disregard for the opinions of those who were analytic and courageous enough to raise questions. The patterns of mistakes repeat over and over from different contexts, and we do not "connect the dots" and learn.

NASA's engineering accomplishments have been extraordinary, but engineers know there are limitations; arrogant managers dismissed limitations as impediments to accomplishing the mission. Cultural problems that run this deep are not fixed with minor changes.

NASA announced some significant changes in operations leadership in July 2003, but only, apparently, in response to pressure from those who provide the funding—the United States Congress. Nothing short of dismantling NASA's management structure is likely to fix a cultural problem this deep.

As this is written, NASA's independent "Return To Flight Task Group" is working. Their charge is to assess NASA's progress on implementation of both the specific and general recommendations in the *Columbia* Accident Investigation Board's report. Their charge is not to determine whether the space shuttle system is too complex, unsafe, or unmanageable to return to flight; NASA seems to have already decided that: "Everything is GO."

Common Cultural Issues

NASA, the operators of space shuttles *Challenger* and *Columbia*, and White Star Line, the operators of *Titanic*, had some common characteristics as organizations. Both built a number of identical vessels for transportation in relatively new ways, one whose passengers and crew existed in spartan functionality and the other with the most opulent appointments money and craftsmanship could provide.

Neither was the first in their realm, but both pioneered new designs. Both began with much excitement and public acclaim and ended in tragedy. Both organizations were respected for their accomplishments and discredited for their arrogance, flawed operating decisions, and complacency.

Sadly, following their brushes with disaster, organizational culture was identified as a significant contributor to their errors and affected the viability of White Star, General Public Utilities (TMI's owner), and NASA. White Star ended up being acquired by another line. NASA will fight for more missions deserving of congressional appropriations, and GPU left the business of owning power generation plants, with the exception of TMI-2. Who would buy it?

Insights

History leaves us with interesting legacies, one of which is a visceral reaction to events with the mere mention of a name that has come to stand for tragedy, human suffering, or victory. In the United States, words such as "Gettysburg," "Iwo Jima," "9/11," and "Normandy" that were once only words evoke meaning, memory, and emotion instantly—even for those who were not present. "Three Mile Island," "*Titanic*," "*Challenger*," and "*Columbia*" are also words that now instantly communicate fear, suffering, loss, and empathy. For those who understand what really happened, there is another reaction—incredulity that these things could have happened at all. But if the chain of mistakes had been broken, those words would still just be words with no message to telegraph to anyone.

Insight #23: Test and retest assumptions—until proven beyond a doubt. Assumptions are at the core of mistakes in physical systems and business. The problem is that we often make assumptions and draw what we think are conclusions on the basis of limited data, and then if nothing bad happens, we begin to view the assumptions as truth. *Titanic* was assumed to be unsinkable. TMI was assumed to be fail-safe under all conditions.

NASA assumed that since foam had been coming off the center fuel tank for more than 100 launches and had never caused any *serious* damage, that it could not cause serious damage. Yet in the investigation of the *Columbia* accident, it did not take long to show that a piece of foam moving at over 500mph relative to the shuttle wing could do enough damage to bring the shuttle down, but only if it hit in just the right place. This is the problem with assumptions, they are just that, and they have limitations that we may not realize. Once we believe them, we closed doors of understanding, killing curiosity and analysis.

Insight #24: Push or ignore engineered safety at your peril. Engineers and designers who build systems of all types build in features designed to enhance the capability of the system to perform the intended function, but they also include features to minimize the chance of damage in the event of partial or full failure. This is true for physical systems from airplanes to zoos and also is important in today's more complicated business world where "systems" include complex human—software—process systems in a wide range of businesses. Do airline reservation systems, manufacturing control and supply chain systems, credit card billing systems, and billing and receivable systems for most businesses have anything in common with physical disasters? The same opportunity to damage a business is there because of the complexity of the design and operations interface of man and machine.

Although designers try to anticipate adverse conditions that threaten the success of the system, they will not always successfully design for every circumstance, and even if they do, human intervention can often overcome the most rigorous safety design. Understanding that built-in safety features are there for a reason should be a cause for understanding limits. Pushing such systems to their limits or ignoring threats that test or evade safety systems should be undertaken only with the greatest care and understanding of the extreme risk involved. *Titanic*, TMI, *Challenger*, and *Columbia* all pushed engineering limits and lost.

Insight #25: Believe the data. "Believe your indications" is something all of us in the nuclear navy learned. Failure to believe information that is staring you in the face is one of the most common causes of catastrophes. In *Titanic,* TMI, and at NASA, operators had warnings of danger and did not heed them. In the case of *Titanic* the warnings were well in advance and could have easily been acted if minds had been receptive. At TMI, damage could have been minimized if warnings that were part of the recovery process had been observed. With NASA, the warnings were repeatedly offered in advance and were analytically sound, but they were dismissed just as routinely as the captain of *Titanic* ignored the warnings he received.

Insight #26: Use available resources. Captain Smith of *Titanic* ignored available resources, other than consulting the ship's designer after the collision, who told him exactly how long it would take the ship to go down. When it was clear the ship would sink, Smith began to seek rescue help.

At TMI, it was two hours before the team on watch seriously sought outside help, apparently believing mistakenly until then that they could handle the situation. Some of the help literally wandered in the door as the next shift reported for work. Others, such as the B&W representative, were sought out, and still others, such as the NRC and Pennsylvania government and regulatory officials, were required notifications.

NASA engineers repeatedly asked their superiors to use DOD capabilities to get close images of Columbia on-orbit and were denied. The debate will go on forever about whether anything could have been done to save the crew, but the opportunity was missed, not once but repeatedly.

Insight #27: Train for the "can't happen" scenario. Those involved with *Titanic, Columbia*, and TMI all thought many things could not happen or at worst were very remote. This mindset is obviously dangerous, but so is an overly conservative "If I don't go outside the sky can't fall on me" attitude. You obviously train for known situations in operating any device from a car to the space shuttle. But thinking about how you would handle something "they" say "can't happen" may be more important than an idle intellectual game.

Insight #28: Open your mind past your blinders. This is extremely difficult. How do you know that your response has been conditioned by the context of your experiences? Perhaps the only defense is to play "what if" games with yourself and your colleagues. Regardless of the business or physical context, these are useful exercises. If you find yourself in a confusing situation, perhaps the proper question when you have exhausted all avenues is, "What's the other right answer?"* This question often opens the mind to looking at whether there is another answer by discarding what you have already thought about without success.

A Note on Big Ships, Big Planes, and Nuclear Power

In the steam age of the late nineteenth century, businessmen pushed for larger ships that could carry more passengers. Safety became a primary concern only when some major disasters, including *Titanic*, changed public opinion and governments demanded reforms through law and regulation. Construction and materials improved, operators complied with new regulations, crews learned, and eventually commerce at sea became relatively safe. There are still disasters at sea, and most of them are man-made, but they are rare by comparison. Man is capable of learning and operating complex systems, but there is, unfortunately, a cycle of learning that is punctuated by the school of hard knocks.

As aviation (and railroads for that matter) evolved, it went through the same technological and operator learning cycles. Man learned to do what he could do with the technology of the time, but accident rates were high. The technology improved dramatically as the jet age came along and safety improved somewhat, but there were still accidents that should not have happened. The operator learning was not complete.

Now Airbus is building the A380 that may eventually carry up to 800 passengers. Have our systems and operations evolved to a point where the safety level will be high enough to please society? I suspect for the 380 and as with the 747, we will see a very low accident rate. The good news is that technological learning, operational learning, systems learning, and attitudes have converged to improve the probability of success at levels that we will find acceptable with minimal shock.

---

* This concept is a good one in many contexts, but I first came across it in Roger von Oech's book *A Whack on the Side of the Head* published in 1983.

What about the nuclear power industry—was TMI a sufficient learning experience? Yes and no. We clearly learned that systems can be designed to save the operators and other stakeholders from dangerous conditions and damage, but they have to be allowed to work. Inadequate training and certification, lax management and regulatory oversight, overly complex sensing, and control systems that provide data but fail to provide useful information all contributed to operator confusion and error that ultimately caused the TMI disaster. The interference and failure to act properly by humans at TMI literally set the nuclear power industry back a quarter century or more in the United States.

The U.S. Navy has proven that similar plants can be operated safely under even more challenging conditions but only with extreme attention to education, detail, discipline, and process. This lesson seemed lost in the public debate that raged after TMI. The technology at TMI worked—just barely. It did not save the plant, but it did not result in any external damage, despite all the incompetent and unintended efforts of people to overcome the built in safety features.

As people, we seem willing to trust technology to help us, but we back away from it when we witness human misuse of that technology, often inappropriately blaming the technology for the outcome. We have allowed those who believe we are incapable of learning to shut down the nuclear power industry that may be more important to our future than ever. We all consume increasing amounts of electricity but do not want to hear that nuclear power generates it. We want to hear that our required power growth is coming from some as-yet-unknown completely clean power source. Over 20 percent of U.S. electricity comes from nuclear sources now, but that will decrease over time as plants age and are taken offline, increasing other environmental problems if we do nothing.

Titanic, TMI, and *Columbia/Challenger* have extraordinary parallels because all involved unfortunate learning about the human role in evolving technologies. All were wakeup calls for improving not only technology and systems but also the training, education, and cultural norms that inform or destroy effective decision-making. We must come to see TMI, *Columbia*, and other disasters as the wakeup call that *Titanic* was—a call for improvement of the way we use technologies rather than the death knell for something that can benefit society.

Business Parallels

As we have seen in case after case, business does not do a good job of analyzing, understanding, and preventing management errors. Those responsible for operating physical systems that have the potential to inflict damage on others do this in a more disciplined fashion but do not always learn what they should.

Business has much to learn from the process of analyzing physical accidents and much more than is acknowledged to learn from the specific findings of physical accidents. People are involved, so the patterns of mistakes are similar. We have repeatedly seen patterns that apply to physical operations and managerial decision-making:

- Failure to believe and act on information
- Decision bias induced by history, culture, or desired outcomes
- Taking shortcuts and/or bypassing proven procedures
- Failure to use other resources that might be able to help
- Absence of impetus for change until there is a major error
- Failure to fully evaluate possible scenarios and consequences of actions
- Failure to analyze decisions and learn from the findings

One of my overriding beliefs, only partially tongue-in-cheek, is

"The world is incompetent."

Those who know me have seen the sign in my office with the preceding saying and have heard me use this in talks since the mid-1970s, and I say it only half jokingly. Examples covered in this chapter prove again that if there is a way to mess things up, someone will usually find it.

Countering these examples are companies who have taken visible proactive actions that are effectively the opposite of the error-inducing behaviors of the preceding companies. That is not to say that the following companies listed do not make errors; they just seem less prone to error chains that become serious, or they have broken a chain that was on the verge of becoming very serious, regardless of the initiating incident source. There are certainly others that exhibit the same effective behaviors and processes but are not as visible. Examples include:

- Johnson & Johnson's 70 years of sustained growth in changing markets and technologies
- Microsoft changing position on Internet strategy (despite mistakes in other areas)
- Southwest Airlines and Dell redefining the playing field in commoditized industries
- Toyota's Lexus and U.S.-based manufacturing for Camry and other models
- Verizon for quickly building the leading U.S. wireless company as a joint venture
- Emerson Electric as one of the most consistently performing "invisible" businesses
- IBM and their dramatic recognition of and delivery on the need for change
- Hundreds of other companies that are delivering results and do not make the front pages

We will explore some of these examples in later chapters, but it is important to understand that we can learn a great deal from the companies and management teams that have made mistakes. It is just as important to understand that, although these examples are abundant, they do not represent the entire universe of businesses.

6

Cultures that Create "Accidents"

"Even if 80 percent of people resist me, I don't care. I'm not a politician, so I don't need to be elected based on popularity."

—Yoichrio Kaizaki, CEO Bridgestone/Firestone, commenting on Firestone's 1994 labor strife that led to quality problems[49]

We have examined a number of mistake chains that were related to execution or strategy in companies. We have also seen examples of physical disasters that were created or made worse by organizational cultures that failed to detect and correct mistakes that led to "accidents" that were really due more to incompetence and neglect than anything accidental.

There were some common traits in the mistake sequences in the physical disasters of *Titanic*, Three Mile Island (TMI), and *Columbia* that we see over and over in business situations as well:

■ Each organization or operating entity thought they knew what they were doing. In fact, they were *very confident* that they knew what they were doing.

- Each was operating a system (or business) that was state of the art for its time.

- Each ended up in a disaster of their own making, created and/or amplified by multiple mistakes.

- Each failed to act on numerous warning signs and thus essentially guaranteed exponential damage from the mistake chain.

- Each created a disaster that left blight so significant that the company (or organization) will be remembered in business history in a negative light for some time.

There is much we can learn from each physical disaster, and yet most business people do not recognize that these accidents have something to teach them, preferring to believe that "they are too far removed from my business."

While the mistake parallels are present between physical and business disasters, the business situations can be more complex because, in many cases, there is nothing physical like a ship or plane to make the problem quite as obvious to those involved. In many business situations, we see that the entire culture of a company becomes supportive of a serious mistake waiting to happen. Observe the examples presented in this chapter and remember the parallels to the physical disasters we have examined.

Myopia as a Fatal Business Disease

For nearly 10 years during the 1980s, I did part-time consulting for a large, growing, multihospital company named American Medical International (AMI) with operations in the United States and the United Kingdom. My work was with a consulting firm, Friesen International, owned by AMI. Friesen had a large team that conducted market needs analysis, program planning and design, conceptual facility planning, and assistance in obtaining regulatory approvals for hospitals and health systems. Friesen did work for outside clients unrelated to AMI, but as the growth in the hospital business accelerated in the early 1980s, AMI needed more time and resources devoted to its growing empire. Friesen ceased doing outside work and became a large planning department with only one client—AMI and its 100+ hospitals and a smaller number of outpatient facilities.

AMI began with one hospital. An entrepreneur in the laboratory business took over a small, less than stellar, for-profit facility in California to satisfy debts owed to him as a supplier. From that humble start, he began to grow a chain of hospitals by purchasing individual facilities from physicians, investors, or local governments looking to exit the business of owning hospitals. He brought in professional management and the growth continued, eventually acquiring other small hospital chains. Typical of the for-profit hospital industry at the time, most of the facilities were located across the southern half of the United States with heavy concentrations in California, Texas, and Florida. Facilities were also scattered across most of the states in between but in lower concentrations. The prime market areas had high growth, and AMI's hospitals in those markets did well while meeting the needs of growing populations.

AMI was number three in an industry that was growing overall but consolidating rapidly. The executives had their sights set on being number one. A few new hospitals were built in higher-growth areas, but they still saw the growth needed to reach the top spot in the industry as coming primarily from acquisitions. The buying spree continued even as the attractive higher-quality, better-performing facilities became harder to find.

By the mid 1980s, it became obvious to a few of us in the planning group that there was a pattern to AMI's overall profitability that was of concern. The team at Friesen conducted a detailed analysis and discovered that about 40 percent of the facilities were providing more than 110 percent of the company's profit. It also turned out that unit profitability was size dependent along with location, classified broadly as rural or urban. This was not immediately obvious because, like many companies, especially in service businesses, a geographic operating organization made the most sense and was in place. This meant that virtually all metrics were tracked and aggregated on a regional basis, in some cases masking patterns.

Each individual regional vice president knew that their larger hospitals generally did better than their smaller ones, but the magnitude of the problem was not appreciated across the company. It turned out, not unexpectedly, that most of the smaller hospitals that did not perform well were in less populated, rural areas. Most were formerly owned by county governments that sold them when they encountered financial difficulty as farm populations continued to decline and the higher quality of medical care in cities made patients more interested in traveling to receive the benefits of larger, better-equipped facilities and medical staffs.

We had the team at Friesen put together some "packaging" scenarios, bundles of assets that might be sold together to a strategic buyer. The results nearly leapt off the page. If you were to create a division with certain hospitals that were small and rural, plus a few facilities located in states where the company had limited operations, it might be possible to sell the whole package since other firms also wanted to grow by acquisition. The result would be a company with only 50 to 60 percent of the current revenues but with dramatically improved profitability. The plan would also release some capital that could be used to invest in existing markets and facilities.

Our group at Friesen believed this was a spectacular business suggestion for AMI. How could it lose? The hospital mergers and acquisitions (M&A) business was hot so there would be buyers, and it would be a real win for the company. We made the presentation and came back to the office to tell our eager and hard-working team what top management had said.

They said "NO"—not politely, not with conditions, not with apologies—an unequivocal "NO." The reason was clearly articulated, "We want to be the biggest company in this business and that means growing, not shrinking. That means buying more facilities, not selling them off. We buy facilities and operate them better than their previous owners; we don't want to see AMI shrink." That was it—the revenue of AMI was the only criterion in the executive committee's sights at that point.

This point of view was not quite as irrational as it sounds since, at that time, most government-funded business (Medicare in particular) was billed on a cost-plus basis, meaning that more facilities with more cost meant more revenue and more profit, albeit limited to a contractual amount. The problem was that our team at Friesen believed the industry was starting to change, likely to move away from cost-plus accounting, and that the changes would accelerate.

Following our presentation, some jokes about career-ending presentations were made, at which the head of Friesen and I laughed since he was very mobile and I was a consultant who had a full-time job in a top business school. The rejection was disappointing, though, because we believed the plan would have left the company in a stronger position for the long run.

The acquisitions continued over the next few years, along with the hoped-for revenue growth. But numbers one and two in the industry were doing the same thing, so there was no net gain in position against the leaders. To make matters worse, the shift away from cost-plus government reimbursement was accelerating with a move to fixed price by condition, regardless of the cost incurred in delivering care. Health maintenance organizations (HMOs) and other delivery mechanisms gained market share from traditional indemnity insurers and became tougher negotiators, driving margins down for hospitals.

Suddenly, having the most facilities with a cost base that could be recovered with a guaranteed profit was not a viable strategy. AMI decided that vertical integration looked good since those controlling access to the system would be in a better position to make money. They made a feeble attempt—that was a complete failure—to enter the health plan/insurance business.

Within three years of our suggestions to management, the head of Friesen and I had moved on to do other things. Our departure was unrelated to the restructuring suggestion, but we continued to believe it had been a great idea.

A few years after our unwanted suggestion to restructure AMI, a group of dissident shareholders began a proxy fight to oust management and replace the board. The company's performance had deteriorated, and while it was a bitter struggle, the dissidents eventually won. Management was ousted, a new CEO was installed, and the turnaround began. AMI was split into two pieces, one of which was sold off and included the smaller, predominately rural hospitals with a couple of attractive jewels thrown in to make the package salable. AMI survived as the larger, more profitable, predominately urban hospitals in higher-growth areas. AMI itself was sold in a takeover a few years later. The shareholders did well, but they probably would have done better if the idea we had proposed had taken place a few years earlier.

To summarize this cultural mistake sequence:

- AMI management was fixated on a previously successful business model and ignored changes in the market that threatened the core of that model—in this case, cost-plus reimbursement.

- Top management firmly believed they knew what they were doing, did not take advice easily, and delighted in management by intimidation.

- Company headquarters was in Beverly Hills, the perfect place for the most senior executives to be completely out of touch with a business that operated in less affluent southern and southwestern cities and towns.

- The executives arrogantly believed they could enter a related, but totally different, industry (health insurance) without understanding that the competencies required were not present in the company.

In fact, this list can be explained not so much as separate mistakes but as one giant cultural mistake that manifested itself in myriad ways. This is the problem with organization culture: It is frequently the most powerful factor in determining the success or failure of an organization, and it often helps both success and failure occur—in sequence.

Knowledgeable employees throughout the company were talking in the halls saying, "We don't understand the strategy." In fact, they understood the strategy, but they also understood that it was the wrong strategy and needed to change. Despite attempts by many, including the Friesen team, top management was the last to realize the mistakes, and it is not clear that they realized what the mistakes had been even after they were ousted in a rarely successful shareholder coup. It was all about mindset and an isolated "We know the right answers and don't need advice" corporate culture that insiders were powerless to change, although many tried and were rebuffed.

This story is typical of companies where culture becomes the worst enemy of success, especially when that culture is one that is driven and controlled from the very top and is out of synch with the reality of the business environment. It is no different than NASA's problems with *Challenger* and *Columbia*. It is repeated in numerous examples in companies and organizations continually, and it is the most difficult form of mistake chain to stop.

Ford/Firestone—When the Rubber Leaves the Road

Today's steel-belted radial tires are a bargain. If you buy a good tire, keep it properly inflated, and drive reasonably, you will get 40,000 to 50,000 miles per set or more. At $100 to $125 or less per tire for most cars, that works out to about one penny per mile for all four tires, probably less than 3 percent of the cost of operating your automobile.

Depending on what and how you drive, you probably spend 10 times that much on gasoline. But even though the relative cost of tires is not that high, they may be one of your most important safety items.*

Most of us take the performance of our tires as a given, expecting that we can drive at, or above, the speed limit for many hours without concern. As a pilot, I inspect the tires on my airplane prior to every flight, but I rarely give the tires on my car more than a casual glance as I walk up to rush off somewhere. I check the air pressure in my automobile tires every three or four weeks, but my observation is that the average person does so even less often.

The biggest enemy of tires is heat, and it builds up significantly when driving at high speed in hot weather. Heat buildup is even more of a threat if a tire is underinflated. Thus, when Ford began to see tread separation problems on the Firestone tires mounted as original equipment on Explorer sport utility vehicles and many light truck models in Venezuela and Saudi Arabia in 1998 and 1999, they likely attributed the problem to excessive heat and speed since both were climates with nearly continuous moderate to high heat conditions.

As failures mounted, Ford did send failed tires to Firestone in an effort to understand the problem. In 1999, Ford replaced tires on Explorers in Saudi Arabia, against Firestone's advice. Ford documents later showed that Firestone had warned Ford against replacing tires in Saudi Arabia in fear of alerting U.S. regulatory authorities.[50]

Ford decided to replace the tires on over 39,000 Explorers in Venezuela in May 2000 with Goodyear tires because there was still no resolution from Firestone on the cause of the problem. Then it got worse—the problem began showing up in the United States. An increasing and disturbing number of fatal accidents involving Ford Explorers seemed to be initiated by the same tread separation Ford had seen overseas. There was no longer any way to rationalize that the problem was due to local driving conditions not present in the United States.

Unknown to Ford, a State Farm Insurance staff member whose job was to look for recurring causes of accidents had noticed, as early as 1998, what he believed was an excessive pattern of tread separation in certain

---

* The differences in tire quality and performance are striking—and confusing. While there are data sources to help consumers make choices, the many consumers simply replace worn out tires with the same brand that was on the vehicle when it was delivered, which is why selling to auto manufacturers is so important to tire makers. Reliable information sources include the NHTSA Web site (www.nhtsa.dot.gov/cars/testing/) and Consumers Union and its magazine *Consumer Reports*.

types of Firestone tires in the United States. He notified the National Highway Traffic Safety Administration (NHTSA) as early as the summer of 1998.

By May 2000, with mounting evidence of Firestone tire failures on Ford vehicles in the United States, the NHTSA announced a formal investigation into tread separation of certain Firestone tire models. Ford finally began their own internal investigation in July 2000 and soon figured out that older tires produced in Firestone's Decatur, Illinois plant had a disproportionate failure rate.

Once the correlations became visible more local data surfaced, and it became clear that especially in warmer, southern states there was an alarming number of Ford Explorer/Firestone tire-related fatal accidents. By late summer 2000, various news reports were attributing 75 or more known deaths to the Ford/Firestone combination. Estimates are that this number eventually rose to 200 or more.

The Ford Explorer SUV is marketed as a family car. Heat buildup, a common occurrence on longer trips in warmer climates, was clearly involved. Thus, many of the accidents were heart-wrenching stories of families on vacation losing a mom, dad, kids, or a whole family in an out-of-control accident. Once the pattern was clear, the press coverage was fast and brutal. State officials, consumer advocates, and the U.S. Congress were all making accusations, holding hearings or investigations, and calling for action.

Ford and Firestone, a unit of Japan's Bridgestone Corporation since 1988, both swung into action but in very different ways. While Ford could have seen the patterns earlier, once faced with the data, Ford understood the need to maintain customer confidence and pushed fairly openly to have the tires replaced, eventually agreeing to have tires replaced on Explorers even if they had to pay for them from manufacturers other than Firestone.

Firestone was not convinced that the problem was theirs and was also worried about production capacity to meet the demand for replacement tires, so the recalls began with priority given to owners in hotter states such as California, Arizona, Texas, and Florida where Firestone claimed 80 percent of the problems had occurred. As the controversy got more press, consumers everywhere demanded replacements, did not want to wait for production to catch up, and were not sure they wanted Firestone tires as replacements.

Other manufacturers saw an opportunity and ramped up production, but even with additional capacity in the system, there were still temporary shortages in meeting the massive 6.5 million tire recall in the specific sizes required.

The continuing pressure from consumers caused Ford to tell all their dealers in August 2000 to replace tires if requested by customers despite Firestone's attempt to limit replacements to the priority states. Under pressure, Firestone began flying tires to the United States from Asia where they were manufactured by parent Bridgestone and authorized reimbursement for consumers who purchased tires from other manufacturers. Despite this, Firestone was perceived as dragging their feet as a result of their attempt to set priorities on exchanges because of supply problems. Significantly, their senior executives were nearly invisible in the process. In particular, Bridgestone's CEO, Yoichiro Kaizaki, did not make any pubic statement on the problem until September 2000, more than four months into the most public phase of the crisis. Even then, while expressing regret for the incidents, his tone was defiant regarding Ford's attempt to shift blame for the crisis to Firestone.

Firestone continued to minimize their responsibility by pointing out how few tires had failed out of the nearly 15 million produced in what was one of the most popular tire models ever manufactured. This effort had little impact, however, as the daily news reports of the problem persisted. As more data emerged, it turned out that the Ford Explorer had a high rollover rate, and Firestone tires had failed in about 10 percent of fatal Explorer rollover accidents. This added some credibility to Firestone's claim that the problem was not solely the fault of Firestone.

In hearings before the Senate Commerce Committee on September 12, 2000, Bridgestone/Firestone testified:[51]

> "The tire failures in Saudi Arabia, of which Firestone is aware, were caused by severe service conditions—damaged tires, improperly repaired tires, and deflation of tires to operate off-road, without re-inflation when returned to 100+ mile per hour operation on the highway.... There are no remotely comparable operating conditions in the U.S. For these reasons and because no defects in the tires could be found, Firestone did not participate in or bear any costs of Ford's Saudi Arabia tire replacement program."

During the same hearing, Bridgestone/Firestone executive vice president John Lampe gave some further clues that Firestone did not accept full blame for the debacle:[52]

> "We are also trying to work with Ford Motor Company to understand the cause. This has led us to understand a key point for the future. The government and others have tended to look at auto safety and tire safety separately. We believe that it is important to look at both issues together. Correct tires must be matched with vehicles; the mutual duties of tire manufacturers and automobile manufacturers must be made absolutely clear."

Implied in this statement are some facts that were not obvious to the public and the news media at the time about a series of mistakes that had led to the problem faced by Ford and Firestone. Those mistakes and others that were revealed later included:

- Ford's design for the Explorer evolved from the Bronco in the late 1980s. The Bronco had a history of rollover accidents, and while Ford wanted an improved vehicle, pressure for time to market led to compromises and the continuation of a number of existing design mistakes that was the likely beginning of the problem chain.

- Explorer's design continued Ford's oft advertised "Twin I-Beam" frame design, touted as making their vehicles tough. The downside was that this design provided less flexibility for engine mounting, resulting in an engine that was higher above the ground than in other vehicles. This raised the vehicle's center of gravity, which was already high in comparison to sedans, making it more susceptible to rollover.

- Criticism of the Ford Bronco from Consumers Union (CU) made Ford sensitive to the need to pass the CU rollover test, so they experimented with various combinations of tires, springs, and other adjustments that could be made without affecting the basic design. After debating the merits of different tires, an internal memo from a Ford engineer was prescient about the fact that the company was taking a risk installing size P235 tires, apparently suggesting that the tires might help pass the test but might not solve the problem under real-world conditions.[53]

■ The Firestone tires that Ford specified met only grade "C" in the NHTSA standard for heat resistance on a scale of ABC, where C is the lowest level allowed by Federal regulation. Of all tires sold in the United States, only 14 percent have a C temperature rating.[54] This rating evaluated tires loaded and properly inflated at 50mph for two hours and then 90 minutes at speeds up to 85mph. This standard seems adequate for a vehicle used mainly for local errands, but the average consumer does not understand the standard. Would you drive a vehicle with tires that said "not suitable for sustained use for more than 3.5 hours?" Many of the families killed or injured in crashes were on long trips and had been on the road for many hours at the time of their accidents.

■ In order to reduce rollover tendencies, Ford stiffened the springs in the suspension and specified inflation pressure for the tires at 26psi (pounds per square inch). Firestone's recommended inflation for the tire was 30psi. Firestone testified that Ford did not request high-speed testing from Firestone at 26psi, choosing to do this at a Ford facility with the understanding that any problems would be reported to Firestone.[55]

■ Firestone did experience manufacturing quality problems for a period in the mid-1990s. This was a period when Firestone was in a very bitter dispute with unions at their Decatur plant. It is clear that some of these deficient tires failed and initiated an accident sequence in many vehicles, but it may have been a survivable sequence had it not been for the vehicle deficiencies noted above.

■ The NHTSA indirectly admitted, through an additional funding request to Congress in September 2000,[56] that it had limited ability and/or authority to gather and analyze information on safety problems such as the Explorer/Firestone situation, on foreign experience with tires (or other products), and on safety information communicated between manufacturers and dealers. This lack of any central information repository contributed to the time it took to identify and understand problems.

This scenario that seemed ready to bury Firestone was a sequence of mistakes made by both companies. Contrary to what the public might have believed from early reports, Ford may have had the larger responsibility for the outcome, but it did not look that way because Ford did a better job of handling the public relations than Firestone. Neither company would have been in trouble without the mistakes of the other, but both companies' mistakes were a result of cultural intransigence.

If we reduce the preceding technical mistakes to something the average person can understand, it might look like the following for Ford and Firestone:

- Ford was facing competitive pressure to bring a new and improved SUV to market. In an effort to decrease development time, minimize cost, and simplify manufacturing, they adopted as many designs and technologies as possible that were already in production, even though they knew these designs had deficiencies.

- Despite warnings about vehicle safety issues from their own staff, Ford engineering managers made decisions to make what they considered small changes in springs and tire pressures to overcome the design deficiencies.

- To minimize ongoing cost, the least expensive tire acceptable under federal regulations for temperature resistance was specified for the vehicle. There does not seem to be any plausible explanation for this other than saving money. Ford also saved some time by not having Firestone test the tires under the conditions that Ford was specifying for operation.

- Ford apparently assumed that consumers would keep tires properly inflated and not drive beyond the limits of the minimally capable tires, a very dangerous assumption given the high proportion of drivers who exceed speed limits and the small number who care about or understand tire ratings.

- Firestone manufactured a tire for Ford that met minimal federal regulations but had limited resources devoted to tracking failures and warranty claims.

- Firestone did have quality problems while attempting to cut costs in the mid-1990s. Firestone resisted union demands and demanded wage concessions during a 1994 labor dispute at the Decatur plant. During the ensuing strike replacement workers were used, many of whom were retained even after the strike was settled. A study published in 2003 proved statistically that there were significantly higher failure rates of tires produced at the Decatur plan during the labor strife than before or after or at other nonstriking plants. The highest failure rates on a monthly basis were associated with tires produced during the month when Firestone made the demand for wage concessions in early 1994.[57]

Significantly, there were Explorer accidents initiated by failures of other brands of tires but very few. It appears that most of the non-Firestone tires on Explorers were replacements purchased by consumers, and these tires from other manufacturers had the higher "B" rating for temperature resistance. Explorers did not have the worst rollover record for SUVs, but their tires were implicated in a significant number of the accidents that did occur.

The bottom line is that the *vehicle system* that was produced with a questionable design by Ford and the cheap tire specified was probably adequate if everything worked perfectly. The problem was there was no margin of error if consumers abused the vehicle or tires in any way or if there were any defects in the tires. Unfortunately, this is what we see in so many mistake sequences—*no margin for error*. How many business situations or plans have you seen where you realized too late that the assumptions made were so narrow and demanding that there was no margin for error?

This multiple-mistake chain resulted from both companies' cultures that sought to "meet customer needs," where the definition of "needs" was minimal. Ford's cost-driven culture produced a vehicle that was attractive from a customer standpoint but minimally acceptable technically. Firestone's focus on cost control caused it to lose sight of the quality responsibility of its business, especially for the legal, but marginal, product they produced for Ford. The problem was that many people in both organizations seemed to know that problems existed, yet no one wanted to take the lead for fear of incurring cost, administrative hassle, and reputation risk.

In this case, the two companies involved traded safety to satisfy customer pressure for price in a very competitive business that was already in serious oversupply on a global basis. This meant that a heavy emphasis on cost control, almost regardless of impact, had begun to creep into these and other organizations in the industry. Automotive original equipment manufacturers (OEMs) began pushing suppliers harder, and suppliers became more compliant in meeting minimum specifications to keep the business.

I observed this firsthand as a member of the board of a medium-size automotive supplier that, along with others in the industry, saw its margins shrink as OEM purchasing departments gained more power than engineering departments through the 1990s. It is quite common in the industry, especially in the United States, for an OEM to award a contract to a supplier with a reasonable starting price for the first year and a *decrease* in price for each of the subsequent contract years. The supplier is expected to improve productivity or find other ways to reduce cost if they wish to maintain their margins or even stay in business.

For industries that are mature, these are normal economic forces at work, but they put companies in serious bind. The question for senior executives in these hypercompetitive industries becomes, "How do I find the money to fund new product development when my margins are shrinking, the competition is moving fast, and customers are demanding higher-quality products at lower prices?" This is the reason that companies in the automotive industry, and others, have little incentive to spend money on anything that does not sell more product. Until recently, safety was in that category.

In fact, it was Ford that first brought seatbelts to mass-produced automobiles in the mid-1950s but pulled them out when they found customers did not care. If it did not sell more vehicles, it was simply an unnecessary cost. The playing field was leveled on seatbelts for all manufacturers when the federal government began requiring them in the front seat of new vehicles with the 1965 model year.

Exciting product design and new features are needed to attract customers, but cost efficiency is needed to make a profit in price-sensitive auto markets. Over time, cost became the mantra for the U.S. auto industry, and other things took a back seat. The real question that cannot be answered is, "Was Ford ahead financially by saving on the design and manufacturing, despite the recall and legal costs?" Probably not, but they may be ahead in other areas where they have skimped that have not been catastrophic.

Throughout 2000 and into 2001, the relationship between Ford and Firestone deteriorated from one of joint responsibility and concern to finger-pointing acrimony. The companies had been linked for almost 100 years, going back to the friendship of their respective founders. Firestone had been the exclusive provider for new vehicle tires for Ford for nearly 75 years, but they were clearly at odds over who was to blame for a significant and growing problem.

In May 2001, Firestone CEO John Lampe fired his customer, ending the long relationship with Ford over what he characterized as significant concerns about the safety of the Explorer vehicle. Ford's CEO, Jacques Nasser, did not shrink from the confrontation, publicly indicating that Ford no longer had confidence in Firestone's tires.[58] Perhaps Nasser should have said, "We were too cheap to buy a better tire or fix other problems, so we are blaming the tire supplier while we quietly fix the problems that should have been fixed some time ago."

On May 22, 2001, Ford voluntarily expanded the recall and announced it was prepared to spend up to $2 billion to replace 13 million Firestone tires. For a time, Ford looked like the good guys, the responsible company that was going beyond requirements to make sure the customer was served well and protected. But as time went on and more investigations took place, the background on Ford's design and decision process began to paint a different picture.

As this is written, Ford and Firestone have settled a number of lawsuits out of court, but many others are still wending their way through the court systems of various states. If they had it to do over again, would Firestone have provided Ford a higher-quality tire at the same price to get the work? Would Ford have made some of the changes to the Explorer's design that they made later to correct the problems? The debacle has cost both companies billions of dollars in direct costs of the recall, lawsuits, and shareholder value as well as adverse publicity that will continue for some years via lawsuits.

Their PR departments would have you believe that Ford and Firestone acted to break the mistake chain. The argument is specious, however, because they were already "in extremis" with damage mounting exponentially by the time they took any serious action, despite numerous early warnings over a number of years.

The cultures of Ford and Firestone worked against doing things that could have prevented the whole mistake sequence. The cultures of the companies also worked against one thing that would have stopped the mistake chain—analyzing and believing the scenarios that could unfold if these somewhat predictable events were to take place and what the likely costs might be. The combination of a dominant and focused culture tends to reinforce its biggest weakness—the inability to look at alternatives.

An important lesson here is that, once something has spun out of control to the point that customers feel panicked about their situation, it is time to stop the excuses and get on with the fix. Regardless of the truth, management has to deal with the reality of perception. But often on advice from lawyers, resistance to this concept is widespread.

One of the recent rare exceptions has been Boeing's admission that ethics principles and perhaps laws were violated in their 2003 Air Force tanker lease crisis. Executives were terminated, and board members Lewis Platt and Harry Stonecipher both came out of retirement to serve as chairman and CEO, respectively. Both immediately went on a public campaign to admit the wrongdoing and get on with rebuilding confidence. This did not erase the crisis or some damage, but it was a definitive step to break the multiple-mistake chain and stop any further damage.

Enron–Living on the Edge and Loving It

Enron management came to believe that they were unique in business and that their company had extraordinary capabilities possessed by no others. Enron was "changing the rules of the game" and, as told by insiders who were there, believed they had developed unique business models that the rest of the world had not been smart enough to see.[59] Between 1985 and 2000, Enron transformed itself from a Houston-based natural gas distribution company into an internationally known behemoth that was the largest trader of electricity and natural gas, with operating entities in or planned in many of the developed and developing countries of the world. Enron was on a roll and believed they could expand their trading prowess to virtually every type of business and become the dominant middleman and market maker to the world.

They were proud of being ranked among the top companies in the world on the basis of market capitalization, and almost everyone in the world was cheering, albeit with a combination of admiration and envy. Almost everyone was cheering—except John Olson, who was the natural gas researcher and analyst with Merrill Lynch who dared to downgrade Enron stock in July 1997. In 2001, Olson, by then working at another firm, told the press that he had become skeptical about Enron because he could not really figure out how they were as profitable as they appeared. He was one of very few analysts who were correct to be suspicious as far back as 1997.

After a 2001 news story published in *U.S. News & World Report*, Ken Lay, Enron's chairman, tore the story out of the magazine and sent it to Olson's boss with a handwritten note that said, "John Olson has been wrong about Enron for over 10 years, and he is still wrong, but he is consistant [sic]."[60] Olson joked with his boss about the fact that at least he knew how to spell "consistent" properly even if Ken Lay did not. The purpose of the note, spelling errors or not, was to make sure that investment bankers understood that criticism by their analysts would not be tolerated by Enron and that lucrative business with Enron was tied to favorable ratings.

A "we can do no wrong" culture had developed with Enron's impressive growth and success, but somewhere along the way it changed from legitimate pride in accomplishment in a competitive industry to arrogance and a feeling of invincibility.

It had not always been this way. In the mid-1980s when deregulation of natural gas first appeared, Houston Natural Gas (HNG), as it was known then, was not on top of the world. Ken Lay was hired as CEO by the board following the founder's death. Internorth, based in Omaha, was the country's largest pipeline company and saw the instability in management at HNG as an opportunity. Shortly after Lay took over at HNG, he was confronted with a very attractive takeover offer from Internorth. The offer was so overpriced that it could not be refused. But Ken Lay's ambition emerged as he skillfully changed what had started as an acquisition of HNG by Internorth into a merger. Additionally, the deal started with assurances that the headquarters of the combined company would be in Omaha but ended up with Lay as the CEO of a renamed company called Enron and based in Houston.

Deregulation of natural gas provided opportunities for Enron, but there were inherent market inefficiencies that limited growth. By 1990, Enron still generated nearly 90 percent of its revenue from the regulated gas pipeline business. Lay wanted more of the potentially profitable deregulated business, and with the help of a McKinsey consultant named Jeff Skilling, began to put together a more complex and aggressive business strategy. Enron would become more than a trader, in essence creating and owning a gas market through contracts with suppliers and purchasers up and down the value chain. Skilling loved the strategies he helped developed and agreed to join Lay at Enron and head up Enron Gas Services, which became the vehicle that propelled Enron's growth, profitability, and stock price in the early 1990s.

By 1993, Skilling and others wanted even more growth and control over their markets, so they put together the first partnership designed to leverage their investments vertically in the industry. The Joint Energy Development Instruments (JEDI) were to be used to make investments that were strategically linked to Enron Gas Services business. In essence, Enron had entered some combination of venture capital and investment banking in the energy field. The best news was that their earlier success as traders had attracted a high-quality investor for the new partnership—CalPERS, one of the largest pension funds in the country representing public employees in California.

But the JEDI partnership was the first mistake in a series where arrogance took the company to places it never intended to visit. The leverage was extraordinary because Enron's capital contribution to JEDI was in the form of $250 million in Enron stock. Since the markets were beginning to believe that Enron was a growth company, the stock was going up, which increased the apparent value of the JEDI investment.

Enron's team believed they were good—really good—and their apparent success in the gas-trading business supported this belief. They began to believe Enron was destined to change the way business was done, and they set out to change conditions that stood in their way. Enron quietly became a significant lobbying organization in a number of states and at the national level. They sought rule changes to reduce regulation on trading gas and electricity, lobbied states to deregulate their utility industries, and lobbied the SEC to change revenue-recognition rules that were favorable to their business.

They understood that there would be opportunities to grow as the rules changed, and they had to be able to raise substantial capital, but the balance sheet would not support straight debt at the levels of investment they envisioned. They were looking for ways to raise capital without affecting the balance sheet, and JEDI was just the beginning.

Off-balance-sheet financing was not a new concept, but the sophistication and complexity of such deals evolved to a new level with the ever-inventive minds of investment bankers and consultants in the 1990s as special purpose entities (SPEs) became popular. Enron found a number of credible and willing investors, but over time their dreams got even bigger, requiring more capital. During the 1990s Enron came to dominate the deregulated gas markets and then moved on to become the largest player in electricity trading. By 2000, Enron believed their "model" could be extended almost infinitely. They began to describe themselves as a logistics company and tried to turn everything into a commodity that they could possibly securitize and, if necessary, transport and deliver. By 2000, over 95 percent of revenues came from wholesale energy services. They saw no limits and entered the water business, believed they would become a huge broadband player, and even considered a venture with Blockbuster to stream movies to the home. All the while they created more SPEs to fund the growth and to drive apparent profits without (apparently) hurting the balance sheet.

There were some who began to question "The World's Leading Company" slogan that Enron adopted. In March 2001, *Fortune* magazine ran an article entitled "Is Enron Overpriced?"[61] pointing out that with a stock price at 55 times trailing earnings, only 7 percent return on capital, and decreasing cash flow, something looked askew. Increasing questions about how they made money and suggestions that the model might not be as profitable as claimed just made Enron executives state even more assertively that their processes were simple but secret and could not be revealed. Many investors continued to buy it—for a while longer.

The financial statements were complex, but the objective was not. Enron wanted to become a growth machine, and the only way they could do it was to do more and more deals. In fact, Enron CFO, Andy Fastow, liked to give out dollar bills with his picture on them, in a western hat smoking a cigar, part of the persona he developed to convince insiders that he would find fuding for their deals.[62] Fastow tried to make the world believe that Enron was conservative and even said that Enron did not speculate.[63] This blatant inconsistency, essentially telling everyone internally that he would fund most any deal and telling those externally that they did not speculate, pointed to the difference between the Enron portrayed to Wall Street and reality.

Enron wanted to be seen by investors as a growth machine but with predictability. The reality was that they did this reasonably well in the early 1990s by taking advantage of changing market conditions. But their aspirations and arrogance, fed by earlier success, got the best of the team, and they set huge expectations, internally and externally. The markets believed it for a while, and then they had to deliver. This led to an internal culture that was "cutthroat, do anything necessary, but get a deal done that makes money." Risk? Enron began to believe they could manage any risk created with financial engineering because they were not just smart but smarter than everyone else. Maybe some of them actually believed they were not taking much risk because the structures used were so convoluted that it isn't clear if management and the board even understood them.

There were warnings, though, beyond the few analysts and reporters who dared to risk their careers by criticizing "The World's Leading Company." One of the most visible wake-up calls (after the fact) was from Sherron Watkins.

Watkins was an Enron VP who found herself in a new job in summer 2001. She was in Fastow's organization and had responsibility for going through the assets Enron owned to help determine which ones might be sold to raise cash that year. She came across a complicated group of assets that had been hedged with funds raised through an organization called "Raptor." When Watkins had others in the accounting organization explain the vehicles and questioned them, her questions were deflected with the defense that the accountants (Arthur Andersen) had approved the transactions.

It was not long before she realized that there was huge risk in the SPE structures that Enron had used serially. Not only did she realize that employees, especially Fastow, were acting in a conflicted capacity on both sides of the transactions, but Enron's financial contributions to the entities was guaranteed with Enron stock. This was not a theoretical risk because, by summer 2001, Enron stock had lost half its value from the previous fall as investors found the P/E ratio hard to sustain on the facts.

Watkins drafted a memo that outlined her concerns about the structure of the SPEs, the conflicts, the use of stock for the capital contribution, the effect on Enron's income statement and balance sheet, and the fact that $500 million or more in unrecorded losses were already lurking in the partnerships. She even drafted a plan for recovery that included hiring an accounting firm other than Andersen to help clean up the mess.[64] She sent the memo, confidentially, to one of her superiors for reaction.

Following much soul searching while others tried to dissuade her, she obtained an appointment with Ken Lay in mid-August 2001 and laid out her concerns. Her meeting ended with Lay's apparent interest in the problem and an offer to help her find another job in the company since she felt she could not stay as part of Fastow's group.

Watkins' warnings had little effect or were too late to have an impact for a company that had already made too many mistakes. A little more than six weeks after Watkins' warning to Lay, on October 16, Enron made a press release that announced a loss of $618 million in income and made no mention of the fact that it had also written down shareholders' equity by $1.2 billion.

On November 8, 2001, Enron announced that it would restate earnings for the last 4¾ years because they had not followed generally accepted accounting principles (GAAP) in dealing with the off-balance-sheet partnerships. Enron executives tried to arrange a last-minute merger with Dynegy, a competitor in some similar businesses, to stabilize the financial situation, but Enron was in too much trouble for anyone to take the risk. The end was nigh, and on December 2 Enron filed for bankruptcy, unable to make multibillion dollar capital calls on its various deals plus debt downgrades that triggered covenants with lenders that it could not fund.

The technical cause of Enron's failure is straightforward—its executives took extraordinary risk by choosing to overleverage the company in an attempt to sustain high growth. Enron's leverage was achieved with off-balance-sheet smoke and mirrors. These actions were blessed by an accounting firm, Arthur Andersen, that was involved in a greater than average number of questionable audits and no longer exists. This convenient assistance from Andersen meant that it took longer for the markets to figure out something was wrong, and the fall and damage was greater than anyone could have ever imagined.

Management's actions at Enron did not completely destroy the company's businesses, a number of which are viable (such as pipelines and local utilities), but they did destroy the ability of the company to function as a viable economic entity. The bankruptcy lead to layoffs, worthless pension plans, massive credit defaults, and ripple effects wherever Enron did business, as shareholders saw virtually 100 percent of their equity wiped out and creditors lost an estimated 80 percent of their claims. Lawsuits will continue for many years, threatening the ability to utilize any remaining assets in a businesslike manner.

Enron is one of the most complex mistake chains imaginable. This was a case of " Multiple Failures to Manage Multiple Mistakes," perhaps represented as $(M^3)^3$ (which would equal M^{27}), which is probably indicative of the damage from Enron when one considers the losses to creditors, shareholders, employee retirement funds, and more than 5,000 Enron employees who lost their jobs. In related events, Arthur Andersen, Enron's accountants, implicated in the wrongdoing, put 10,000 or more employees out of work worldwide when they went under as a result of their Enron-related activities.

There were multiple examples of mistake chains at Enron, each one of which included multiple mistakes in such significant numbers that this can be considered only a representative list:

■ **Desire for growth**
  ◆ Ken Lay had aspirations for Enron to be a high growth/high profit company. He and Skilling initially saw the deregulated gas industry as the engine. With some success there, they began to lobby heavily at federal and state levels for changes that would allow them to grow. It is not clear that Enron had any unique value to add in many of these businesses or geographies, but they had ambition. Enron seemed to see lobbying as a significant success factor in their business plan, something many businesses would see as necessary but not a central part of the strategy as it was at Enron.
  ◆ The need for growth pushed them to believe they could securitize almost anything, leading them to aggressively push technology-enhanced trading businesses.
  ◆ Enron came to believe much of the dotcom mantra about broadband and made huge bets that they could rapidly control much of the market by becoming a market maker for broadband capacity.
  ◆ They believed that many of the same plans would work in other countries and aggressively sought large overseas acquisitions and deals—solely for the sake of growth.

■ **Aggressive financial management**
  ◆ The growth objective was so overpowering that they took on huge risk through the SPEs.
  ◆ There seemed to be little concern that there was any risk to increased leverage, other than the fact that rating agencies might downgrade their credit rating if they knew about the true exposure Enron had, so it was hidden in the SPEs.
  ◆ Buying CalPERS out of an SPE (JEDI) at a profit through another SPE (Chewco) on a leveraged basis amounted to a Ponzi scheme but with the use of Enron stock as collateral.
  ◆ Recognizing fees paid by the SPEs to Enron in Enron's statements, when the money came from Enron's guaranty of loans

the SPEs had taken from an unrelated third party (Barclay's Bank), without any mention of the contingent liability that was assumed, was not only aggressive, but illegal.

◆ Recognizing "management fees" paid to Enron as income without accounting for the proper period over which they should have been earned was also a violation of generally accepted accounting principles. Worse, the source of these fees was once again the same borrowed funds that Enron had guaranteed off the books.

◆ The SPEs (JEDI and others) held Enron stock as collateral for Enron's investment in the partnerships Enron formed. Enron recognized revenue as a result of the increase in value of this "investment" when Enron's own stock price was still going up. In the first quarter of 2000, this increased Enron's income by $126 million. By the third quarter of 2000, Arthur Andersen, which had approved the earlier transaction, had decided that recognizing income in this way was not appropriate.

◆ Enron, through the SPEs, wrote puts and calls on commodities, equipment, and entire power plants, all done with little legitimate business purpose other than managing earnings.

■ **Unfailing belief in a new business model**

◆ Enron's management really began to believe they could enter virtually any business and find a way to dominate it through clever trading and market making.

◆ Beyond the traditional natural gas business, Enron found itself in electricity, water, pulp and paper, fiber networks, retail broadband, and finally Enron Online, a general-purpose online trading site.

■ **Push boundaries to win**

◆ Fastow substituted a lower-level employee (Micahel Kopper) as a principal in some transactions to get around proxy disclosure requirements regarding conflict of interest for senior officers.

◆ Enron pushed its auditors, Arthur Andersen, hard, and they seemed to acquiesce regularly to aggressive, and often incorrect, opinions.

◆ Enron regularly pushed a number of the world's top banking organizations to rate their stock favorably or risk losing investment banking business. Most caved to the pressure and hyped Enron stock.

- **Lack of oversight**
  - There was an unbelievable lack of oversight by the board and its committees, which asked few questions about transactions put before them, approved transactions that put Fastow in conflict of interest situations, and even approved an exception under Enron's Code of Conduct to allow Fastow's participation as general partner of an SPE (LJM1) because the management team told the board it was good for Enron and they did not see a problem.[65]
  - The board failed to see patterns in the large number of SPEs that seemed to have little legitimate economic purpose other than to manage earnings.[66]
  - Fastow allowed Kopper to be paid huge fees for his role as partner in SPEs, clearly a serious breach of fiduciary responsibility on the part of both.
  - The executive group broadened the group of subordinates who were allow to "invest" in the SPEs, with extraordinary returns essentially guaranteed on a preferred basis over the company.
  - The board's Audit and Compliance Committee was assigned the duty to oversee the transactions the board knew about and approved, but the committee failed to exercise its oversight responsibilities in anything but a mechanical fashion.[67]

Every one of these mistake chains was a direct result of a culture of supremacy that was built consciously by Skilling, Fastow, and others. They believed that the management team at Enron was simply more intelligent, insightful, and skilled in all business matters than anyone else in the world. The supremacy culture began with some large egos (Skilling, in particular) and developed further as a result of legitimate business successes on a modest scale. The outsized egos grew and led these executives to feel that they really knew what they were doing and that competitors were truly ignorant and oblivious to the changes taking place around them. Although Enron was not a dotcom business, the mentality was similar and actually made worse because Enron really did have revenues and profits.

The result was the belief that Enron had found the Holy Grail of business, or what I call the "Silver Bullet Effect."* It is surprising how many naïve business people believe there is magic to be found. Based on many years of designing, teaching, and overseeing executive education programs, I would estimate that 5 percent of executives really believe there is a "silver bullet" answer somewhere to their business problems, and if they can just find the right guru or analyze hard enough, they will find it.

This searching for the silver bullet is more damaging than amusing. It leads to the delusional belief that if you find the silver bullet, you don't need to worry about competition because your advantage will be unquestionable. The fallacy with this line of thought is that, even if you find a silver bullet, the time it takes others to acquire them is nil in a hypercompetitive world.

This is what happened culturally at Enron. Senior management believed they had silver bullets, they told the troops down the line that the company had lots of silver bullets, and the board, outside investors, governments, and magazine editors believed it as their faces showed up in articles and cover stories.

Unfortunately, the silver bullets turned out to be the same lead everyone else used with some silver paint that began to peel off. Worse, when everyone looked a little deeper, they found Enron was a bunch of kids scaring people with toy guns, doing a lot of damage in the process.

There is a fine line between world-class motivation to achieve and destructive arrogance. Good leaders encourage a management team to believe that they are good, that they are capable of doing things they never imagined they could do, that their sights should be higher, that they can do substantially better than competitors, and that they can overcome obstacles others see as roadblocks. Leaders who put their own egos, personal victories, and compensation above the organization's success cross the line from productive motivation and encouragement to destructive arrogance.

Once arrogance became the dominant behavior for senior management at Enron, another very dangerous effect took place that had to do with pushing boundaries. Enron got so used to believing they could change

---

* For many of us who grew up in the 1950s, the weekly episode of *The Lone Ranger* was a must on television and a source of negotiation with parents since it appeared on a school night (Thursday). The Lone Ranger's silver bullets were unique and identified him not only as the best at what he did (finding bad guys) but as someone who always won.

the rules of the game through lobbying for legislative or regulatory changes that they pushed the principles of influence and negotiation to accounting and legal interpretations. They pushed accounting issues with Arthur Andersen, for example, meeting only minimal requirements to justify the treatment of their SPEs. Even these minimum requirements were ignored later through the use of structures and transactions so convoluted that the only conceivable purpose was to give the appearance of improved performance while obfuscating the truth. This behavior was so out of control that is it unlikely that anyone fully understood what was going on any longer, even Fastow and the other perpetrators of the fraud and deception.

> **Insight #29: Culture is powerful —what creates success may kill you.** The cultures of AMI, Ford, Firestone, and Enron worked for and against them. There are many examples, typically in the early stages of successful companies, where culture helps organizations see things in markets that others miss, get past survival challenges, grow faster, and weather competitive threats. The same powerful, but hard to define, force that binds an organization together for success can also be a catalyst for, or even a cause of, failure.

Ford and Firestone started a century ago as entrepreneurial companies based on unique visions of their founders. They succeeded against great odds and over time became huge corporations. But the cultures that created the successes became bureaucratic and focused primarily on operating efficiency, to their detriment in changing competitive markets.

In the case of Enron, the entrepreneurial visionary spark and culture that created early success rapidly became a fleeting flame. The flame was smothered by the actions of senior executives who took risks to support their egocentric needs for outsized success beyond the laws of economics, and once that line was crossed and they saw the flame being extinguished, they did not know how to stop the process and save their egos. The destruction could have been stopped earlier, in time to save something of the company, but that would have involved personal admissions of imperfection and poor judgment. As a result it became all or nothing—huge success or one of the largest failures in the history of business. Dysfunctional culture and ego lost, as they usually do. The laws of economics won again.

No matter what the culture or circumstances, however, it still generally takes multiple mistakes to cause serious damage. This means there are still chances to break the chain, but it is difficult, if not impossible, when the nearly automatic cultural reaction is to reject any effort to break the chain.

7

Mistakes as Catalysts for Cultural Change

"I have traveled the length and breadth of this country, and have talked with the best people in business administration. I can assure you on the highest authority that data processing is a fad and won't last out the year."

—Editor in charge of business books at Prentice-Hall Publishers, c. 1957[68]

One of the difficulties with mistakes is that they are often grounded with "certainty" in good intentions. As we have seen in a number of examples, overconfidence often develops because an individual or organization has avoided bad results in the past. Jolting organizations out of an experience-induced comfort zone and asking them to radically change their culture is a very difficult task, and it usually requires a catalyst. These catalysts come in a variety of forms, but two of the most likely are as follows:

- **A naturally occurring event,** such as a customer service issue, a lost contract, a product problem, or some other similar situation can be used as an object lesson to push a broader agenda to raise standards and performance in an organization. One of the jobs of senior leaders is to provide a sense of unease about the future as a constant reminder that complacency is an insidious path to the loss of competitive advantage. "Inventing" a crisis to mobilize an organization is rarely a good idea; smart people will see through this manipulation, and it is likely to work only once, if then. But most effective leaders use naturally occurring events to help their organization see the need for change.

■ **One or more dramatic failures,** in which many in an organization suddenly see the need to begin a change process. It is unfortunate that we need a disaster as a change agent, but in some cases, even those who see the need for change may need additional "evidence" to garner support from those with the power to initiate change or the broader group that wants to understand the need for change.

The signals and events that have been used to stimulate cultural change are as different as industries and people. The most successful organizations tend to be more effective at seeing early signs of the need for change through naturally occurring events rather than waiting until crises, failures, and other events with dramatic consequences make the need for change blatantly obvious. Companies that fail usually have confused messages, strategies, and priorities that shift frequently, confusing staff.

Fast Food: Customers Will Have It Their Way— Whether You Want Them to or Not

McDonald's Corporation did not invent the hamburger. Ray Kroc did not even invent McDonald's—he just grew it into one of the most successful businesses on the planet. The McDonald brothers invented efficient delivery of limited-menu fast food, and Kroc was a 52-year-old distributor of milk shake machines when he came across the McDonald brothers in 1954 in San Bernardino, California. McDonald's had eight locations in southern California, was charging 15 cents for hamburgers, and happy customers were standing in line to be served.

Kroc badgered the McDonalds to let him franchise a store and sell franchises to others. Within 10 years, there were over 700 stores. McDonald's did not even invent the Big Mac and Egg McMuffin; they were invented by franchise operators. But McDonald's did develop and refine operational procedures, equipment, a supply chain (before people called it that), and marketing that standardized McDonald's as the most effective and efficient global operation in the fast-food business. Many would argue that McDonald's really taught the high-tech, automotive, and consumer goods businesses the virtues of a well-managed, tightly integrated supply chain.

This emphasis on standardization, speed, mass production, and value has now produced a number of generations of young people whose first job experience was "flipping burgers." But the McDonald's experience, driven by a culture with conscious objectives, was also a lesson in standardization to provide the customer with exactly the product he or she expected on every occasion of service.

Burger King was also formed in the mid-1950s as a number of fast-food entrepreneurs saw opportunities to capture the post-war interest in burgers, fries, and shakes in an efficient fashion. There were plenty of competitors in the hamburger/fast-food space, including Krystal, White Castle, and thousands of individual drive-in restaurants with carhops on roller skates. But the McDonald's and Burger King models were scalable and more profitable.

The downside, just as it was when Henry Ford developed the first standardized, mass-produced automobile, was that although standardization reduced cost, bringing value to the customer, it limited choice. Any variance from the standard product introduced cost and complexity. While most customers were happy with the standard manner in which McDonald's prepared its burgers, some wanted different combinations of condiments.* Most stores would actually accommodate a special request, but it took too much time because it disrupted the normal operating routine.

In an effort to differentiate itself, in 1974, Burger King came up with the "Have It Your Way" marketing campaign to offer customers some deviation from the standard McDonald's approach to its products. Despite Burger King's aggressive use of this campaign for some years (recently revived), they still remained a solid #2 behind McDonald's.

This culture focused on standardization, and "we'll deviate for the customer, but only if we have to" served McDonald's well for decades. But as the 1990s drew to a close, consumer tastes were changing rapidly.

* The most frequent request was to leave the onions off the sandwich.

Aging baby boomers realized they had gobbled a few too many Big Macs and Whoppers, were overweight, and also were looking for something more akin to a dining experience. Add to this a variety of diet fads from grapefruit to Atkins and McDonald's growth started to slow.

The cultural reaction was interesting. While Wendy's grew with a shift in menu by adding salads and Burger King added experimental sandwiches, McDonalds doggedly stuck to their tried-and-true formula—standard products, rarely changed, produced in a way that was efficient for the company. They also kept building new stores at a torrid pace, in the United States and abroad.*

Sales slumped and franchisees became unhappy as owning a piece of the "Golden Arches" was not nearly as attractive as it had been. The stock, a growth stock for decades, declined as revenues and earnings turned down, declining from a peak of nearly $50 per share (split adjusted) in late 1999 to $12.50 in early 2003, when McDonald's posted the first quarterly loss in its history.

Where was management? The board? The world was changing around them, the signs were there, but McDonald's seemed stuck. There was little product innovation, and stock analysts pointed out that they seemed to be able to compete only by discounting, and even that was losing its appeal to customers.

This was not a simple business downturn; the culture that served McDonald's well for nearly 50 years had somehow faltered. Double-digit growth through delivery of value-based standard products delivered in standard settings, while adding as many new stores as possible each year, was at an end. The board of directors realized that McDonald's had problems and acted.

The board called James Cantalupo out of retirement and made him CEO, replacing Jack Greenberg, who had beaten Cantalupo for the CEO job in 1998. Upon returning, he put together a revitalization plan and immediately began:[69]

■ Closing underperforming stores

■ Selling off some brands (such as Donatos Pizzeria) that were not central to the core business

■ Focusing on basics: clean stores, friendly service, and hot food

---

* McDonald's global success is so strong that *The Economist* magazine uses its "Big Mac Index" to measure the "true" purchasing power parity of currencies around the world.

- Pushing new products, including McGriddles and salads, that were actually initiated by previous management
- Stopping price wars
- Slowing expansion

Like many high-performing companies, McDonald's grew at double-digit rates for years and then began to ask, "How can we keep up the growth rate?" The answer had been constant opening of new stores, global diversification, and then product-line diversification. McDonald's culture of operational excellence was intact, but the growth and diversification efforts got off track.

Franchisees had begun to complain that their most serious competition was McDonald's opening new stores too close to existing stores. Management thought they could get growth with acquisition of hot product areas such as pizza (Donatos), Mexican (Chipotle), and more traditional meals (Boston Market), but these flattened out and became a drag on core earnings.

McDonald's went back to basics and found out their core competence is operations and marketing in a fairly narrow area, and extending those competencies to similar but different product areas was more difficult than imagined. They refocused on the basics of a business that they had taught the world. This was something that the organization and its culture knew how to do well, and the execution worked, with performance turning around in a year. The old saying "Don't forget who brought you to the dance" sometimes applies in business as well.

Unfortunately, James Cantalupo died of a heart attack only fifteen months into the revitalization effort. In that short time however, he accomplished so much that it proved once again that a powerful culture can accomplish many things, especially when there is leadership that knows how to leverage the organization's true capabilities.

Insight #30: Culture is powerful, but be sure you understand where to extend it. As McDonald's found out, their core culture is built around attention to detail, standardization, and discipline in operations and marketing. This is a tremendous strength, but it cannot be extended easily to other businesses or even other food businesses. Other food businesses are different enough that extending the same detailed procedures did not work well. This was predictable because the McDonald's culture thrives on standardization with minimal adaptation. Going into new businesses requires rapid learning and adaptation. This is not to say that McDonald's cannot get results in other food areas, but it will do so less efficiently or will have to develop teams with different competencies.

Some years ago, Michael Treacy and Fred Wiersema postulated that successful companies must be focused on one of three things[70]: customer intimacy, operational excellence, or product leadership. But it is very tough to be focused in three different directions.

It is an exaggeration to say that you can only do one or the other, but for the most successful companies this is usually true. Companies that serve high-end markets rarely go down market well because the competencies and disciplines are different. Companies that assemble and market well are not always the best at research and development (R&D) (for example, Dell). Boeing and the automobile companies have all been slowly moving operations to partners as they realize they need to be focused on product leadership.

In the Treacy-Wiersema structure, McDonald's entire culture is focused on operational excellence, including their thought processes, employee selection, training, operating procedures, and customer relationships. They returned to what made them successful, took advantage of the power of their culture instead of fighting to change it, and for the moment seem to be doing well.

Rapid Culture Change in the U.S. Navy Submarine Force: No Second Chances

They are called "boats" because the first submarines were tiny compared to the ships of the line a century ago. As traditional as blue and gold, we still call modern nuclear submarines "boats" even though the ones I "drove" while serving as an officer in U.S. Navy submarines from 1965 to 1970 displaced as much as 8,500 tons submerged—as much as a World War II cruiser. Today's generation of Trident missile submarines displaces 18,750 tons. The attack boats, like the new *Seawolf* and *Virginia* classes, displace up to 8,000 tons. They are fast, stealthy, carry the most sophisticated weapons systems ever devised, and cost up to $2 billion each.

Operating submarines has never been easy, but today's size, complexity, and interdependence of systems means there is an even higher premium on executing correctly every time. The old navy saying we discussed in Chapter 1, "There's no partial credit in the Fleet," applies in submarines as much or more than any other situation in the world. You'd better be good because you will be a winner or a loser; there is no in-between.

This is especially true in the unforgiving environment hundreds of feet below the surface of the ocean and thousands of miles from home. The depths of the ocean are just as unforgiving as outer space. In space, the vehicle that man travels in must withstand the lack of an external atmosphere. In a submarine, the first enemy is the extraordinary pressure of deep water.*

When *USS*† *Nautilus* (SSN-571)‡ went to sea in 1956 with a nuclear power plant, the nature of submarines changed forever from surface ships that could submerge to true underwater vessels that could surface. This fundamental change in capability meant that new submarines could be designed to stay underwater nearly all the time, surfacing only to enter port—usually for crew rather than mechanical needs.

The reason that nuclear power changed all the assumptions and operating parameters is that nuclear fission releases energy, in the form of heat, without combustion and thus consumes no oxygen in the process. This capability to produce power endlessly in an enclosed environment shifted the emphasis for submarine development. A wide range of systems and capabilities from power generation to environmental control were developed, along with more capable weapons systems, advanced materials, construction techniques, and new hull

---

* Seawater exerts a pressure of 44 pounds per square inch (psi) for every 100 feet of depth. Thus, the pressure on the hull of the deep submersible that went to the bottom of the Marianas Trench, the deepest spot in the oceans at 36,000 feet, was approximately 15,840psi. This is more than 1,000 times atmospheric pressure at sea level.

† In 1907 President Theodore Roosevelt issued an Executive order that established the present usage: "In order that there shall be uniformity in the matter of designating naval vessels, it is hereby directed that the official designation of vessels of war, and other vessels of the Navy of the United States, shall be the name of such vessel, preceded by the words, United States Ship, or the letters U.S.S., and by no other words or letters."
—Executive Order 549, 8 January 1907.

‡ A navy designation in which SSN is a nuclear-powered attack submarine and SSBN is a nuclear-powered ballistic missile submarine.

design. The convergence of these technologies and devices led to faster, deeper-diving, more capable submarines, literally with the ability to circle the globe without surfacing*—as long as you could carry enough food.

As a submariner, you are trained to deal flawlessly, sometimes by rote, with routine and emergency situations that you know will happen at some point or another. But a lot of time is also spent learning to interpret signals, both about the systems and machinery and about the external environment. Synthesizing and interpreting information from a variety of sources is an important skill, particularly since you cannot see what is going on outside the ship.

In uncertain environments, such as a submarine or a business, interpretation of signals and leadership becomes more important. The job of leader is not telling those you work with to do the obvious; that's the part they should know and execute flawlessly, if you have trained them well. No, during uncertain times, the most important job of leaders is synthesis. The highest value added for leaders is helping a team figure out what the signals in an uncertain environment mean and devising strategies and plans that will win. Winning can mean a number of things—from safe operations to tactical or strategic victory or all of these—and this is where it gets complicated because sometimes there are unavoidable tradeoffs.

Uncertainty in submarines arises internally with respect to the operation of your own systems or externally with respect to the environment, enemy actions, or even the actions of allies. Unlike Jules Verne's *Nautilus*, submarines do not have a big glass window in the bow. They receive continuous information about the environment from a variety of sources, of which sonar is the most important tactical external sensor. This data has to be interpreted with great skill. Is that noise in the ocean biologic or a small freighter in the distance? Is that occasional hum random noise or (during the Cold War) a Soviet submarine?

The development and pace of change in U.S. nuclear submarine capabilities in the 1960's was truly extraordinary. The commitment to deploy the finest technology in the Cold-War environment led to an

---

* The most common question I hear as a former submariner is: "What's it like to live in a submarine that stays submerged for 60 days? Don't you go crazy?" Day-to-day existence isn't that difficult, though the time away from home is a different story. The modern nuclear submarine offers her crew a well-controlled internal environment, good food, an adequate (albeit tight) place to sleep, and on the attack boats, all the excitement you can handle.

unprecedented peacetime investment in new ships. Development was pushed rapidly as the United States moved toward a goal of an all-nuclear fleet of 42 Fleet Ballistic Missile (FBM) submarines (each carrying 16 nuclear missiles) and 100 attack submarines—all bringing together not only nuclear power but hundreds of other new or massively redesigned systems of one type or another.

Admiral Hyman Rickover, known as the "father of the nuclear submarine," reigned with an iron fist, mandating extremely rigid and uncompromising procedures for the operation of "his" submarines and their power plants. Initial training for all officers and enlisted men was lengthy (up to 18 months following college), rigorous, and continued on a regular basis aboard operating ships.

Despite all the training, emphasis on safety, and "no cost is too great" engineering, there were problems. On April 10, 1963, the attack submarine *USS Thresher* (SSN-593) sank in 8,400 feet of water approximately 220 miles east of Boston with the loss of all hands. *Thresher* was engaged in deep-dive testing (approximately 1,300 feet)* accompanied by an auxiliary ship from Portsmouth Naval Shipyard on the surface. *Thresher* sank in water too deep for recovery, but the navy used a bathyscaphe for observation of the wreckage. This, along with a review of records and interviews of personnel involved in the design and construction process, led the navy to conclude that the likely causes (multiple mistakes) of the loss of *Thresher* included:

■ Deficient specifications

■ Deficient shipbuilding practices

■ Deficient maintenance practices

■ Deficient operational procedures

Two particular deficiencies in design and construction were critical in the loss of the ship and were egregious mistakes, as noted in Navy testimony before Congress:[71]

> "*Thresher* had about 3,000 silver-brazed piping joints exposed to full submergence pressure. During her last shipyard maintenance period, 145 of these joints were inspected on a not-to-delay vessel basis

---

* The navy does not release the "test depth" of its submarines, but this estimate has appeared in a number of newspapers and magazines.

using a [then] new technique called ultrasonic testing. Fourteen percent of the joints tested showed substandard joint integrity. Extrapolating these test results to the entire population of 3,000 silver-brazed joints indicates that possibly more than 400 joints on *Thresher* could have been substandard. One or more of these joints is believed to have failed, resulting in flooding in the engine room."

"The main ballast tank blow system failed to operate properly at test depth. We believe that various restrictions in the air system, coupled with excessive moisture in the system, led to ice formation in the blow system piping. The resulting blockage caused an inadequate blow rate. Consequently, the submarine was unable to overcome the increasing weight of water rushing into the engine room."

What could be more important in a submarine than the ability to keep high-pressure seawater connections from breaking and being able to safely blow ballast tanks? As in other cases we have discussed, no one set out to design or build systems that would not function properly, but in the rapid arms buildup of the late 1950s and 1960s, Cold-War environment mistakes were made. As in many other situations, the precipitating events that led to the loss of *Thresher* were independent of each other but did share common origins. When combined, the seawater piping failure and the failure of the ballast tank blow system created an event sequence from which there was no recovery.

It is speculation, but *Thresher* might have survived the seawater leak if she had been able to blow her ballast tanks properly. The flooding would have continued, but with the engine room isolated* and pressurized, the flooding would have slowed or stopped as she neared or reached the surface.

Had the seawater leak not occurred or been minor, the failure of the ballast tank blow system might not have been life threatening. With the rest of the ship operating properly, *Thresher* could have reached the surface without the ability to do a full blow. Just as with an airplane, if she had propulsion, she could have used the stern planes† and fairwater

---

* As the world learned when the Russian submarine *Kursk* sank in the Barents Sea in August 2000, submarines have a number of watertight compartments that can be isolated from one another to try to save the ship if there is damage.

† Planes used primarily to control the angle of the ship mounted with the rudder, just forward of the screw.

planes* (adjustable surfaces like elevators on an airplane) to drive herself to broach the surface (part of the ship above the surface) while sorting out the problems with the ballast system. Even if the blow system failed permanently (which was unlikely), she could have headed for shallow water and grounded relatively safely.

Once again, we see the essence of multiple mistakes—that you can often survive one or two problems caused by mistakes but not a whole series of such problems. The failures in the seawater connections and the blow system were different manifestations of similar mistakes in design, construction, testing, and quality control.

Note that the *type* of mistakes we see here can also be found in business. Whether in physical systems or manufacturing or services businesses, we design our systems and operations in certain ways and provide standard procedures that may or may not be correct. The personnel operating business or physical systems may make mistakes or not. Over and over we see that the specifics may differ, but the patterns leading to disaster are similar, and yet we fail to learn that systems design and understanding, data sensing and analysis, operating procedures and feedback mechanisms, and organization culture all have an impact, regardless of setting.

The navy saw the problems as serious and interrelated and believed the situation required massive cultural change to ensure that such deficiencies in submarine quality never cropped up again. They needed rigorously controlled design, construction, inspection, and quality-control mechanisms, and they needed improvements quickly. The newer, more complex, deeper-diving submarines had less margin for error than the less-sophisticated, shallow diving boats of World War II. The interesting thing about the navy's response to the *Thresher* accident was not just the magnitude of the changes that were mandated, but the rapidity with which they were implemented and became part of life in the submarine community.

Navy brass, unwilling to accept any compromise of safety in the future, mandated the SubSafe program, which required dramatic improvement in quality standards and positive tracking of each and every part going into the construction of a submarine and its critical systems. Every part became attached to a history of the material, the manufacturing process, testing, and operational experience, including repair and replacement associated with it and the system it supported.

---

* Planes mounted on the sail of the submarine that help to control depth.

Additionally, substantial changes were made in quality control, tracking, and testing of welds, critical pressure piping, and the hull itself.

An interesting part of the process was that, although shipyards performed the construction or modification of submarines, the ship's crew had to personally witness and attest to results of critical tests. Safety was something in which the crew had a personal interest and through which they became part of the process of accountability.

When I joined the *USS Woodrow Wilson* (SSBN-624) in 1969, she was in the Newport News Shipyard being overhauled. Shortly after arrival, I came upon the captain sitting in a lawn chair on deck above the aft end of the missile compartment, smoking a cigar and watching a large pressure gauge. I asked him what he was doing and was told that one of the required tests prior to leaving the shipyard was a reactor compartment pressure test. Apparently someone had messed one up in the past, so Admiral Rickover had mandated that when such a test took place in the future, the commanding officer of the submarine would personally witness the eight-hour test and observe the pressure gauge. This seems extreme, but there are times in organizations when it must be made clear that personal responsibility for important actions is not optional. Rickover had decided that this was one of those situations. The lesson was not lost on any of us.

By December 1963, eight months after the loss of *Thresher*, the navy formally issued SubSafe certification requirements. Between 1963 and 1974, the requirements were constantly modified and improved, resulting in the publication of the Submarine Safety Requirements manual that continues to guide the design, specification, and construction standards for U.S. submarines today.

The navy believes that SubSafe has been a success and offers the fact that between 1915 and 1963, there were 16 submarine losses for noncombat reasons. Since SubSafe went into effect in 1963, there has only been one sub lost in noncombat conditions.[72] But therein lies a still-unexplained loss that brings us to a lesson of the difficulty of rapid implementation of massive change in large organizations with conflicting priorities.

The *USS Scorpion* (SS-589) sank off the Azores in May 1968. *Scorpion* failed to return to her homeport of Norfolk, Virginia following a routine three-month deployment to the Mediterranean. Families of the crew literally waited on the pier for *Scorpion* to return, and the ship simply never showed up. The navy did not know exactly where the ship was, which is not unusual in the submarine force.* Sadly for the families, it took six months to find *Scorpion*. She had sunk about five days before her due date in Norfolk in 11,000 feet of water off the Azores. The deep water precluded recovering the wreckage, but navy deep submergence vehicles did obtain pictures, most of which remained classified until recently.

The navy conducted two investigations over 25 years into the loss of *Scorpion*. The extant theory, until recently, was that *Scorpion* had been lost as a result of a torpedo malfunction. One theory postulated that a malfunctioning torpedo exploded inside the ship. Another idea was that a "hot run" torpedo† was jettisoned and then doubled back, acquired the ship, and sank it. As a former submariner who also spent a tour as the weapons officer on a boat, I find both of these theories hard to believe.

A series of newspaper stories in the mid-1990s cast doubt on this theory. While we will likely never know the truth, there is information that suggests *Scorpion* may have suffered a fate similar to *Thresher* for maintenance or design/quality reasons.

Implementation of SubSafe was a massive undertaking. With Cold-War pressure and the Soviets building submarines rapidly, the navy faced pressure to build boats and keep them at sea as much as possible. There were dozens of submarines under construction or in overhaul in the 1960s. The navy did retrofit submarines built before the SubSafe program to the new standards, but it was impossible to get it all done at once. Submarines that were not yet modified had operational depth restrictions placed on them, and *Scorpion* was one of four remaining boats that was not SubSafe certified at the time she went down.

Interviewing family members and former crewmen, the *Houston Chronicle* put together a picture of a boat that was not only not SubSafe but had a host of other mechanical problems, including significant chronic external hydraulic leaks‡ that were difficult to track down and fix. There is even the story of Electrician's Mate Dan Rogers, who was so afraid of the condition of the ship that he voluntarily offered to give up his submarine qualification in order to get off the boat. Rogers would

---

* Navy submarine movements are classified as secret. The objective is for all submarine movements to remain undetected. Families were told the day the ship was to arrive in homeport but little more. The boats do not routinely report positions or communicate while en route to minimize the chance of detection.

† A torpedo in which the motor, driven by electric batteries, starts running while in the torpedo room or inside a tube.

‡ The stern and sail plains on the outside of the hull were powered by hydraulic actuators.

not have called it that, but he was trying to break what he perceived as a chain of mistakes in process, a series of maintenance problems that troubled him enough to put his career in the navy on the line. He was transferred a few weeks before the ship set sail on the fatal cruise, but he was on the pier to see his former shipmates off when they set sail on February 15, 1968. He went on to serve on a number of other submarines until he retired.[73]

One author, a former submariner who writes submarine fiction, speculates that *Scorpion* suffered a sheared main propulsion shaft (which drives the screw), allowing catastrophic flooding in the engine room.[74] This accident continues to pique the interest of many who would like to know the real story, but we simply do not know the real story. There is no "black box" as in airplanes.

There was great concern in the 1960s about how many subs we could keep at sea to cover all the operations that were a priority during the Cold War. We were building ships as fast as possible and increasing the length of deployments for attack boats to cover the missions. For those based on the West coast (as I was), deploying to the western Pacific (WestPac) for seven to nine months at a time was not unusual.* In this high-pressure environment, it was unlikely that any admiral commanding a fleet of submarines would say that he could not meet requested commitments because some of his subs were unsafe, yet many believe that was the truth in the case of *Scorpion*. It is alleged that the pressure to keep ships at sea contributed to loss of *Scorpion* in the form of a shortened overhaul in which only those things that were considered critical were addressed and that she went to sea on her final deployment with many deficiencies.

When viewed this way, this story begins to sound like NASA/*Columbia* in an undersea environment. At the time that *Scorpion* was lost, the navy was on its way to dramatic improvements in quality. But operational demands may have clouded judgment about whether it was safe to deploy submarines that had not been modified to SubSafe standards.

Thousands of deployments and missions have been conducted safely since all submarines became SubSafe certified. It is important to note that the SubSafe organization has a limited and focused charge. It does not bear total responsibility for all aspects of safety aboard submarines.

---

* Exciting as it was, I left the navy when my five-year commitment was up because it was clear that I would spend my life at sea for years to come with little chance of a normal family life.

It is concerned with the "SubSafe Certification Boundary—those structures, systems, and components critical to the watertight integrity and recovery capability of the submarine."[75]

The navy designed the organization specifically to change culture and procedures related to managing the environmental risk as it relates to the fundamental survivability of the submarine. Other safety and operational issues were left to other departments for oversight. This razor sharp focus on mission is an important part of the success of the program. This does not mean that the program has been without problems. It has been recalibrated and tightened up a number of times over the years, but it still appears to be doing what it was designed to do: make submarines safe against their first enemy—the pressure of deep water.

Insight #31: Rapid culture change designed to obliterate mistakes in super-critical areas is possible, but sharp focus, extra diligence, and continuous training are necessary for success. These standards cannot be relaxed if you wish to maintain performance.

The navy changed the culture toward quality and safety in submarines rapidly with SubSafe. However, conflicting priorities for meeting operational demands allowed rationalization that, despite the loss of *Thresher*, the problem was not universal or so serious that the subs could not be used as long as some operational restrictions were imposed. We do not know if *Scorpion* was lost to a SubSafe deficiency, but the possibility lingers that this was a case of multiple mistakes in which an attempt to break the chain (SubSafe and Dan Rogers complaints) was correct, but the impracticality of instant implementation across the entire fleet resulted in one additional accident.

It is important to point out that the other extraordinarily successful major submarine safety program has to do with nuclear power. The Naval Nuclear Propulsion Program has enjoyed special status* in the navy ever since the brilliant but eccentric Admiral Rickover made it a reality in the 1950s. There are nuclear-powered surface ships as well, but the program initially developed its design, discipline, and procedures around the more demanding requirements of the submarine environment.

---

* The Director of the Naval Nuclear Propulsion Program reports directly to the Chief of Naval Operations, an unusual structure indicative of the importance of its mission in the navy.

There has not been a serious accident involving a shipboard navy nuclear power plant in nearly 50 years of operation. This record is extraordinary and is a testament to the rigor that Rickover developed and left as a legacy for the program.

Navy "nukes" have always been held to high standards. Beyond the required knowledge and demonstrated practical understanding of plant operations under all normal and emergency conditions, one of Rickover's most important tenets was "believe your indications." He understood that all too often, when we see something unexpected or off the norm, our first tendency is to dismiss it as unlikely or impossible. As we have seen in nearly all the examples in this book, failure to believe information as valid is the first and often the most serious mistake in an accident sequence.

Rickover's personal influence created a culture that was fanatical about following procedures, improving on them, and continuously teaching the new and improved procedures to all involved. This culture survived without Rickover's personal influence after he retired and later died, resulting in the safest, most effective submarine force (perhaps even any ship force) in the history of the world.*

Each one of us who served in nuclear submarines at times hated the detailed adherence to procedure, especially in initial training when the volume of information to be memorized was huge. This extraordinary attention to understanding where problems could occur and careful documentation of the steps necessary to stop an accident sequence not only ensured our safety but left each of us with a life-long appreciation of the need to detect anomalies and break the chain early.

Lest you think SubSafe, nuclear power, navy procedures, and discipline have little to do with business, consider the following:

■ "Believe your indications" would have worked for Intel's 386 problems, and it did work for Tylenol.

■ Brokerage firms' compliance programs should look a lot like SubSafe if they are to ensure an envelope of safety around their relationships with their customers.

■ Hospital infection-control programs are as important for patient care as SubSafe is to the safety of submarine crews, and other programs to

---

* Neither *Thresher* nor *Scorpion* is suspected of having suffered a failure of the nuclear plant itself. Obviously, in *Thresher*, the piping for the seawater cooling system for steam (secondary) system was involved.

reduce mistakes for healthcare providers could benefit from the extraordinary discipline discussed in the preceding examples.

- Many industries, such as chemicals, mining, and others with dangerous physical situations, operate programs similar to those previously mentioned.

Sadly, many of the operators at Three Mile Island were originally trained as navy nukes but apparently lost the rigor in a less demanding, more monotonous environment. Success is not achieved in the ongoing battle to avoid mistakes with complex systems simply through procedures and training.

Success requires an organizational culture that sets non-negotiable, irrefutable standards at the highest level and a mindset on the part of individuals that adherence to standards is not optional. Success in avoiding mistakes is about vigilance and never forgetting to "believe your indications" and that "there's no partial credit in the Fleet."

What aspects of your business could benefit from a shift to a culture that demands more discipline, more protection through design (products, process, organization), or more thorough analysis of the reasons that mistakes happen?

The Grand Canyon Changes Air Traffic Control

According to the Federal Aviation Administration (FAA), in the year 2000, U.S. commercial air carriers made 12.6 million departures, flew 21 million hours, and carried 693.7 million passengers, consuming 202 million gallons of fuel in the process[76]. With an accident rate of 2.9 accidents per million hours for Part 121* scheduled air carriers[77] in 1999, commercial aviation in the United States is one of the safest forms of transportation in the world—but accidents do happen.

Aviation accidents are visible, often sensational, and can cause a threat to others beyond the passengers and crew. But they receive attention in the press that is far out of proportion to the actual risk to passengers or those on the ground. It is also an area where regulation, equipment improvement, and procedural standardization all help improve outcomes. The FAA and National Transportation Safety Board (NTSB)

---

* Refers to Part 121 of Title 14 of the Code of Federal Regulations (14 CFR), the federal regulations that govern regularly scheduled air carriers, excluding charters and general aviation aircraft.

have various responsibilities for regulation, accident prevention, and investigation. Across the industry, manufacturers, equipment makers, and operators have been striving to reduce accidents, accident rates, and injuries since the airplane became a reality 100 years ago.

Aviation technology advanced steadily for more than 50 years following the Wright brothers' first flight at Kill Devil Hills, North Carolina on December 17, 1903. During this time, with impetus from both civilian and military interests, we saw the evolution of sturdier airframes, higher powered and more reliable engines, improved navigation, and instruments and equipment that made flying possible in most weather conditions. In short, there was an amazing convergence of technologies from a variety of sources that made flying a more reliable and effective means of travel, commerce, and military activity.

While aviation achievements in the first half of the twentieth century were exciting, pioneering, and numerous, the second half of the century yielded extraordinary simultaneous advances in technology, safety, speed, and comfort. For those of us growing up in the 1950s, it seemed there was always a movie about an airliner in a storm over an ocean that might not make it. Most Americans had still not flown, and while aviation was accepted, most chose to take the train or bus because it was less expensive and perceived as safer.

As the jet age blossomed in the 1960s, it was suddenly all about the ability to get around the world in comfort and style, and more people were flying than ever. Safety and confidence was improving, largely as a result of the technology embodied in newer, more capable jet aircraft. Beyond the technological improvements in aircraft, there were other system improvements that, like regulation following the *Titanic* investigation, required the catalyst of a tragic accident to bring about the required changes.

Some of the greatest improvements in air safety received their impetus as a result of an unnecessary airline crash on June 30, 1956. A mid-air collision of a United Airlines DC-7 and a TWA Constellation over the Grand Canyon killed 128 people. Controllers in those days did not have radar coverage over the whole country and, in many cases, simply coordinated requests from aircraft rather than "controlling" them. The two aircraft left Los Angeles a few minutes apart on instrument flight plans, with altitudes assigned by the "hemispheric rule."*

---

* Separation was achieved by assigning flights on courses to the east of north-south headings odd altitudes (such as 17,000/19,000/21,000 ft.), and those west of the north-south heading line were assigned even altitudes.

In the days when much of the population was new to flight, the airlines took every opportunity to point out the sights along the way. The crew of both flights wanted to maneuver over the area of the Grand Canyon for the benefit of passengers and requested deviations off the airway.* The weather was good except for some towering cumulus clouds.

The United flight was at its assigned altitude of 21,000 feet and was clear of clouds, but the TWA flight at 19,000 feet could not stay clear of clouds and requested a higher altitude. This was either for sightseeing or passenger comfort in the vicinity of the clouds but was not required. Because the United aircraft was assigned 21,000 feet, the request was denied. (Remember that the controller did not have radar, so he only knew the approximate position of the two planes.)

The TWA pilot then cancelled his instrument flight plan, leaving him free to go where he wanted to under visual flight rules (VFR, requiring him to stay clear of the clouds). Apparently, while maneuvering near clouds and trying to let the passengers see the sights, the two aircraft collided. The accident report faulted the pilots for not seeing and avoiding the other aircraft in, what was at the time, "uncontrolled airspace." The airplanes literally fell into the Grand Canyon, where some of the pieces still litter the landscape at the bottom of the Canyon.†

This crash and the investigations and analysis that followed brought the realization that our system for aircraft control was woefully inadequate for the day[78], much less the dawning jet age. The result of this and other crashes in the next year stimulated Congress to act, yielding the Federal Aviation Act of 1958. This legislation set up the Federal Aviation Administration (FAA) and gave it responsibility for safety rule making, as well as the development and operation of a system of air navigation and traffic control to serve both military and civilian aviation interests.‡

The establishment of the FAA and, in 1967, the NTSB signaled the beginning of a more formal approach to the analysis of the causes of accidents and recognition that there were rarely simple, one-cause accidents of any consequence. The quality and safety of aircraft, navigation, and communication systems, air traffic control (ATC)

---

* An "airway" is an electronic highway in the sky defined by an electronic signal that the aircraft follows.

† Because of numerous local sightseeing flights, the airspace over the Canyon is heavily regulated today.

‡ The FAA also received responsibility for promoting aviation in the national interest, a mission that some still question as being in conflict with its regulatory oversight requirements.

systems, and procedures and weather information continued to improve. Over time accident rates improved, but for the last decade of the twentieth century it was evident that one area that was not improving as rapidly as others was the performance of the humans involved. This has been the subject of much study, analysis, and training on the part of the industry for many years, and while improved, human error is still most often responsible for aviation accidents because the technology has improved so much.

Flying into the Ground–with Everything Working

Have you ever been in a business situation where everything seemed to be going just fine, right up until the moment that you found out there was a horrible problem that you were powerless to stop? Think about Gateway Computer as it suddenly found itself uncompetitive, some of the airline bankruptcies, or Wyeth Pharmaceuticals with their diet drug problems. In these and other cases, things were going reasonably smoothly and then, in a blink of an eye, something changed the world for these companies. There are analogies from which we can learn in aviation.

The aviation accident classification known as "controlled flight into terrain" (CFIT) is among the most persistent, difficult to understand, and difficult to correct since it involves pilots flying an aircraft into the ground because they lost track of where they were in relationship to surrounding terrain. NTSB statistics show that you are 20 times more likely to have a CFIT accident than a collision with another aircraft in flight.[79]

Quite simply, this means that pilots fly a perfectly functioning airplane into the ground while completely under control because they did not understand where they were in relationship to the ground, usually hills or mountains. Unfortunately, the examples of CFIT are numerous. Even more sobering than the statistics are the accident reports where cockpit voice recorders allow us to eavesdrop on pilots who we hear going about their duties casually, usually in a distracted or uniformed fashion that is about to lead to their death.

CFIT is a specific case of what is more broadly called "loss of situational awareness" (or in a business context "lack of market awareness"). While loss of situational awareness is found in a number of different types of accidents, CFIT is the most prevalent and should be easy to fix. Unfortunately, CFIT, almost by definition, also shows a failure of crew resource management (CRM, discussed in Chapter 3, "Execution Mistakes and Successes as Catalysts for Change") since it is clear that, with at least two crewmembers and sometimes more in the cockpit, someone should understand where the ground, especially dangerous ground, is located.

From the many examples, most of which involve a sequence of multiple mistakes, there are some that have particularly important lessons. Korean Air flight 801 (KE-801) departed Seoul, Korea about 9:30 PM local time on August 5, 1997 en route to Guam. A few hours later, the aircraft crashed into a small hill on final approach to Guam International Airport, killing 228 of the 254 persons on board. Guam's airspace is under U.S. jurisdiction, thus the investigating agency was the NTSB. A portion of the abstract of the final report[80] on the accident reads as follows:

> "The National Transportation Safety Board determines that the probable cause of the Korean Air flight 801 accident was the captain's failure to adequately brief and execute the nonprecision approach and the first officer's and flight engineer's failure to effectively monitor and cross-check the captain's execution of the approach. Contributing to these failures were the captain's fatigue and Korean Air's inadequate flight crew training. Contributing to the accident was the Federal Aviation Administration's (FAA) intentional inhibition of the minimum safe altitude warning system (MSAW) at Guam and the agency's failure to adequately manage the system.
>
> The safety issues in this report focus on flight crew performance, approach procedures, and pilot training; air traffic control, including controller performance and the intentional inhibition of the MSAW system at Guam; emergency response; the adequacy of Korean Civil Aviation Bureau (KCAB) and FAA oversight...."

By the time a long investigation of a disaster like this is boiled down to a short summary, it looks pretty sterile. (The full report is more than 100 pages.) The reality is that there is much to be learned from the more specific details of this accident that makes it a classic case of failing to break a sequence of multiple mistakes. By the time KE-801 disappeared from the Guam approach controller's radar as it crashed into a hillside on the final approach course, there had been a chain a half dozen or more mistakes and contributing factors that resulted in the loss of 228 lives:

- **Fatigue.** The chain starts with the fact that the captain flying on 801 was originally scheduled to fly to Dubai but was reassigned to the Guam flight because he did not meet the rest requirements for the longer flight to Dubai. He likely started the flight tired and can be heard on the cockpit voice recorder (CVR) saying that he is "eh … really … sleepy." This comment came just 21 minutes before final impact as the most challenging portion of the flight, the approach phase, was beginning.

  Fatigue is a risk factor in operating any vehicle from a bicycle to a 747, but it is insidious because it is dependent on the individual, hard to quantify, and may affect thought processes as well as physical function such as reaction time. Even when fatigued, most individuals can function if they are alerted to danger. The problem is that, when fatigued, you may miss the signals and thus not be in a mindset prepared to react until it is too late. At one time or another in our lives, most of us have felt too tired to continue driving, writing, reading, or some other activity. (My wife could not understand how I could fall asleep during the second act of *Les Miserables*, but in doing so I did not harm anyone.)

  When mentioning that he was sleepy, the captain might have said, "I'm really sleepy. Let's all look at this procedure closely and double-check each other to make sure we do it correctly." But the reality is that this likely did not occur to him for reasons related to his mindset.

- **Mindset.** This is not identified directly in the report, but the captain was apparently expecting a fairly easy approach into Guam. While on an instrument flight plan and expecting to make an instrument approach to the runway, the crew had information that the weather at the airport was VFR* (good weather), and they were expecting to see the airport early and make a visual approach. Fully expecting one thing to happen and seeing another can make one slow to adapt to the unexpected situation.

---

* Visual flight rules, meaning that the ceiling (clouds) is at least 1,000 feet above the ground and the visibility is three miles or greater.

- **Changed conditions**. The crew was expecting an approach in clear weather but received a recorded report a few minutes before commencing the approach indicating that there were rain showers in the area. Once beginning the approach, a small rain shower between the aircraft and the airport obscured any visual clues from lights on the ground that might have helped the crew while flying an unfamiliar approach, although this should not have had any bearing on their ability to execute the procedure.

- **Equipment problems at Guam**. The "glideslope" portion of the instrument landing system (ILS) was out of service. While still usable for horizontal guidance to the runway, this meant that the aircraft autopilot could not automatically track the correct altitude during the final approach, requiring the crew to use a different procedure and make manual altitude corrections on a number of phases of the approach. This is a "nonprecision approach" that all pilots learn and practice. However, large aircraft like 747s usually go into airports with the best instrument approach equipment, so these crews rarely fly this type of approach that requires more action on the part of the pilot.

  Additionally, the minimum safe altitude warning system (MSAW) that is part of the Guam controllers' radar system had been inhibited by the FAA because of a high number of "nuisance" false alarms. According to the NTSB final report, within 17 days after the KE-801 accident, the system had been recalibrated and was working, albeit it with 18 false alarms daily. Most pilots, myself included, would prefer to have a system helping to monitor our altitude during an approach even if it occasionally results in a false alarm. Had this equipment not been purposely inhibited, it held one potential key to breaking the accident chain.

- **Authoritarian captain**. Korean Air has had a well-documented problem with a very authoritarian culture and cockpit manner. In this case, the captain did not properly brief the rest of the crew on the nonstandard approach to be flown, and his manner was consistently autocratic and intimidating to other crewmembers.

The result of this chain of mistakes was a completely preventable CFIT accident that, through the 1990s, was one of the most serious accident types facing commercial aviation. This and other accidents at

Korean Air finally caused them to quietly hire other airlines and safety organizations to help them learn ways to improve safety, especially changing the command and control culture to reduce accidents.

While difficult, the CFIT type of mistake can be intercepted. One example occurred in England on May 20, 2002 as a flight from Copenhagen to East Midlands airport was on final approach. The 727 was somewhat high and fast before reaching the final approach course as a result of avoiding thunderstorms in the area. Approach control ordered the aircraft to descend to 2,000 feet and slow to 180 knots. This required the crew to extend the "speedbrakes" to get the aircraft down fast.

It was turbulent and dark (about 10:30 PM), and as the aircraft rolled out of the turn onto the final approach course, the flaps were extended in preparation for landing. At this point the aircraft stick-shaker activated, indicating an incipient stall. The crew increased power and pitched the aircraft down, normal procedure to recover from the coming stall, but the stick-shaker continued as the aircraft lost altitude. A number of audible alarms were going off in the cockpit, including the ground proximity warning system (GPWS), indicating the ground was coming up fast.

The mistake sequence was broken as the flight engineer (in this case also a pilot) noticed that the speedbrakes were still engaged and called out to disengage. The two pilots did not hear the first warning, but the engineer persisted a second time, and the pilot then disengaged the speedbrakes.

Once the speedbrakes were disengaged, the aircraft climbed rapidly, circled, and made an uneventful approach and landing, but this was almost another CFIT statistic. The aircraft came as low as 800 feet above the ground before recovering, so there were only seconds remaining between success and disaster.

The problem was that the 727 is not supposed to be operated with both the speedbrakes and flaps extended simultaneously. This causes excessive loss of altitude, exactly what happened in this incident. The need for a rapid descent and slightly abnormal approach in turbulence caused the crew to overlook the extension of both devices simultaneously. While an alarm sounded to signal the problem, the crew initially missed this, but an alert nonflying officer in the cockpit broke the mistake sequence.

The value of an additional human cockpit resource is a point that pilots' unions have made for decades as the industry has moved from a three-crew cockpit to two. On the other hand, many of these technical conflicts have been removed with newer technology in aircraft. The Airbus aircraft with "fly by wire" (all but the oldest models) are "impossible" to stall because computer systems automatically initiate actions to keep the aircraft from getting into a configuration/situation that will allow the stall to occur.

While human errors continue to be primary cause of CFIT, additional technology is being mandated to provide more information to crews in an effort to reduce these types of accidents. Beginning in 2002, the FAA mandated that newly manufactured turbine aircraft for passenger service be equipped with Terrain Awareness and Warning Systems (TAWS) and retrofitted to older aircraft by 2005. TAWS provides a visual picture of upcoming terrain based on current position, a digital terrain database, and the projected flight path of the airplane. The system then provides warnings when a potential conflict is projected.

The regulatory change requiring TAWS took many years and many accidents acting as small catalysts. When those who study accidents realized that, as safety increased in other areas, CFIT had moved up the list to be one of the top causes of loss of life in aviation, regulatory approval was fairly rapid. It could have been attacked sooner, but until it moved up to the top of the list of accident causes, there was simply not enough focus on the problem to get action.

CRM and other approaches to reducing human errors will continue, but technology has much to add and will continue to be added to airplanes in an attempt to "outthink" the human mind and its tendency to create errors where no one imagined they would be possible.

What are the monitoring systems that you can put into your business to warn you of the equivalent of CFIT—going down in flames while feeling like everything is under control?

Cultural Success: Working Together to Learn in an Emergency–United 232

The extraordinary story of United Airlines flight 232 (UA-232) on July 19, 1989 is one of the great success stories for CRM as a way to minimize damage in a nearly hopeless situation. It illustrates a concept that applies directly in business as well—how a team that has practiced at working on problems together can even learn together when they see a problem they have not encountered or trained for previously.

The flight was en route from Denver to Chicago at 37,000 feet over Iowa in good weather. At 3:16 PM there was a loud explosion, and the cockpit lit up with warning lights and alarms. The #2 (center) engine on the DC-10 had suffered an uncontained failure of the six-foot-diameter fan disk* that caused shrapnel to tear through the tail section of the airplane, severing enough hydraulic lines to completely shut down all three "redundant" hydraulic systems on the airplane. These systems are used to operate all flight controls,† landing gear, flaps, nosewheel steering, and brakes. Three redundant systems were built into the airplane to make it possible to fly normally with any one of the systems working. They are not interconnected, so designers believed that there was virtually no accident, short of a crash, that could take out all the systems. This assumption was obviously wrong.

Captain Al Haynes was one of United's most experienced senior captains and was nearing the FAA mandatory retirement age of 60, beyond which pilots may not fly as pilot in command on regularly scheduled airlines. During the next 30 minutes or so, Haynes and his crew, along with the help of Dennis Fitch, a senior United captain and DC-10 check pilot who happened to be flying onboard as a passenger, did an amazing job of learning to fly an airplane in a configuration that had never been done before. They were lauded worldwide for their skill in a successful crash landing in a fiery cartwheel into a cornfield adjacent to the runway at Sioux City. While 111 passengers and one flight attendant died, this extraordinary ability to "break the chain" saved the lives of 185 passengers and crew.

Following the engine explosions, it did not take the crew long to figure out they could not control the airplane, even if they did not at the time fully understand what had happened. First Officer William Records was flying the airplane from the co-pilot seat at the time of the accident. He realized he had lost the #2 engine and concentrated on flying the airplane while Haynes and Second Officer Dudley Dvorak started the engine shutdown checklist. They found they could not close the throttle on the #2 engine (the engine was torn apart, not just dead), and the fuel supply valve would not move either. Another valve, further up the fuel system, was used to stop fuel flow to what was left of the engine.

---

* The first stage of the engine compressor system that you see when looking into the front of an engine. An "uncontained" failure means that shrapnel and larger parts come off the engine and are not contained within the engine nacelle (covering).

† This includes the ailerons (roll), elevator (pitch), rudder (yaw), flaps (for landing), slats (lift devices for better landing control) and spoilers (to reduce lift) for descent or on landing.

Within 15 seconds of the explosion, Records told Haynes he could not control the airplane.[81] Haynes immediately grabbed the yoke on his side of the cockpit and found that with both pilots holding full left aileron, the airplane was still turning to the right. As the aircraft came to 38 degrees right bank, likely going toward rolling all the way over, Haynes instinctively pushed the throttle on the #3 (right) engine all the way forward while closing the #1 (left) throttle. This asymmetric thrust caused the airplane to stop turning and slowly righted the bank angle.

With little or no function in the flight controls, the two pilots began learning how to control the airplane using only differential power. This was not something they had ever practiced for control purposes. All pilots who fly multi-engine airplanes must learn how to compensate for asymmetric thrust when an engine is lost on one side of the airplane with another one functioning on the opposite side. The difference in this case was the use of thrust as the only control available to them. Additionally, because of damage to the airplane, it "wanted" to turn right constantly, so their progress was marked by trying to reach Sioux City in a series of advancing right descending turns toward the airport.

While Haynes and Records "learned" how to fly the airplane in its current state of disrepair and talked with air traffic controllers, Dvorak was on the radio with United's maintenance staff in San Francisco trying to find out if they could figure out anything to help them.

About 15 minutes into the accident, the crew found out that Fitch (the DC-10 check pilot) was on board and invited him to the cockpit to help. After some experimentation, they settled into a routine where Fitch, in addition to helping discuss options with the crew, handled throttle adjustments desired by Haynes and Records from behind the center console that is between the two pilot seats.

Manipulating the power on the remaining two good engines had become the only means of control for the aircraft, but it was trial and error with Haynes and Records trying to navigate and observe the aircraft response and asking Fitch to make throttle adjustments. At one point they experimented with Fitch and Dvorak changing places, but by this point Fitch had "learned" the throttle movements in this new control mode and operated them more smoothly than Dvorak, so they switched back to their previous roles.

The differential power method of control they used worked adequately in flight, but more precise corrections were needed for landing. Unfortunately, the state of the airplane was not going to allow those more precise corrections as a result of the airplane's unfortunate tendency to roll to the right following the initial damage. This could be corrected with higher right engine power, but for landing, the power had to come off at some point or the airplane would be going too fast. Additionally, since they could not operate flaps and other lift control devices, they would have to approach at higher speed,* pull the power at the last moment, and hope to stay in control. This speed requirement and control difficulty meant the final approach speed was about 215 knots instead of a normal 140 knots for that aircraft.

To make matters worse, the damaged controls left the airplane with a consistent slow longitudinal oscillation (phugoid) with a period of 40 to 60 seconds. This slow up and down motion similar to wave motion was not a problem in flight, but it complicated landing. The crew got the airplane to the airport, was aligned to try to land on runway 22, but at about 300 feet one of the phugoid cycles started to push the nose down and the airplane crashed. Upon "landing," the aircraft broke apart and cart wheeled down the runway engulfed in flames. Though they suffered serious injuries, the cockpit crew survived, partly because the nose literally broke off the airplane and landed in a different area away from the fire.

A total of 111 persons died and 185 survived the crash landing, but all might have died had not this crew, controllers, and rescue personnel done such an outstanding job. Haynes also points out that there was a lot of luck involved in making this a serious accident rather than a total catastrophe:

- First, the location of the accident was good luck. Had they had been mid-ocean en route to Hawaii, they would not have made it.

- The flatlands of the Midwest meant that they did not have to worry about navigating around terrain obstacles.

- The good weather also made controlling the aircraft much easier. Since they could see outside, they did not have to try to fly the airplane with their crude control system while relying solely on instruments to understand aircraft attitude.

- The outstanding work of the controller, Kevin Bauchman, who worked the flight for most of the time during the emergency, eased their workload by giving them constant vectors and distances to the airport.

* To avoid a stall, which would result in an out-of-control crash and more damage.

- Sioux City had run a disaster drill two years earlier in which the scenario was that a crippled DC-10 made an emergency landing off the runway at Sioux City and the local community has to deal with 150 survivors. Gary Brown, the director of emergency services at the time, was not completely satisfied with the drill and made some changes to their plans afterward. This meant that not only was Sioux City well prepared, but that their emergency teams had essentially practiced the specific scenario that occurred when UA-232 showed up that July day. This preparation improved the survival rate.

The key elements in the United success, which are almost the complete opposite of the mistakes made by the Korean Air crew at Guam, included:

- Very effective crew resource management and coordination: inside the cockpit, with the cabin crew, and via radio with controllers and United technical staff
- Ongoing discussion and analysis of the unusual situation
- Focus on the objective—getting on the ground as much "under control" as possible
- Continuous and effective help from controllers
- Prepared and effective emergency rescue personnel and plans

One huge difference between this situation and the Korean Air flight is that the Korean Air pilots did not realize they had a problem; they were oblivious to the fact that they had started a mistake sequence. Recovering from the mistake sequence in the Korean Air situation would have been a very minor issue if the crew had been alert enough to understand what was happening. This reinforces again the importance of continuous monitoring of operations as a necessary competence and practice, but such practices are developed as a result of the values advocated through a culture.

Haynes discounts the accomplishments of the crew in the incident, saying that they just did their job. Yet the public and the aviation community have made him a hero because we all realized that keeping the severely damaged aircraft reasonably stable was an extraordinary accomplishment. No one would have blamed a crew that could not land it.

The flight of UA-232 is an outstanding example of CRM in action. Haynes credits the training that he and others at United received as the company adopted CRM and made it a part of the operating culture during the 1980s. This crew's performance is something you hope any group of professionals would be able to do with precision, yet the fact that many others have not been able to handle crises when required highlights the importance and power of good CRM.

As in all aviation accidents, the summary of the probable cause(s) by the National Transportation Safety Board is factual, cold, and terse:

"The National Transportation Safety Board determines the probable cause(s) of this accident as follows:

"The inadequate consideration given to human factors limitations in the inspection and quality-control procedures used by United Airlines' engine overhaul facility which resulted in the failure to detect a fatigue crack originating from a previously undetected metallurgical defect located in a critical area of the stage 1 fan disk that was manufactured by General Electric Aircraft Engines. The subsequent catastrophic disintegration of the disk resulted in the liberation of debris in a pattern of distribution and with energy levels that exceeded the level of protection provided by design features of the hydraulic systems that operated the DC-10's flight controls."[82]

It is believed that the crack in the fan disk was the result of a manufacturing defect that was not caught when the fan was manufactured or on any of the required inspections. The disk flew on the airplane for 17 years and underwent six inspections that failed to detect the small defect that eventually led to the fatigue crack that led to catastrophic failure of the fan disk. This was, in itself, a mistake sequence that should have been stopped. Al Haynes and his crew had the last chance at stopping the sequence, and while they did not stop it without damage, they did an amazing job of mitigating the severity of the accident.

By the way, despite the examination of some high-profile aviation accidents in this book, commercial aviation in the developed world is still a very safe mode of transportation. UA-232 was the first actual engine failure that Captain Al Haynes had seen in his 29,700 hours as a pilot. His skill in handling the situation is an indication of the value of flight simulator training that is required every six months for airline transport pilots.

But even simulators can only train pilots for the things that the operators think to program, and complete loss of control surface systems was not in the curriculum prior to this accident. A number of studies by NASA and others of the most effective techniques to use for "propulsion-controlled aircraft" evolved out of this accident. One of the most critical initiatives in managing multiple mistakes is the desire, interest, and capacity to learn and distribute knowledge gained from past mistakes effectively.

One is almost afraid to say it, but there is one major U.S. airline, of those that have operated for a decade or more, that has never killed a passenger—Southwest. They came close in Burbank, California in March 2000 when a 737, with a few mistakes by the pilots, ran off the end of the runway and taxied into a Chevron station, looking like it needed a fill-up. A major part of the safety record at Southwest is equipment and procedural standardization. Using only one type of airplane—the Boeing 737 series—helps reduce complexity for pilots,* maintenance staff, and schedulers and simplifies overall operational issues.

The UA-232 scenario shows that, despite extraordinary circumstances, cultures can be built that keep individuals focused on the objective of operating safely, avoiding mistakes, and having the ability to "break the chain." Southwest's long history without a serious accident reinforces this point, in stark contrast to Korean Air that has had an unenviable safety record.

In business it is rare that executives have to make these kinds of "save the plane" or "save the company" decisions in real time with the verdict on performance delivered in under 30 minutes, but the parallels are real. Look back at consumer product companies that handled unexpected crises effectively like J&J with Tylenol or Pepsi's product tampering hoax involving a syringe in a can of soda (discussed in chapter 10, "Making M³ Part of Your Culture for Success"). Contrast this to those handled less effectively like Intel, AmEx, and others. What was the difference? The difference was preparation around how to handle problems. Not every specific problem, but how to handle problems in a

---

* Pilots have to be "type rated" and current for each specific airplane type they fly, so having only one type improves scheduling and standardizes everything from operating procedures to casual conversation about airplane handling characteristics.

cultural context that makes priorities and responsibility to customers clear and actionable. The use of culture to avoid mistakes and a willingness to learn—even if that learning had to occur on-the-fly—is often the difference between success and failure in a company, just as it can be in a cockpit.

If pilots can get teams to work together effectively in emergencies in a half hour, and if consumer product companies can get results from teams in a half week, we would expect any capable company to be able to solve a strategic challenge in a half year. Most of the big ones do not happen that fast, but the transformation to believing the change is necessary and getting it well under way can and should take place that quickly.

Marketing Your Culture Change

One of the most significant and successful culture changes of the last decade was inside IBM. What a difference! In the early 1990s, we ran some 30 executive courses at Wharton that were attended by 1,500 IBM managers and executives. Every person I met that attended those courses was dressed in the standard IBM dark suit, white shirt, and muted tie. Every one of them had a "25 Year" lapel pin. When running courses in 2004 for executives at similar levels in IBM, I noted that not a single one showed up in a tie, and when we went around the room for introductions, the average tenure (for those in the room) at IBM was about seven years.

There was a time when IBM, DuPont, and other large companies hired staff only out of college. You got in when you were young and stayed forever. That thinking has changed, but that is a small reflection of the change that took place since IBM hit rock bottom and was declared dead by most pundits in 1993, with its stock at lows it had not seen in 20 years.

IBM had done well in mini-computers even though DEC had invented the category. They had done very well in PCs even though Apple beat them to market. But they faltered as they stuck to mainframes as the profit engine when the world shifted to client-server and other platforms. In a sense, they were like Kodak a decade later, stuck in a profit model they could not shake because they could not see anything else that could make so much money.

It took guts for the board to choose Louis Gerstner as CEO, a nontechnician who was a strategist and marketer with successes at companies that did not look at all like IBM, other than they had great brands. His strategy and marketing experience at McKinsey, American Express, and RJR Nabisco soon became respected as relevant when he dug in to change the culture at IBM to make the people, products, and services more consistent with a market that had changed faster than IBM had realized.

Over a decade, IBM has shifted to the point that hardware is no longer a majority of revenue. The mantra is for solutions, not products, and the people come from all sorts of backgrounds. The acquisition of PricewaterhouseCoopers Consulting in 2003 made the shift in philosophy and orientation clear if it had been missed previously.

IBM is still a top-notch technology company, with divisions that make everything from chips to high-powered mainframes, but that is no longer the positioning IBM wants with customers and potential customers. Solutions are front-and-center, and that is clear in their communications and conversation with any of their employees. The culture has changed. Making the culture work to fit market needs was a massive task, but more importantly IBM has now found ways, through marketing and behavior, to make the world believe that their culture is a strength reflective of the needs of their customers rather than an anachronism of the past.

IBM has marketed its culture change well, but they are not the only company to use culture to advantage in marketing. It is standard practice in the airline industry to pull all advertising when an accident occurs. If your airline is on the evening news with passengers in body bags, you do not want to remind people who you are—at least for a few weeks. We hear a lot about price competition in the airline business, but despite the amazing overall safety record of the industry, if you ask most travelers they will mention safety as one of their top concerns. Airlines do not advertise their safety record, though it is available from government sources if you want to go to the trouble of searching for the information. Yet they do advertise safety, albeit quite indirectly.

I remember an American Airlines television commercial a few years ago in which a mechanic is seen observing a maintenance operation on an aircraft in a hangar, and the scene then shifts to a passenger terminal. He says something to the effect of, "Every time I want to know how important my job is, I just wander over here to the terminal and see all the people that depend on me." Subtle, but it gets the point across—your safety is one of our major concerns.

USAir (now named U.S. Airways) suffered two fatal crashes during the summer of 1994. On July 2, a DC-9 crashed on approach to landing at Charlotte, North Carolina, killing 37 of the 57 passengers and crew in an accident that was the result of poor judgment on the part of the crew in the vicinity of severe thunderstorms. On September 8, a Boeing 737 crashed while descending on approach near Pittsburg, killing all 127 people on board. This accident was likely the result of an equipment failure that caused a "rudder hard over"*, rapidly rolling the airplane in a way that makes recovery almost impossible, especially at low altitude.

Regardless of the cause of those crashes, USAir's safety record became a question in the minds of travelers as they chose airlines. On November 21, 1994, USAir announced that they had hired retired Air Force General Robert C. Oaks in a newly created position of vice president, corporate safety and regulatory compliance.[83] The same day, the company printed a letter from the chairman about USAir's commitment to safety in full-page advertisements in newspapers across the country. They needed to make the public believe they were serious, but this public display was also about making employees believe they were serious about safety as a priority in the culture.

USAir had a cultural problem that was typical of companies born of multiple mergers. In this case, over a number of years, the company grew through the integration of Allegheny, Piedmont, PSA, and others. Each had its own culture, way of doing business, flying procedures, and different types of airplanes. USAir at the time operated more different airplane types than any other airline, which increased costs and made standardization of any type, from seating to safety, more difficult.

The campaign to market safety as a value and an important element of the culture worked. The company's traffic recovered (although it eventually ended up in and out of Chapter 11 for other reasons). They did not have another fatal accident until early 2003 when a commuter plane operated by a partner airline under US Airways colors crashed on takeoff from Charlotte, the result of a maintenance problem.

Customers develop confidence in their suppliers for many reasons: high quality products, good service, fair dealings, ethics, personal relationships, and in other ways unique to specific industries and

---

* The rudder is driven to its maximum deflection very rapidly, causing the airplane to roll.

companies. It is increasingly clear, however, that culture can be a differentiator because customers want a reason to believe they are doing business with winners—people who know what they are doing and will treat them properly. A powerful culture, embraced across an organization, has the ability to produce good results and make customers feel good about dealing with your organization.

> **Insight #32: Most cultures develop by accident; those that are designed to accomplish a purpose are more effective.** Whether we look at McDonald's, Southwest Airlines, the navy's submarine force, or IBM, when you see successful organizations, you find strong cultures with teams that understand what they need to focus on and reinforce it over and over again. Successful companies design cultures through consistent priorities and behaviors. This does not mean that priorities remain unchanged, but when they do change, the changes take place in a considered and deliberate fashion and are communicated very well.

Unclear messages and frequently changing strategies and priorities confuse staff and lead to confused or ill-defined cultures that are often associated with failure. Culture is difficult to define and is difficult to build and maintain, but it is a reflection of values, principles, examples, and behavior of leaders at all levels in organizations. It is one of the most powerful forces in an organization, for better or worse. Culture can facilitate mistake sequences, be the force that prevents them from ever starting, or be an engine for change when you realize you have made a mistake or series of mistakes that needs to be stopped and rectified.

Companies/Industries in Need of Cultural Change–for Different Reasons

Sadly, there is a long list of companies with distinguished histories that are in need of a culture change. We can ask if these are cases of bad strategy that has caused morale to slide and drive the best people away, but we can also ask whether lack of attention to cultural values has caused people to underperform, leading to ineffective strategies and/or poor execution.

This is a classic chicken-or-egg discussion, though, because after looking at hundreds of examples of organizations that make serious blunders, I am convinced that the two go together. It is hard to find an organization doing badly that does not have some kind of culture problem inhibiting its ability to perform more effectively, and it is hard to find an organization doing well that does not have a culture that contributes significantly to its success.

How did Boeing get into trouble in the commercial air transport side of its business?

- Was it arrogance bred of success that caused them to misread market shifts and customer preferences?
- Was it bureaucracy built up over much of a century that made them slow to adopt new technology that became important when a younger, more nimble competitor came along?
- Was it distraction with the mergers of McDonnell-Douglas and a number of smaller companies and/or the difficulty of integrating different cultures?

How did AT&T go from being one of America's most respected to least respected companies in a decade?

- Was it the arrogance and bureaucracy built of a century of protected markets?
- Was it because they could not learn how to function in a deregulated environment fast enough?
- Did they get distracted with abortive efforts to enter the computer business by acquiring NCR and joint venturing with Olivetti?
- Were they slow to sense shifts in customer preferences?
- Did they sell off their greatest strength when they spun out Lucent and with it Bell Labs?

These are just two important and accomplished companies searching for a better future. There are others, but the questions are similar to those you could have asked about a variety of other companies that no longer exist. These might include Bethlehem Steel, Packard Motors, Pan American World Airways, and others.

Avoiding the ultimate mistakes that lead to the death of businesses is still about strategic vision and flawless execution. The specifics change, but the principles have been the same since the industrial revolution. The ability to use culture in an organization to facilitate these basic needs may be the most important way to avoid the most life-threatening mistakes of all.

8

Economics at Work: Watching Entire Industries Lose It

"We're losing a little on every sale but making it up on volume."

−Anonymous

Economics works. I was not sure I believed that the first time I took an economics course as an undergraduate many years ago because I did not have the experience to relate to the principles being illustrated by curves and equations. But eventually one realizes that there are real relationships between business reality and terms like market structure, indifference curves, marginal rates of substitution, production functions, price elasticity, income elasticity, supply and demand curves, equilibrium price, and so on. I believe, more than ever, that the principles are real and that they affect real businesses in real ways. What surprises me is how few business people relate industry-level economic principles to the realities they observe in their businesses every day. Perhaps they feel isolated from Adam Smith's "invisible hand of the market," but they seem to believe that unless they happen to be in a pure commodity business (such as soda ash used in steel making), the principles do not apply.

Long-cycle economics can hide mistakes—temporarily. If your analysis is not deep, you can blame poor performance on any number of current factors such as "seasonal patterns," weather, raw material shortage, labor strife, dust storms on the plains, and others from a Chinese-menu litany of excuses some executives always seem to have handy. Economic mistake chains often start when executives make short-run decisions that seem prudent or expedient without realizing the that symptoms they see may be part of a longer-run, broad, industry, or country economic cycle. Understanding and evaluating the potential impact of the economic cycle can provide context that makes it easier to see mistakes before they lead to economic destruction.

The World Automobile Industry—Trying to Defy the Laws of Economics

The automobile industry may be one of the world's best examples of how the laws of economics work with brutal indifference as to who is affected. The industry is more than a century old, but it has only been 75 years or so that the masses in most developed countries have had access to private vehicles. Some might argue that having 20 million registered vehicles in a state like California with 35 million inhabitants is not necessarily a sign of progress, but growth in personal vehicles is inextricably linked with economic growth and prosperity around the world.

As economies develop, consumers acquire more disposable income, and the desire for luxury goods increases. In the case of the automobile, what was once a luxury became a necessity as living, working, and commuting patterns changed. This pattern accelerated in the 1950s in the United States and other parts of the world with the post-war growth explosion in suburban areas of larger cities. The pattern of rising affluence driving automobile purchases has played out over the last few decades in areas like Southeast Asia, Latin America, Eastern Europe, and most recently, China.

The automobile industry developed in many places around the world about a century ago, particularly as more reliable internal combustion engines were developed. During the first half of the twentieth century, the industry was regionally based with significant manufacturers located in North America, Europe, and Japan. The industry matured fairly rapidly in the United States as it became clear that it was becoming a business of scale. Henry Ford's development of the assembly line reduced the cost of production dramatically, making vehicles more affordable and thus increasing income-driven demand as a larger segment of the population found that they could afford what was, at the time, a luxury.

Industry consolidation between the world wars continued to reduce costs and increase the ability to design, manufacture, sell, and service vehicles in broader geographic areas, although the industry was still localized in the major developed countries of the world. By World War II, the "Big Three" in the United States—General Motors, Ford, and Chrysler—were well established. The remaining smaller companies, including Packard, Studebaker, Nash, Kaiser, and Willys, merged with one another, died, or were absorbed and disappeared by the 1970s. The Jeep, originally a product of Willys, survived as part of Chrysler, which merged with Daimler-Benz in 1998.

In a hundred years the industry went from hundreds of small makers of personal vehicles to a dozen or so global powerhouses and some smaller niche players. Today four of the ten largest companies in the world are auto manufacturers (GM, Ford, DaimlerChrysler, and Toyota), and three are oil companies whose fortunes are heavily tied to the automobile (Exxon Mobil, Royal Dutch/Shell, and BP).

Economically, the industry evolved like most new technology-based industries. Initially vehicles were hand made, costs were high, and only the rich could afford the product. Manufacturers moved quickly from providing basic transportation to cater to the needs of the more affluent. Cars were built to accommodate a chauffeur and had special appointments for the owner. But Henry Ford clearly understood economics and proved it when he made reducing cost a priority so that he could reduce price, which in turn would drive higher volumes allowing him to make money. Consumer appetite for freedom via personal transportation drove industry growth, and as economies grew, vehicle sales grew as a result of positive income elasticity of demand. In the United States, the industry grew further as income elasticity of demand for two cars per family rather than one shot up with incomes in the 1950s.

The economic cycle of the auto industry has passed through many phases as the industry evolved over its first century. As shown schematically in Figure 8.1, this broad pattern has included:

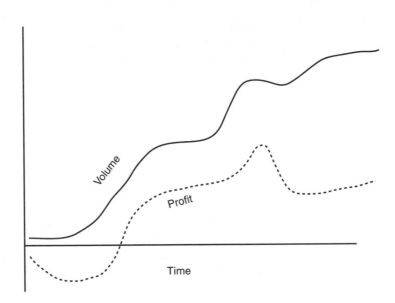

Figure 8.1 Auto industry economic evolution.

- Many early entrepreneurs and innovators who had trouble making money because competition was significant, the technologies were crude, and costs were high when early models were hand built. Experimentation went on with a variety of technologies (such as steam, electric, and gasoline power).

- Innovations in production to lower costs (such as the assembly line, standard parts, technology standards), leading to mass-market demand and volume growth.

- Technological improvements (such as engines, electric starters, better transmissions, lights, tires, safety glass) made the vehicles more reliable and easier to operate.

- Design improvements (such as enclosed compartment, windshield wipers) broadened market appeal.

- Marketing innovations (such as new models, model cycles, financing) helped grow volume significantly.

- Industry consolidation in various regions continued to bring efficiency to the industry, lowering prices in real terms, broadening markets, adding features, and improving quality.

- The impact of broad economic conditions (such as the Depression, wars, recessions, fuel crises) moved the industry sideways at times, but overall it continued to grow nearly unabated through each decade of its existence.

- Industry expansion as incomes rose, especially post-World War II as the car became part of the American dream and culture.

- Rising profits from good times in the industry allowed rich pay and benefits packages for labor that were affordable at the time but later came to be millstones for the companies.

- Incorporation of extras as standard features. In the 1950s, it was common to buy your radio and air-conditioning as an after-market add on. Today it is difficult to purchase a car without these "basic" items.

- Continued consolidation to achieve scale and scope economies as the remaining smaller, weaker players could no longer compete.

- Industry expansion with new model types (such as station wagons, pickups, sports cars, SUVs) as the industry learned that annual model changes were not enough; consumers expected something very different every few years.

- Globalization of the industry with intensified competition as manufacturers all over the world began to believe they could sell something in other than their home markets, making use of production capacity and increasing revenue.

- New niche entrants (such as Tucker, DeLorean, Samsung) came along from time to time, promising a "new" type of vehicle and company and usually failing rapidly as the laws of economics proved once again that as industries mature, scale matters with the exception of some very high-end niches (such as high-end sports cars such as Lamborghini, many of which are no longer independent).

- Increased regulation (such as safety, fuel economy, and pricing disclosure) that provided value to consumers but increased costs for companies.

- Competition based on price became the norm as major companies fought for market share to keep their plants running efficiently.

- Competition intensified on features; quality and safety became the norm, especially after foreign manufacturers began to set new standards in the United States in these areas.

- Diversification into financing, emphasis on after-sale service, related businesses (such as GM's OnStar), and loosely related businesses (such as Ford's Hertz Car Rentals or GM's Hughes Electronics) as companies looked for ways to make money other than in the cutthroat new vehicle part of the business.

- Major emphasis on cost reduction as competitive pressures increased, companies realized that they had settled into the mature phase of an oversupplied industry.

- Consolidation of the supplier base as OEMs became disciplined purchasers and, in many cases, began to treat their suppliers as profit centers, wringing everything they could out of the suppliers' part of the value chain.

Despite the laws of economics playing out as they have over the industry's history, global manufacturing capacity still exceeds demand by as much as 20 million vehicles per year[84] or a third of current demand. This is where we get to the real economic issues driving the industry. U.S. auto companies are not adding to their manufacturing capacity. Quite the opposite—they have excess capacity that is often not suitable for building the platforms or working as flexibly as needed for today's markets. This does not mean that auto manufacturing has not grown in the United States. The North American domestic market is so huge that foreign manufacturers have built manufacturing capacity here to serve local markets. Honda, Toyota, Nissan, Mercedes, and BMW all operate auto-manufacturing plants in North America.

Non-U.S. companies have excess capacity, especially in Japan and Korea, and are more than happy to produce for the world, especially for the world's largest single market—the United States. Therein lies an economic conundrum that we have seen in many industries in developed countries ever since the industrial revolution.

Innovation leads to developing and selling new products to the world, raising local standards of living, raising consumers' purchasing power, increasing their consumption, improving the economy, attracting competition, raising wages (in the presence of barriers to immigration or training), raising costs, stifling investment, making manufacturers less competitive. Thus begins a downward spiral that we have seen so frequently. Of course, this gets even worse and proceeds more rapidly if competitors show up in a market with better products of higher quality produced more efficiently, as both the Japanese and now the Koreans have shown U.S. manufacturers.

The U.S. auto industry finds itself in something of a very long and slow mistake sequence that has been achieving momentum and destroying value for nearly 50 years:

- Believing that profitability and market share were God-given rights
- Failing to take foreign competitors seriously
- Allowing others to redesign the competitive playing field around quality and features
- Forgetting that selling cars is about excitement
- Making short-term decisions that increased long-term, fixed costs (such as job guarantees and retiree benefits)
- Failing to modernize manufacturing
- Allowing manufacturing efficiency to dominate decision-making
- Confusing the appropriate role of prices and incentives, leading to price competition with average rebates like GM's $3,000 to $4,000 per car[85], which has trained the market to never pay full price, leaving unanswered the question of what the appropriate price point is for any of their products
- Killing off suppliers by demanding concessions*
- Falling behind on product cycle times

All of these errors add up to a U.S. auto industry (the Big Three) that finds itself in the unique position of having paid so much attention to the competitors that looked just like themselves that the rest of the world snuck up on them and blindsided them with cars that are more exciting, of higher quality, more reliable, longer lasting, and perceived by customers as better value for money.

The inroads of the Japanese, the Germans, the Swedes, and now the Koreans in the U.S. market have been staggering. We can only presume that the Big Three believed what they read in newspapers and magazines in the late 1960s when it was fashionable to say that the Japanese would never gain a foothold in the U.S. market because the Big Three were so powerful.

---

* It is not unusual for suppliers to receive a contract to produce a part for an OEM for $100 in year 1, $95 in year 2, and $93 in year 3 and beyond. The suppliers are expected to figure out how to get the increased productivity or material cost reduction on their own. If you are unwilling to accept such terms, you do not get the contract.

A failure to anticipate and believe the economic cycle of the industry and a series of mistakes over the last 35 years has brought the Big Three to a point where the profit they make comes primarily from financing vehicles and selling spare parts. GM, Ford, and the Chrysler portion of DaimlerChrysler are still very large companies that produce a lot of cars, but they do not even return their cost of capital on a consistent basis.

There is an important point here that has to do with long industry cycles—every industry has two breakeven points. The first occurs early in the evolution of the industry when competitors are all losing money while figuring out how to make the industry work. From there, many companies improve production (whether physical products or services), increase volume, and produce profits. The second breakeven point occurs as industry profits are declining because of excessive competition and/or changed markets. Business people inherently understand the first breakeven point and pour investment into companies trying to accelerate the time to industry profitability. This makes senses because they realize that, in most cases, a healthy industry stimulates broad-based demand and gives all competitors a better chance to grow and prosper.

It is the second (downward) breakeven point that executives are loathe to admit exists. In the first case, early in an industry's evolution, if you are reasonably competitive you can ride the growth wave and survive for some period. But in the second case, late in an industry's life, you have to be great because only one or two firms usually survive the shakeout.

Economics has taught us repeatedly that, even in brutally competitive industries, there is almost always a winner who does fairly well compared to others. Winners see different opportunities, have different philosophies, have a better understanding of industry directions, or are more careful in business-development decisions. In the auto industry, these characteristics are found in Toyota, BMW, and to a lesser extent, Mercedes.

These lessons occur over and over again, and if you prefer a more recent example of the same principle, remember the example of the networking industry in Chapter 4, "Strategy—How Do You Know It's a Mistake?" Technology was developed at Xerox PARC and commercialized into an industry by 3Com and many others who did well for some years, but the industry is dominated today by Cisco with 3Com on life support.

In 2003, Toyota passed Ford to become the world's second-largest vehicle manufacturer with a *profitable* market share of 11 percent globally and 11.2 percent in the United States. How has Toyota grown, in a relatively short period, from a Japanese-focused car maker, to an unknown maker of inexpensive imports for the U.S. market, to a broad-based global manufacturer and one of the most successful and respected companies in the world? Many books have been written trying to answer this question, but it is fundamentally about a single-minded focus on providing value for the customer. Other non-U.S. manufacturers have pursued this strategy as well, but none has done it with the breadth, scale, success, and longevity that Toyota has achieved.

A few years ago, I began hearing from my mother that she was spending a fair amount of money every few months maintaining her American-brand automobile, one of the best-selling models for the previous ten years. The car had 125,000 miles on it, so some maintenance was to be expected, but I told her that the amount she was spending was excessive and, from what I had read, was not likely to improve as time went on. She decided to buy a new car and asked for my recommendation:

Mother: "What should I buy?"

Me: "Buy a Toyota Camry. They're highly reliable and inexpensive to operate."

Mother: "Oh, I couldn't buy a *foreign* car."

Me: "Okay, would you buy the most reliable car made in the United States?"

Mother: "Yes, that's exactly what I'm looking for."

Me: "Then buy a Toyota Camry; they're made in Kentucky."

Toyota's design and production systems are legendary, and they have even surpassed quality levels in Japan at their U.S. manufacturing plants, something the pundits said could never be done because "U.S. culture is so different." Look at *Consumer Reports*, J.D. Power, or other organizations that conduct surveys of customer experience, and you consistently see the fewest problems with Toyota of any brand in the world.

Mother bought the Camry and has been happier with it than any car she has ever owned, not an unusual sentiment if you look at surveys of customer loyalty and satisfaction. The Camry does not have the elegance of the '56 Packard or the excitement of the '56 Thunderbird that she and Dad had when I was a kid. No, she's happy because it is has reasonable features, has decent power and room, and is more reliable and less expensive to operate than any of the cars the family ever owned. Multiply her sentiment by similar realizations on the part of millions of other Americans, and you understand why Toyota can command a price premium unavailable to other manufacturers.

For other segments, Toyota does have some exciting cars for those who want exhilaration while driving. Toyota's capabilities and reputation are the antithesis of the problems most of the U.S. auto industry has had for the last 20 years: poor quality, with resulting maintenance hassle and cost, no excitement, and fewer small features that make a difference to customers.

Toyota is not the only non-U.S. car company to succeed by changing the rules. Volvo did well for decades with safety as a major emphasis in vehicle design and marketing. But doing well with a safety strategy does not mean you will grow large. This relegated Volvo to a niche market of 3 percent or less in the United States, and Ford recently acquired Volvo, paying $6.5 billion, as part of its luxury-brand strategy.

Other manufacturers, including Mercedes, were decades ahead of U.S. manufacturers on safety as part of design, although it was rarely trumpeted in the marketing materials. Mercedes is a high-end manufacturer that can afford to engineer their vehicles beyond minimum requirements. The mass market has always had the challenge of competing on price, and that creates a culture that affects every decision in the company. Low price means low quality in many industries, but as both competition and regulation increased requirements, the auto industry found itself having to produce higher quality and compete on price. This has usually been good for customers, except in dramatic examples like Ford/Firestone where the tradeoffs were disastrous.

A few years ago, I became acquainted with the CEO of a company that makes seals for engines and transmissions in the automotive industry. One day I casually asked him, "Why does every American car I have ever owned leaked oil onto my garage floor by the time it had 100,000 miles on it, and no foreign car I have ever owned has done this, even if I kept it for 200,000 miles?" I was surprised when his immediate answer was, "$7.50." He went on to explain that was the difference in cost of the higher quality seal package he supplied to American and foreign auto manufacturers to seal their engines. It doesn't seem like a lot, and I would gladly pay the difference, but the manufacturer whose culture is dominated by cost rather than customer value looks at $7.50 as an unnecessary cost. Ford/Firestone was just that simple but with different designs, parts, and more serious consequences than a puddle of oil in your garage.

The U.S. auto industry has been on the defensive for the last decade. Their answer to their lower quality, fewer features, and few exciting models when compared to their foreign competitors has been to improve a little bit and discount a lot. This has not been a great strategy as market share and profitability have continued to slide.

It appears, however, that the U.S. industry has awakened and is raising the competitive stakes. The 2004 Detroit Auto Show saw more exciting new models and realistic concept models from the Big Three than have been unveiled in many years. More emphasis on manufacturing quality seems to be showing up in better statistics for selected nameplates such as Cadillac, which placed second only to Lexus in a 2003 survey of initial quality.[86]

The world automotive industry will continue to be brutally competitive, but economics works. As new entrants have entered the market with investments in additional capacity, the more established players tended to compete on cost. In theory, the "rational" manufacturer will continue to increase capacity or reduce price to stimulate demand until the marginal cost of production is equal to price. This is an equilibrium state for a competitive industry, and when it happens consolidation is not far behind.

The problem with this line of thought is that it assumes demand is elastic—that lower prices will stimulate greater consumption. But what if people have all the cars they want? And what if there is no compelling reason for replacement because the quality has become so high that consumers are willing to keep vehicles longer? It is at this point that companies begin to get a sick feeling in the stomach as they realize that demand has become inelastic—unresponsive to price.

The "rational" thing to do would be for the whole industry to limit production at a level that maximizes economic return for all players. This is called a cartel, the most visible example being OPEC, and is illegal in the U.S.

With every competitor acting in his or her self-interest and no one watching out for the industry as a whole, there are no "rational" competitors. Price becomes the major competitive weapon, and products become undifferentiated or commoditized. Investment in new products, plant modernization, new technologies, and market expansion will be put off. When competition really gets bad, managers shift from thinking about long-term marginal cost to short-term marginal cost, looking only at cash flow and ignoring past capital investment that should have a return.

The next, and desperate, stage is when companies begin producing, regardless of losses, on a marginal basis to keep plants running "efficiently" because the labor contracts or plant operational requirements make it necessary. This is always done with the hope that the situation is temporary and that "demand will turn around any day now." Overproduction results in the need to discount further, in turn increasing the losses.

Older, mature industries typically have high employee costs and, if unionized, also have minimum flexibility to manage wages, benefits*, and work rules affecting productivity. The law of the economic jungle is often that the new competitor can design a more efficient manufacturing environment, and the old competitor, who may have invented the industry, is unable to compete economically.

As the losses progressed in this manner in the auto industry, there was a move to "decapitalization" where plants were sold off to suppliers, usually with the labor force, in the hope that someone else could find a way to increase productivity while giving the OEMs more flexibility. The manufacturers also shifted to buying built-up modules with suppliers doing more "value-added" work.

Large, independent companies like Johnson Controls and Magna have grown on the basis of not just making parts but outsourcing significant major module manufacturing and assembly. Two large parts suppliers became "independent" companies when Ford spun off its parts business as Visteon and GM did the same thing with Delphi. The growth of these mega-suppliers doing much of the integration that the OEMs used to do also delineated the clear distinction between Tier 1 (highest) suppliers and those less broad Tier 2 or 3 companies. This increased competition in the supplier world as more Tier 2 and 3 suppliers had to sell to the Tier 1s. The net result has been a reduction from 30,000+ auto-industry suppliers to fewer than 8,000 in the last 10 to 12 years.

Strategically, the industry is moving away from a century-long march toward full integration, believing that the only way to be profitable is to focus on the things where each company really adds value. There was a

---

* GM spends about $1,400 per car for health benefits, making this the largest single cost the company incurs. This extraordinary amount provides benefits for more than a million active and retired GM workers.

time when no one would think of outsourcing manufacturing. In fact, Henry Ford pursued a strategy of full vertical integration for many years, attempting (unsuccessfully) to get all the way down to growing rubber trees to yield rubber for the tires. He abandoned this approach as it became obvious that the control gained over supply was less important than having the lowest-cost supplier. Additionally, these were essentially different businesses requiring different skill sets and competencies.

OEMs have finally realized that competition in the auto industry is now about design and marketing, not just cost control. Manufacturing is a cost of doing business when you have to deliver a physical product, and there are specialists who can do it well at reasonable cost. Final assembly has stayed inside the car companies as a means to control quality, but there are some who believe that might even move out at some point.

The U.S. auto industry seems to have rediscovered design excitement, higher quality, new features, and new technology as competitive weapons. Toyota, BMW, and a few other foreign manufacturers have used these strategies well in the last decade to differentiate themselves and grab dramatic pieces of global market share. The question now is whether the Big Three can transform themselves as the competition intensifies.

Some argue that the demise of the industry has been predicted for 20 years, and there have been a number of books and essays arguing that the Big Three have been on a slippery slope to irrelevancy for a long time. No one really believes that Ford or GM will go away anytime soon. It is just that without a massive transformation involving new ideas and attitudes even more than capital, neither one is likely to ever be seen again as the company to beat. In the 1930s, when Bethlehem Steel was so important and powerful that it fabricated all the steel for the Golden Gate Bridge and shipped it across country, no one would have bet that they would end up insolvent and broken up 65 years later.

Lately, the U.S. auto industry is showing signs of life. Perhaps they have a shot at avoiding the total death of some other industries, but understanding that the laws of economics encompass not just dollars and cents but changing consumer tastes and preferences is part of the cure for the commoditization disease. Understanding the economic cycle of businesses is fundamental to long-term survival. The same generic cycle is repeated in industry after industry, but we always think it is new and unique:

- Invention with small volumes and high costs
- Mass production with high margins
- Increased competition
- Consolidation
- Commoditization and lower margins
- Differentiation and specialization
- Relocation, replacement, or extinction, depending on the industry and circumstances

We have seen the same cycle in steel, textiles, automobiles, aircraft manufacturing, heavy machinery, machine tools, and even higher tech areas like semiconductor manufacturing. Those cycles will not stop; they will continue and affect every industry over time. The most fundamental characteristic of a truly vibrant economy, or company for that matter, is the ability to reinvent itself periodically.

> **Insight #33: Economic forces and laws are real, and industry changes are real.** They are not as unexpected as most people believe; it is usually only a matter of the timing. The mistake chain in which entire industry changes occur is driven by a failure to recognize the need to make fundamental changes in a business model early enough to avoid being consumed by the natural laws of economics.

Number 1 or 2 in Your Industry—Where Did It Come From?

There is a huge caveat that applies to the discussion of the growth, prosperity, and decline of the preceding industries. There are almost always one or two very good companies, despite industry upheaval, that find ways to differentiate themselves and not only survive but prosper, even in an industry in decline.* Even if you pay attention and make most of the right strategic and operational decisions, there will still be things that surprise you in the economic cycle. Thus, if you are truly one of the

---

* An exception would be a technology-driven area such as the proverbial buggy-whip or steam locomotives, where demand simply ceases for lack of function and all companies die unless they change businesses.

very best in your business, you have a better chance of getting past the challenges that surprise you than if you are a mediocre competitor.

One example is Caterpillar, which has survived and prospered despite the kind of industry cycle and global competition just described. Similarly, a shining example of a company that has emerged from nowhere and dominated discussion as an industry leader in one of the most rapidly changing industries in history is Dell Computer.

Who knows who first articulated the idea that in economics only the fittest survive, but the need to be #1 or #2 probably did not originate with Jack Welch. However, he was certainly responsible for recognizing the principle and making it part of the very successful evolution of GE's businesses. From those successes, "being #1 or #2" became the business mantra of the 1990s.

This is precisely what we have seen in the preceding examples. Economics has shown since the time of Adam Smith that there are winners and losers and that, in most industries, the strongest can survive. Of course, this may leave some room for interpretation that could get you in trouble. It is not clear that being #1 in red quarter-inch shirt buttons will get you far.

The concept is a reflection of the laws of economics. If ignored, you may succeed for a period, but in any industry your viability will be in doubt at some point.

Insight #34: Being #1 or #2 really does matter, not because it was the much heralded rallying cry at GE, but because it is a reflection of the laws of economics that will bite if you are not a leader in your field. Having a vision that includes an understanding of the forces at work and the time you have available is a must.

Old and New Companies: Convergence, Specialization, and Evolution

One of the oldest continuously operating companies in the western world is based in the United Kingdom. The company, GKN plc, has over $8 billion in revenue and is primarily an automotive and aerospace parts supplier. That is its business today, but it certainly did not start there when it was formed as an ironworks in 1759 in Wales. It has been in a lot of different businesses in more than 200 years but has managed to have only one full-year period during which it lost money in its history, and that was in 1979.

As chronicled in a recent article,[87] this is a company that has reinvented itself numerous times over the centuries and always found a way to make money. In the early and mid-1800s, GKN was the largest iron and steel producer in the world. The only time it has really been in trouble was when it strayed from its metal manufacturing roots into totally unrelated businesses. This company has always seen its capabilities in the area of making metal parts and, importantly, has a history of looking for new applications for those capabilities and abandoning old markets before they become life threatening to the enterprise.

Somehow this is a company that has understood, for its whole history, that you cannot win with a "last man standing" strategy.* Evolving from making iron and steel nearly 250 years ago, to screws and nuts 150 years ago, to being the world's largest supplier of automotive constant velocity joints† and jet fighter parts today is an amazing accomplishment. This two-and-a-half century transformation included a number of significant leaps of faith about the future.

GKN is a good example of the transformation process needed to stay ahead of normal economic cycles. It seems obvious in retrospect: They foresaw that coal would be a more effective and available source of heat for iron-making before others, they foresaw that in an industrialized society automated (for the day) manufacture of nuts, bolts, and screws was important, and they saw that someone had to make specialized parts for automobiles and later aircraft. But it was not that obvious because others failed and died with the cycles.

Did GKN succeed or fail in the steel industry? They succeeded, not because they are still in the industry but because they rode the cycle late into the twentieth century, with other businesses developed and viable for diversification when it became natural to exit the steel industry. They did the same thing with screws and evolved into higher-tech fasteners and eventually left that business.

We might say that GKN started with a fairly narrow focus, broadened it with the capabilities it had developed as technologies converged,

---

* There are those who believe that there is money to be made if you can be the last company to survive in a dying, or even heavily consolidated, industry—an obviously risky strategy.

† A part that is necessary to allow front-wheel drive automobiles to transmit power to the wheels smoothly.

specialized in higher value-added areas as competition intensified, and evolved with divestitures. The detailed history of GKN appears to have many fits and starts, but overall it was a fairly smooth evolutionary process that worked in tandem with the technological and economic cycles of society. The commonality that runs through GKN over history is that most things they have done have something to do with metal and metal components, with everything from powdered metal for specialty parts to complete helicopters.

A modern version of this phenomenon that has evolved rapidly is Dell Computer. Perhaps our eighth generation descendants will see if Dell survives as long as GKN, but Dell has done an amazing job so far of anticipating the shifts in their industry and adapting rapidly.

Dell's transformation and redefinition of the personal computer space is its greatest protection against the mistakes others have made in a cutthroat competitive industry. This is a classic "grow or die" scenario in an industry where prices go down every year while value goes up. There is dramatic value being transferred in the personal computer industry, but the industry is so competitive that the customer is the primary beneficiary—except for Dell, the one company that has redefined the business and is benefiting as a result.

The PC business has evolved dramatically over the last 25 years from a hobby for techies to a "must have" business and personal productivity, communications, and entertainment device. The industry has gone through all the classic economic cycles, except that what we saw happen in automobiles over a century happened in PCs in one-quarter of the time. The general stages we use to describe the process in most industries and the PC examples are:

- **Invention with small volumes and high cost.** Apple II (at $2,500 in 1981), Tandy TRS-80, Commodore, and others.
- **Mass production with high margins.** Apple Mac, IBM PC.
- **Increased competition.** Compaq, HP, DEC, Gateway, eMachines, many generics, Dell, and foreign competitors (such as Acer from Taiwan and Legend in China) enter the market.
- **Consolidation.** Commodore, DEC, and many others fail or abandon the market.
- **Commoditization and lower margins.** Gateway and Dell push their direct-to-consumer and "build-to-order" systems without a presence in physical stores, resulting in lower prices.

- **Differentiation and specialization.** Apple sticks with its proprietary operating system and focuses on education and graphics markets, IBM eventually focuses on the business market with only laptops at retail, and Dell takes charge by becoming the most efficient producer and marketer in the world and drives prices down to levels where others cannot compete.

- **Relocation, replacement, or extinction.** Dell becomes so powerful that they define the market and others must respond. Dell manages customer relationships better than anyone in the industry and expands heavily into its own branded peripherals, breaking partner ties (such as HP) and further increasing their strength. Compaq and HP merge, Gateway buys eMachines and starts to push hard into consumer electronics (such as high-end TVs), and Apple moves into selling music devices and online music distribution while maintaining a small, but loyal, niche PC business.

As the competitive dynamics of the PC industry evolved, Dell went through a number of stages where they changed the economics of the industry by changing the model:

- **Build-to-order with supply chain management.** This reduced inventory, which in turn reduced production backlogs, increased cash flow, and eliminated obsolete inventory. Initially, this was a simple strategy to reduce cost to be able to compete on cost, but it evolved into the basis for an entire new business model, not with reduced inventory but with no inventory at all.

- **Minimize R&D by being a fast adopter.** GKN didn't do a lot of R&D but was quick to adopt technology from others. This included being the first licensee of the Bessemer steel process in the early 1800s and the first to license automated screw manufacturing machines in the United Kingdom. Two centuries later, Dell has applied the same principles as it adds new features and peripherals to its products and sales process with everything from CD drives to printers to networking equipment to digital cameras—all made by someone else, albeit with a Dell label in most cases.

- **Use of the Web for configuration, ordering, and many service functions.** This improved staff efficiency but also increased customer satisfaction because the service was standardized and there were no wait times.

- **Solve major problems for corporate customers and get them to do the work.** Dell set up special corporate accounts and Web pages (Premier Pages) to facilitate ordering and outsource machine configuration. If desired, this even includes installation of customers' proprietary software so that machines ship in a truly network plug-compatible setup. This saves customers time and money on delivery and ensures that employees order to a company standard, thereby improving the purchasing and standardization process.

- **Improve forecasting and track results.** This is actually easier with a build-to-order system since you do not make the mistake of trying to sell what you have instead of what customers want to buy.

- **Study customers and incorporate what they value into your products or services offerings.** Dell found that customers valued not only leading-edge products and competitive prices but easy ordering, flexibility in configuration, after-sale service, hassle-free setup, and the ability to add peripherals now or later with ease. They did not figure out how to put all this into the business model at once, but over time it evolved to an integrated model for the PC market that is unparalleled in the industry. This allowed Dell to be broadly competitive and be seen as adding value for an entire package of products and services. Once established, this meant that they do not always have to have the lowest price on individual items. After establishing themselves in the personal and business PC space, they went after related, but different, markets such as servers and networking.

Some would say that Dell had it easy because they came to the industry late and could easily invent a new model since they did not have an old model to destroy. There is some truth to this since HP and Compaq both had traditional retail-distribution models in place and believed they could not change to a Dell model and be competitive. Yet others like Gateway started with the same model that Dell did and were unable to compete. There were a variety of reasons for this, but the primary one is that Dell came to embrace its model like a religion—faith, belief, dedication, and evangelism internally and externally with customers.

The net result today is that Dell looks a lot like Southwest Airlines or Wal-Mart—the player that defines the playing field in their sector and has the highest margins as a result. Like Southwest, Dell does not do everything that its broader competitors IBM or HP do, but it now makes the rules in its space.

Economic Business Visioning–the EBV Model

The ability to avoid the mistakes that lead to destruction by economic cycles is dependant on the ability to understand economic cycles, synthesize signals, and sense changes while developing ideas about what might work in the future. Some might call this being a "visionary," but I think it is more about being curious and analytic about what you see around you. Synthesis of weak signals is an almost impossible skill to teach if those running a business are not interested. The ability to understand and evaluate where you are in the economic evolution of your industry is required, however, to survive in the long term, as shown by what GKN, Toyota, and Dell have accomplished in very different industries.

When we look at companies like GKN and Dell, we see that their leaders have not been "visionary" as much as observant. They simply see, a little earlier than others, what will be described as obvious after the fact. They see signals and react with good ideas a little quicker than others—but not too far in advance. In fact, there are many examples of visionaries who were far enough ahead of their time that their ideas took a great deal of time to develop (such as Carlson and Xerox from Chapter 4 or the invention of television and aviation) or were failures because the market was not ready.

The ability to be ahead just enough to win is what I call "economic business visioning" (EBV). Every business claims to have a mission, and every executive claims to have a vision for accomplishing that mission. But many of those visions are driven more by aspiration than an understanding of where the business stands in the underlying economic cycle of the industry and the broader environment. This emphasis on the word *economic* as part of the visioning process means that the process must include:

- **An understanding of the industry economic cycle** and what is driving cost, price, volume, and the level of competition.

- **A diagram of the growth and profitability** cycle for the industry to date with explanations for the changes in absolute values, slopes, discontinuities, and general trends, along with scenarios for how the curves will behave in the future (see Figures 8.2 through 8.5).[88]

- **Analysis of subcycles for specific products** within the overall industry cycle.

- **An understanding of what customers value,** or valued at different points in the cycle, and whether you can deliver things they value directly or can provide alliances or partners to do so.

- **Identification of points in the past where new competitors or substitute products affected the cycle** and where you predict that will happen in the future.

- **An explicit understanding of the role of productivity** in your cycle and how much it needs to grow to avoid margin erosion.

- **An analysis of which costs are truly fixed and variable** and scenarios that might shift them to provide additional flexibility (such as outsourcing).

- **An analysis of what economic factors are driving R&D in related areas that will affect your industry** (for example, biotech and genomic R&D are not part of the traditional pharmaceutical industry but will affect its future).

- **Competitive modeling and gaming,** including product cycles, costs, pricing, capabilities, strategic intent, vulnerabilities, and ways you can help competitors hurt themselves (legally) by competing in a way that is difficult or expensive to match.

- **A timetable by which the EBV process functions,** with dates and/or conditions that should cause refinement or new creation of the business vision.

- **A commitment that the objective is not to stay in the business you are in** but to be able to generate value in a business that will be in demand, where you have a plan for superiority, and where you have or can develop the competencies required to win.

My experience has been that companies look at most of these things, but the analyses are buried within silos of operations, marketing, product development, or finance. It is rare to see all the factors brought together in an effective strategy process. This is not to say that detailed, even exhaustive, analytic processes do not take place, but most of these processes are flawed because of the assumptions made either directly or implicitly. Many of these assumptions violate the laws of economics and economic cycles that we have been discussing. Some of the most common are:

- **There is no substitute for our product,** such as tetraethyl lead in gasoline to reduce engine knock. This was true until the invention of computer-driven engine control systems that solved the problem in other ways, without the additive, and improved engine performance while reducing emissions.

- **That move will kill us (or save us).** Sometimes things work differently than expected, like the concern on the part of the movie studios that demand would drop when people acquired VCRs. In reality, the opposite happened, as more people saw a need for movies to view both in their homes and theaters.

- **Our (quality, price, design, cost, whatever) is the best in the industry.** There is always a new gunslinger looking to beat the established player, and they will seek you out.

- **Our price is high, but customers will pay for quality (or service).** Sometimes they will (Tiffany), and sometimes they will not (all the small store owners put out of business by Wal-Mart or Home Depot), and their definition of quality may change over time (Dell).

- **We understand that we need to change, but we have time.** Never underestimate how fast a market can change once it goes past the tipping point—just look at Kodak.

- **You can't differentiate a commodity.** Wrong—look at the loyalty to brands of gasoline.

- **People are our greatest strength.** Maybe, but it is the abilities that those people possess and how they apply them that is important and that can get out of synchronization with market needs quickly.

There are many other potential assumptions that management teams make explicitly or implicitly, but a vigorous EBV process can help identify which of the assumptions have veracity and which ones do not. The EBV model can be applied to virtually any industry. The time frames, competitors, cycle dynamics, and economic relationships will be different, but the principles apply. Failure to pay attention to these broad principles is the reason that multiple companies and entire industries end up in trouble as more nimble competitors replace them. The U.S. airline industry provides an interesting case for deeper analysis of EBV.

Flying High and Broke–Applying EBV in Undifferentiated Cutthroat Competition

Airline industry analysts will tell you that the airline industry is broken badly, but economists will tell you it is just the market at work. Competition is fierce, companies have a hard time making money (many of the remaining companies have operated under bankruptcy protection, some more than once), airports are crowded, the air traffic control system is straining under the load, and most airlines have resorted to selling sandwiches onboard to make a few extra bucks.

But it has never been better for passengers. Fares are low, flights are frequent to most cities of significant size, and safety is better than ever. Despite the aftereffects of 9/11, more people are traveling than ever, and more than 90 percent travel on a discounted fare.[89] This is another case of a competitive industry where all the benefits are being competed away to the customer.

The EBV model is a useful structure for examining this industry, and as with PCs, there is one major beneficiary and a number of smaller ones. The financial winner in the airline industry for over 25 years has been Southwest Airlines, a company that, like Dell Computer, invented a different model of the industry based on a detailed understanding of industry economics and customer preferences and priorities. For many years, Southwest was seen as a small niche player that the major airlines looked down on as providing discounted air transportation for those customers who were willing to sacrifice quality for price.

Over time, however, the Southwest model survived, gained respect, and made money predictably, while the major airlines saw wild variance in profitability. Like Dell in its industry, Southwest has seen copycats in the industry that have come and gone in the form of People Express in the United States and Laker Airways in the United Kingdom, both during the 1980s. Recent more successful imitators include JetBlue in the United States and Ryanair based in Dublin.

One advantage of examining a regulated industry is that there are public sources for a great deal of data. We cited safety data earlier but will now look at some of the economic history of the air transport industry and its relationship to EBV. The industry followed a pattern similar to the auto industry prior to World War II as airlines fought to bring costs down and bring reliability and safety up to make their services available and attractive to a broader market. Most credit the development of the Douglas DC-3 aircraft in the mid-1930s as the machine that most helped the fledgling industry become a business.

C.R. Smith, the president of American Airlines, wanted an airplane that would allow passengers to sleep in berths on long, overnight flights. Airplanes were the fastest form of transportation available but were still relatively slow and had limited range. The trips were long, and some required intermediate stops. There was thus a need to accommodate passenger comfort, so it seemed natural to put berths in an airplane since the affluent customers who could afford an airplane ticket were used to the comfort of the Pullman railroad car. The first DC-3 delivered to American accommodated 14 passengers with fold-down berths or 28 in a daytime configuration. While a small, low performance airplane by today's standards, the DC-3 turned out to be the most used, most reliable airliner for nearly 25 years, with a fair number still in service today in remote locations.

Following World War II, the economy improved dramatically, aviation technology improved, and businesses and consumers had more money to spend. A lot of aviation entrepreneurs saw the opportunities at the same time, and after the war there were a surplus of pilots who wanted to continue to fly. The industry was regulated and fares were high, but as shown in Figure 8.2, the industry grew in passenger miles and revenues fairly smoothly along with the overall economy. An EBV process, if they had called it that at the time, would have said that economic growth, advancing aircraft technology, and higher disposable income for consumers would predict a bright future for the airlines.

As seen in the longer-term chart in Figure 8.3, however, this growth in passenger miles began to look a little choppy as a function of a number of important economic events. In the long term, the most significant event was industry deregulation in 1978. The impact was not immediate, partially because of the rising fuel costs during the 1970s, a large shock in oil prices in 1979, the early 1980s recession, and the one-two punch of inflation and high interest rates (called "stagflation" at the time).

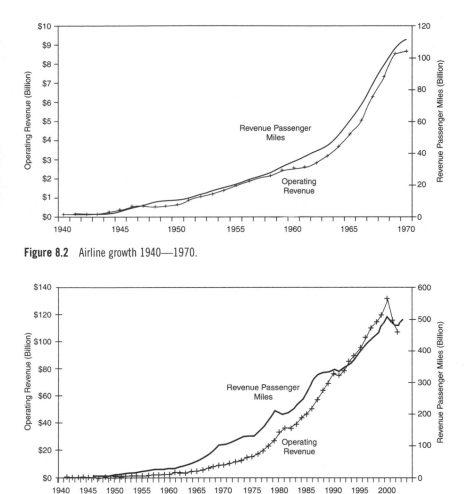

Figure 8.2   Airline growth 1940—1970.

Figure 8.3   Airline growth 1940—2002.

The interesting thing about the airline industry since deregulation is the different views of an EBV model. Most competitors have continued to slug it out on the same basis ever since deregulation in 1978. The last great innovation was frequent flyer programs, first brought to market by American Airlines in 1981 as a means of building loyalty by rewarding their most active and loyal customers. The programs worked, but once every airline had adopted a loyalty program, the benefits were largely neutralized, except that the airlines were able to track their customers travel patterns and habits more effectively.

As the economy recovered in the early 1980s and interest rates declined, more entrepreneurs saw the growth opportunity in the deregulated industry, and discounters arrived in the form of People Express and others. The majors were concerned, but business was good and they viewed the discounters as something other than "real airlines." They saw little reason to change their business models, especially when they saw that their price-insensitive business customers were responding to the benefits of "silver" or "gold" status.

Over the years following deregulation, the airlines learned to compete on price because any other differentiation was very difficult. The late 1980s and early 1990s saw a brief stock market crash, the savings and loan crisis, and a recession, all of which hurt the entire industry. By the mid to late 1990s, though, the economy was booming, airfares had crept up, and good business conditions meant that there were lots of passengers flying on full-fare coach, business, and first class tickets and were happy to collect frequent flyer miles.

Every once in a while, following the pattern previously discussed for other competitive industries, an airline like Midway would come along and differentiate with airplanes equipped with only first class seats as a means to try to lure full-fare business travelers. All of these initiatives eventually failed, and pure price competition prevailed. American's late 1990's program to increase seat pitch (spacing) called "more room in coach" seemed well received, but it was not enough to save them from significant financial difficulty in the early 2000s.

I happen to believe that airline service quality differs, and I have my own preferences, but there is not widespread agreement on this subject or certainly not enough agreement that it has any substantial effect on business success. In short, like the auto industry, there is very little real differentiation across providers of commercial air service.

But trouble was brewing for the industry as the dotcom crash and a broader market decline presaged the recession that began in 2001. Businesses began cutting back drastically on travel, and the airlines were in serious trouble, even before September 11, 2001 when their fortunes changed dramatically. In today's world, the only real difference in this industry that operates on such thin margins, especially post-2001 recession and post 9/11, is the ability to be the lowest cost provider, a role that Southwest has played successfully for 25 years* while the majors laughed.

---

* Southwest has been displaced in the low-operating-cost derby recently by the smaller, but growing, JetBlue.

Southwest's model has prevailed with consistent profitability and growth across a number of economic cycles, competitive onslaughts, and changed strategies by others. Why have they prevailed with an EBV process that has clearly been very different from their competitors, has been successful, and has, until recently, had little imitation? If you listed the top three things about their planning process that has facilitated their success, as viewed from the outside without the benefit of and inside knowledge, what would they be?

I believe that Southwest's EBV is simple. They created a visioning process based on sound economic principles and, except for minor changes, have not deviated from it:

- If you create true value, customers will come.

- If you treat employees well, they will make sure you achieve the vision.

- You can engineer value drivers into the business design early more easily than looking for them after the fact.

The problem with this list is that it is so generic that anyone in any business could do these things. Why haven't others copied it sooner or as effectively? The answers lie not just in the concepts but in a deeper EBV that includes understanding the principles and executing against them consistently and almost flawlessly.

- **If you create true value, customers will come.** Value comes in many forms, but many business people believe consumers narrowly equate value only with price. What about consistency, reliability, and even the context for delivering value? SW delivers value that consists of more than just low price:

  - Most consumers know that Southwest has low prices, but they also know they can depend on them to almost always have the lowest prices, not just when you happen to catch them on the day they are having a sale.

  - Southwest operations perform reliably well, including on-time performance, baggage handling, and customer service as measured by a number of surveys and indicators.

  - Southwest has, from the beginning, sought to deliver value enhanced by a culture where employees are known for the "can-do" attitude, humor, and believability.

■ **If you treat employees well, they will make sure you achieve the vision.** Most individuals want to do a good job and feel satisfied by the work they perform. Southwest has a high-performance culture that produces results through people. This does not happen by accident. It is built through disciplined recruiting, training, performance management, and reinforcement. Southwest has great discipline but has also built a loyalty among employees who feel like they are on a mission that matters and are part of a family effort to be the best in their business.

■ **You can engineer value drivers into the business design early more easily than looking for them after the fact.** Critics and competitors of Southwest, Wal-Mart, Dell, or any other successful, low-price, value-oriented organization like to complain that such companies have a competitive advantage because "they started that way—they don't have to change a lot of long-standing bad or expensive practices." As most of us have told our children from time to time, "Life isn't fair." It is not easy to compete against a successful but radically different model, but compete you must. Much of the Southwest business design is easy to understand, but tough for competitors to emulate once they have taken a different path:

  ◆ Southwest generally chooses to fly to less congested airports near larger cities. Smart move—this improves on-time performance, and such airports have lower landing fees. Competitors could do this. Why don't they?

  ◆ Southwest flies one type of airplane, the Boeing 737 (with some variance across versions), which reduces cost for maintenance, training, and service. Competitors could do this. Why don't they?

  ◆ Southwest does not sell tickets through agents and has the highest proportion of tickets purchased online in the industry. These two things save them a great deal of money. Competitors can do this but have only recently caught on and are trying to train their customers.

The list could go on, but the point is that the elements of an EBV must have the following characteristics:

- Be based on sound economic principles that are proven to drive customer behavior
- Be internally consistent (not in conflict)
- Be robust enough to work for a variety of scenarios, not just the current one
- Be related to execution and have the capacity to create the desired effect

This is the real secret of the EBV at Southwest—it all works together. All their competitors want to keep their costs low, but they are not willing to reinvent themselves in a model that has a chance to emulate a lower cost model. Why? Because they have a fundamentally different view of industry economics; they clung too long to the view that there was a big segment of price-insensitive customers to support a higher cost/higher service operation. The reality is that, once the costs are built into the operation, they become cultural and nearly impossible to remove.

Like most airlines, US Airways evolved from a series of consolidation mergers but never got their costs under control. As a result, they operated at little or no profit in the boom times of the late 1990s because they had the highest cost structure in the industry. You can't violate the laws of economics—when the downturn came, they ended up in bankruptcy.

A pilot at US Airways told me that he and his colleagues would gladly take a contract to operate like Southwest, but the unionized US Airways flight attendants and mechanics are so overpaid by comparison that he believes they will "fight to the end," and the airline will never be able to change or compete. Similar behavior by mechanics at Eastern Airlines was the final blow that brought the demise of that organization.

The biggest warning sign that assumptions around price insensitivity in the industry were changing came with the growth of the business jet industry. The growth of this segment has been substantial for the last decade, and the pace actually accelerated after 9/11 as the hassle factor associated with commercial transportation increased. The customers who were previously most likely to pay high prices found a substitute product—a private airline in the form of business jet time-sharing, or what is called "fractional ownership." At the end of 2003 there were 6,217 companies or individuals who owned fractional shares in business aircraft,[90] nearly all of which are very capable jets. This number underestimates the number of affected travelers since the airplanes rarely depart with only one passenger.

When the cuts came during the 2001 recession, it was upper-middle management that was no longer paying the high fares as their companies forced them to travel less or with restrictions to obtain discounts. The EBV of all of the major airlines failed—and failed with clearly visible trends and facts that were not consistent with their implicit assumptions for the last decade. A couple of airlines (Delta and United) made half-hearted attempts to enter the fractional ownership and/or charter business, but the truth is there is little profit there. It is just a competitor that eats away at margins, with the benefits (time and convenience) going to the customer.

British Airways made a serious attempt to use EBV as a means to improve their plight in the industry. BA's vision in the 1999 to 2001 time frame was to reduce capacity, especially over the very competitive North Atlantic, by reducing the number of deep-discount coach seats and increasing the number of business class seats on its airplanes. To do this, they also planned a shift to smaller 777 aircraft, reducing the use of their very large 747-400 aircraft.

At the time, this seemed like a great plan that recognized the realities of the market. The business traveler was the source of great revenue and profit, and if you could use a less expensive airplane and fill it with a greater proportion of business travelers, you could actually make more money flying fewer passengers. Additionally, the North Atlantic was not as accessible for the business jet threat because only the top few models have reasonable nonstop transoceanic capability.

It was a reasonable risk, but the scenario that was not considered was a combination of a business downturn and 9/11 and its aftermath. However, it turned out that having lower-capacity aircraft flying was the right strategy after 9/11 as traffic declined, so BA was as well positioned as anyone else, even thought the result was not at the profit level they had hoped.

The difference for Southwest turns out to be that their EBV can produce success even under the scenario that unfolded in the world in 2001 and beyond. The other visions and assumptions, even BA's innovative approach, were not robust enough.

The small number of airlines that have had any financial success over any period of time is an indication that the industry operates at economic equilibrium—just enough money made to keep a very competitive industry afloat but not so much profit that an "average" competitor can enter and survive. Delta Airlines had a reputation for being well run, fiscally conservative, and consistently profitable, but they fell from grace in the aftermath of 9/11 as well.

The net result, as shown in Figure 8.4, is an industry that has been so competitive that over its history it has been profitable only for moments in time. The attractiveness and necessity of the industry have made it both highly effective for consumers and brutally competitive. Its sensitivity to the economic cycle and outside input variables (such as fuel costs) make it vulnerable, which is all the more reason to have a robust EBV.

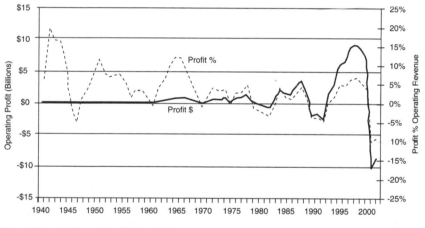

Figure 8.4   Airline profits 1940—2002.

Intelligent people who want to succeed run the major airlines, but they have had trouble coming to grips with economic realities. Everyone wants to believe they can differentiate their product in a way that will provide a competitive advantage. They are all trying, but the market is finally bringing the realization that Southwest discovered some time ago—intense competition and the economic cycle eventually turn most businesses into some form of commodity.

Continental has been in bankruptcy twice but has emerged as competitive because their CEO, Gordon Bethune, understands the economics of the industry and the need to find ways to provide high service levels and keep costs under control. Bethune used many techniques to get cost down and service up, but one of the most effective was giving employees monthly bonuses based on measurable outcomes like on-time departures and customer satisfaction. He may not have called it by the initials EBV, but that is effectively what it was— understanding the economics of the industry and finding new ways to compete to change the no-win outcomes of price-only competition.

One telling story of an EBV that was ahead of its time and then later behind was Pan American World Airways. The short flight from Key West to Havana became the first route for Pan American Airways (original name) in 1927 and the first "international" route by any U.S. airline. It took over an hour to fly the 90 miles carrying mail sacks.

Pan Am's founder, Juan Trippe, had an economic business vision, and from that inauspicious beginning on the Key West to Havana route, he went on to a series of firsts as Pan Am became one of the most respected names in international aviation. Pan Am opened transpacific and later transatlantic routes with its Clippers*, flying boats made to Pan Am's specifications.

In the 1930s, Trippe enlisted the help of Charles Lindbergh as an advisor and board member to help him understand where aviation was going in the future. In 1933, Lindbergh wrote to Trippe, urging him not to think about today's routes but to try to think about which routes would be the best to have in the future.[91]

Trippe made a habit out of pushing the limits of aircraft technology in going to more places at greater distance under challenging conditions as aircraft evolved. Pan Am started around the world service in 1950, was the first U.S. airline to enter the jet age with the 707 in 1958, and was the first to order Boeing's new 747 when it was announced.

Pan Am developed a near monopoly on international travel among U.S.-based airlines, and part of Trippe's vision was to operate an "economy class" to allow the masses to take advantage of air transportation. Following World War II, he tried to introduce discounted fares at a time when the International Air Transport Association (IATA) set fares on international routes. In a protectionist move, the United Kingdom actually blocked his flights if they had economy seats. Trippe responded by flying to Shannon, Ireland, but the entrenched anticompetitive environment continued for many years.

Despite this bureaucratic and protectionist setback, government mail contracts and protected status (through the process of granting routes)

---

* The first flight from San Francisco to Manila took six days with a number of stops en route.

allowed Pan Am to become an international powerhouse. In return, however, the U.S. government would not grant Pan Am domestic routes. By the 1960s, other airlines were granted international routes to blunt Pan Am's control, but Pan Am did not acquire domestic routes until the deregulation of the industry after 1978. Pan Am acquired National Airlines for its domestic service, hoping it would smoothly feed Pan Am's international routes.

The dream of a seamless domestic and international airline was not to be, even as it became obvious that this structure was precisely what one would need to be competitive in the new, deregulated environment. National and Pan Am did not create a smooth operating organization, could not get their costs down, did not market effectively, and by the mid-1980s began to liquidate assets by selling off coveted Pacific routes to United Airlines.

The economic environment had changed. Despite Trippe's EBV, he and his company adapted to the economic environment of the time and could not change back at later date when the environment would allow the vision he had well before its time. Being a great operator serving the business or wealthy private travelers of the world in a regulated environment was very different from competing for customers on routes with tough competition and no price controls.

The airline that had been a powerhouse with a global reputation was sliding down the slippery slope to economic doom as one of the casualties of true competition. Nostalgia over the colorful history of Pan Am and its founder, Juan Trippe, was not enough to save it when it became clear that the problem was its failure to see how quickly and deeply it needed to change its culture and get costs under control. Pan Am was already on the ropes by 1988 when it was the victim of a terrorist bomb that left pieces of a 747, with the Pan Am logo visible in pictures flashed around the world, littering the ground in Lockerbie, Scotland. By 1991, Trippe's vision of dominance of the international air transport market with service across the economic strata to a wide range of destinations came to an end when Pan Am declared bankruptcy.

Add to this the history of Eastern, Braniff, and others that sold assets (routes, planes, gates) to pay creditors as they went out of business, and the air transport industry followed the same path as many other industries that grew from nothing to greatness in the twentieth century. Consolidation was brutal and often only a delaying action in advance of failure. As in a number of other industries, only one or two players came out as consistent leaders in creating value for shareholders, and those one or two winners are not always the ones who invented the industry.

The industry has become more efficient over time. Figure 8.5 shows the revenue per seat mile since 1941. It has doubled, but that is in nominal terms. If the data were adjusted for inflation, the real cost to the consumer would likely be dramatically lower than it was 50 to 60 years ago. This is what has driven the growth and success of the industry. It is also what makes it difficult to achieve lasting success. This industry is no different than dozens of others; you must constantly improve productivity through any means possible to be among the handful that will do well.

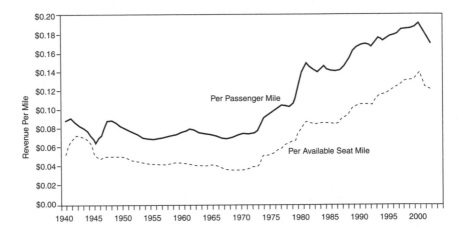

Figure 8.5   Airline unit revenue 1940-2002.

Industry models, competitors, technologies, customer preferences, input costs, and productivity all change over time. Failing to understand that your business model will have to evolve is the deadliest mistake a management team can make. Having a position as a leader in your industry or, better yet, being the leader of the revolution is the only place you want to be when discontinuity occurs. You will need the flexibility to be able to lead a new model, change the businesses, or exit the business successfully.

The personal leadership required to avoid mistakes of the economic cycle is substantial. It is much easier to keep slogging away, fighting the battle that we know than it is to ask the tough questions about the scenarios that might unfold. It is very difficult to acknowledge that your industry has seen a structural change that is not likely to reverse itself to the "good old days."

Are there signs in your industry that you are ignoring? Are there indications that the fundamental value equation is changing? Do you have new competitors who operate with a different model, or have your customers substituted you out of the picture? Asking the questions of yourself and your team is the first step. You may not like the answers, but recognizing the need to change is first step on the road to success in most businesses.

Earlier in this chapter, we discussed two important insights about the timing of economic changes and company positioning:

Insight #33: Economic forces and laws are real, and industry changes are real. They are not as unexpected as most people believe; it is usually only a matter of the timing. The mistake chain in which entire industry changes occur is driven by a failure to recognize the need to make fundamental changes in a business model early enough to avoid being consumed by the natural laws of economics.

Insight #34: Being #1 or #2 really does matter, not because it was the much heralded rallying cry at GE but because it is a reflection of the laws of economics that will bite if you are not a leader in your field. Having a vision that includes an understanding of the forces at work and the time you have available is a must.

The final insight for this chapter has to do with the fact that there must be a process to structuring and analyzing the economic insights that guide your business:

Insight #35: EBV is not optional, but few companies, except perhaps pure commodity businesses, factor such a process into their planning. The usual set of assumptions in most planning cycles revolves around a range of economic assumptions from "a little better" to "a little worse," with "a lot better" and "a lot worse" thrown in to make the set look complete but with little belief that either will occur. For both the short and the longer term, designing a process for analysis and spending time understanding the shifts in the industry economic issues will help avoid mistakes that are deadly.

All the industries we have looked at or referenced in this chapter have provided extraordinary value to their customers. The real question and responsibility for management is to figure out how to provide both extraordinary value for customers and decent returns for shareholders. EBV is one tool that can help in the quest.

9

Mistakes Aren't Just for Big Companies—Small Company Chains

"Don't gamble; take all your savings and buy some good stock and hold it till it goes up, then sell it. If it don't go up, don't buy it."

—Will Rogers

One of the best-known business stories in the world is how a very talented and visionary college dropout founded a software company and in 20 years, became the richest man in the world. For every huge success like Bill Gates and Microsoft, there are millions of hopeful entrepreneurs who would be happy if they could achieve even a more modest level of success.

We have focused on large enterprises in this book and, we hear about them in the news daily, but much of the world's economy is driven by small businesses. In the United States, the impact of small business on the economy is dramatic:

- Nearly 90 percent of all U.S. businesses have fewer than 20 employees, employing about 18 percent of the nongovernment workforce.[92]

- Over 99 percent of all U.S. firms have fewer than 500 employees,* employ 50 percent of the workforce, and produce approximately 50 percent of GDP.[93]
- However, less than 5 percent of businesses generate revenue in excess of $1 million annually.[94]

The U.S. economy would not be as strong as it is, domestically or globally, without the relatively small number of large firms that represent a large share of GDP and are part of a smooth system of global commerce. But the number of small businesses and their importance and impact on the overall economy is much greater than the average person realizes.

Small business is very different than large business, but small business owners and mangers find themselves in mistake chains in much the same way as larger company managers and executives. They miss signals, ignore or do not seek data and information, bypass systems, or allow short-term thinking to obscure their longer-term vision. These are classic drivers of mistake scenarios for all businesses, but there are some other situations that are unique to startup or smaller businesses that should be examined separately.

Most small company owners and entrepreneurs measure their success on the basis of profit but express it openly in terms of employees and/or revenue. From the preceding data, we might conclude that a very large number of small companies and proprietorships generate a middle-class living for their owners and employees, but very few generate substantial wealth. But the ability for anyone to build a business that earns them independence and the possibility of a good living, or perhaps wealth, is what drives entrepreneurs to start and operate small businesses. It is the dream that has been realized millions of times and has driven America for most of the last century.

The odds of success as an entrepreneur are not as small as they are for making it to the big leagues as an athlete playing a major sport, but the road to business success is littered with those who were not able to complete the journey for one reason or another. But the probabilities are high enough to make this ability to achieve independence and wealth the reason that many around the world admire the United States and seek to come here.

---

* U.S. government, Small Business Administration definition of a small business.

Governments around the world have initiated efforts to improve the environment for new business creation and foster a culture of entrepreneurship to stimulate economic growth. The systems that support and foster such efforts are both straightforward and very complex. There are many requirements to make such a complex system work smoothly, most importantly the rule of law and protection for intellectual property. One part of the equation that we take for granted in the United States, because we are so used to it, is the ability to easily incorporate and raise risk capital from unrelated parties whose liability is limited to their capital invested.

Most of the beneficiaries and would-be beneficiaries of this system do not realize that the legal underpinning of the ability for anyone to have an idea, start a company, raise capital, and succeed is only about 150 years old. There were large trading empires earlier than this, but business beyond what an individual could accomplish, as a sole proprietor, was somewhat unusual unless the business had government or sovereign sponsorship. The need for structures to accommodate growth was present in early society. Some assert that at least one example of a venture-capital partnership goes back to the Assyrians around 1800 BC.[95]

The structure was more formalized by the 1600s when the English East India Company began trading missions, but to form a company one had to seek permission from the crown for a charter to operate. Investors could then be sought, but these were most often investments targeted to a specific short-term objective, in this case funding a trip to the Indian Ocean to retrieve spices for sale through London markets. Loose agreements often led to misunderstandings about when and how funds would be returned. In 1603, some investors in the company thought their money should be returned after one voyage, albeit one that met with only modest success because of a temporary oversupply of pepper. But the controlling investors voted to reinvest the funds for other voyages.[96] The illiquidity of pre-IPO venture investing is not new.

What is relatively new is a simple legal structure that provides the ability to incorporate easily and raise money from investors for long-term purposes, with accountability to shareholders. This has not come easily. By the mid-1600s in England, joint stock companies were permitted but fell out of favor after the excesses and scandals of the "South Sea Bubble" in the early 1700s caused investors to lose a great deal of money and faith in the structure.

Industrialization and the need for massive amounts of capital brought the realization that a stock ownership system was necessary for growth, with controls to deal with the "agency problem."*

One of the most significant challenges that drove change in the systems of capital formation was the building of the railroads in the United Kingdom and United States in the mid-1800s. The new technology had obvious public benefit but made business people and politicians realize that the massive need for capital required to build and operate large-scale operations was making extant business models obsolete. At the time, the predominate business forms were still sole proprietorships or partnerships, which made it very difficult to raise the required capital for large projects that were not funded by government.

The United Kingdom enacted the Joint Stock Companies Act in 1844. Corporations were permitted in Connecticut as early as 1837, and over the next century, corporate law evolved differently in the individual states as they realized that having corporations locate, or at least incorporate, in their states was advantageous.

The system is still not perfect, and the "agency problem" still has weaknesses, as we have seen so visibly in corporate scandals at least a few times each century for the last 300 years. But for all its weaknesses, this is the system that allowed General Electric, Ford, Kodak, Wal-Mart, McDonalds, Microsoft, and thousands of other successful companies to grow from an idea to prosperity over the last century.

Not all companies go from an idea to dramatic success in a decade or two. In fact, over the lifetime of businesses, some estimate that 39 percent are profitable, 30 percent break even, and 30 percent lose money.[97] Many of those that break even are likely to be S-corporations, limited liability companies or partnerships designed to distribute all income to the owners so that the corporate tax return, from which this kind of data is drawn, shows no income or loss. This means that roughly two-thirds of all companies are at least providing a living (or more) for the owners.

We will examine many common mistakes that I have observed personally in working with and investing in small companies over the last 25 years. While these mistakes are described in small company terms, I can also say that I have seen variants of these mistakes in larger companies as well—they just look more sophisticated and are on a larger scale.

---

* The idea that professional managers were agents of the owners (shareholders) and that safeguards had to be put in place to protect owners from agents' conflict of interest.

The mistakes and potential mistakes described in the following sections are often independent. They are not always a chain of mistakes where the next mistake is somehow related to the previous one. The mistakes can be made individually or in concert; it is simply a question of how many mistakes are made before there is damage and how rapidly it all plays out.

The consequences may be smaller scale, but they are no less challenging for small businesses than for large. There are some entrepreneurs who seem to have nine lives, an amazing ability to repeatedly slide to the precipice, hang on by their fingernails, and find a way to recover. This survival instinct and ability to always find a way out of a jam is unique to the most talented entrepreneurs, probably the upper quartile or less. There are many others who find themselves in situations where a few mistakes that would not damage a larger business significantly will kill a small business very quickly.

Choose the Right Idea–Then Change It

To paraphrase Will Rogers' quote about the stock market, "Starting a company is easy: get a good idea, raise money from some investors, make the business very profitable, then sell it and retire—if it's not profitable, don't start it." This is easier said than done.

I was teaching an entrepreneurship course many years ago and was discussing the mindset of entrepreneurs with a more experienced colleague. A real entrepreneur, he said, "Starts a company because he or she has a vision for how to create a business to meet a need that they can feel viscerally. They're *entrepreneurs of the heart*—it makes them physically excited when they describe their vision to you."

He went on to explain that too many students wanted to start companies because they are *"intellectual entrepreneurs*—they know how the process will get them the success they want if it goes well, but they don't have a passion for any particular market or product." The passionate entrepreneur of the heart does not always win, but he or she is more likely to win in my experience because he or she is more deeply committed.

I have seen some of these "intellectual entrepreneurs." The Wharton Innovation Center offered market research services to entrepreneurs considering new ventures. MBA students who wanted to learn how to evaluate new ventures did most of the research work. An entrepreneur came to visit one day with some technology-based ideas for improving HVAC (heating, ventilation, and air-conditioning) systems' efficiency.

We pulled together a team, and the group got to work doing a market and competitive technology review. A couple of weeks later, the students came to give me an update and were clearly troubled by their findings. Their concern was that more sophisticated and proven solutions were already in the market for the purpose our entrepreneur envisioned; he just did not know about them. The students thought the entrepreneur would be crushed but decided that the only thing to do was to call the guy in and tell him the competitive facts of life.

The entrepreneur came in, and the students very tactfully got around to the fact that the market was not as big as he thought and that competitive technologies already had a significant lead on his concept. After sitting quietly for about 30 seconds, our entrepreneur said "You know, I never did think that was much of an idea anyway. I'll call you when I get a better one."

We had two reactions. The first was that we were pleased that he realized the idea was not good and that he had saved himself a lot of anguish by not trying to start a business around a weak idea. The second reaction was that we realized he had never been particularly committed to it in the first place. He lacked the emotional attachment and excitement that is necessary to carry you through the tough times in a new business, usually in the face of competition where one must figure out how to be better. He had avoided a mistake, but his first mistake was that his level of commitment was simply not deep enough to start a new business.

I can honestly say that the most stressful time over my entire career was not associated with nuclear submarine operations, running mid-size organizations, or being a member of a board in a tough situation. It was the first year of a startup that I co-founded. You do not understand stress until you have been in a situation where you realize that, if you do not have enough receipts this week, you will not pay yourself so that you will be able to pay your programmers. Worse, this may go on for some time, and you may have to remortgage your home to lend your company money. This is what separates the entrepreneurs of the heart from the intellectual entrepreneurs. Those with passion find a way to succeed— often over and over again in the first few rough years. This does not mean, however, that if you just hang in there you can pull a bad idea to market successfully.

What do you do if you go forward with an idea and six months or a year later you find out that the market is not what you thought? You get a sick feeling in your stomach as you realize that what you just knew was a great idea is not receiving the acceptance you thought it would—or a competitor with much greater resources has beat you to market and is picking up customers fast. Is it time to stick it out, hunker down, and work harder, or is it time for a new plan?

Very often a small company will go down the drain, sticking dogmatically with the entrepreneur's original idea, rather than shift to an area that will keep the business alive. This is the difference between idealism and pragmatism. There is no easy answer here because there have been cases of those who stuck with something and made it successful, often creating markets where no one initially saw a need (such as Apple, Xerox, Polaroid). But the big mistake is to fail to reevaluate where you are and come up with a concrete plan of some sort. Here are two specific examples:

- **"The finest image on a CRT"** was the subject of a new venture named Innovative Solutions & Support (IS&S) in 1988. The entrepreneur, Geoffrey Hedrick, was a serial inventor who had more than 40 patents issued in his name. He was an electrical engineer who had already built and sold a very successful company in the avionics business and had developed a technology that would make the standard cathode ray tube (CRT) capable of producing a much brighter, better-focused image while reducing power consumption.

- His reputation was good, and he quickly raised $500,000 in an "angel round"* of financing from friends and acquaintances. He predicted in 1988 (later proven to be correct) that the monitor would become the most expensive part of the PC, not because it would go up in price but because there was no way the price of the monitor could fall as fast as the components of the PC going forward.†

- The market for monitors in 1988 was big and growing, and certain high-end applications (such as CAD/CAM) where high resolution was important had customers willing to pay more. But the company

---

* Typically, the earliest outside funding for a venture is from those who believe in a person and his or her ideas enough to invest when plans and organization are still in the formative stages.

† This has happened recently with advances in LCD display technologies, but he was correct for 12 to 14 years.

was not in the monitor business, nor was it feasible to enter that business on a small scale, so the technology would have to be licensed.

This presented a major problem: "other people's timetables." This is one of the greatest challenges that an entrepreneur or small company faces. When you have only one product or service with which to generate revenue, it is your lifeblood. When you have few customers, you need to generate the business quickly. Your larger customer or partner marches to a different drummer and takes longer to get your project on the agenda, much less make a decision.

While the technology was very good, the companies that were potential partners, such as Sony, saw the new technology as a minor improvement that, while valuable, did not have value for their entire customer base. Reluctantly, the entrepreneur decided to return to his roots and compete again in the avionics market where he knew he could generate revenue in a reasonable time frame.

He rapidly reoriented the company toward avionics, and over the years, IS&S grew, went public in 2000, and continues to do well.[*] The original investors still own the CRT patent, but it has not been commercialized. Now, 16 years later, LCD and plasma displays have improved quality at lower prices and are beginning to replace CRTs even in higher-resolution applications. In this case, the decision to change directions was a wise one. Had the CRT business been pursued as the primary product line, it would likely have consumed a great deal of time and capital in a market that was not ready for the innovation. The specific technology opportunity was lost, but the thought process led the entrepreneur to other display applications using newer LCD technology in innovative ways. In really successful smaller companies, ideas are not always lost; they often hibernate until the world catches up with the innovator.

- **Improving medical office and clinic management was the objective** when two partners, a physician and I, formed Intellego, Inc. to develop a medical office management system in 1985 as PCs became capable enough to do real work. Many saw the potential for PCs to replace more expensive mini-computer systems or mainframe time-share services. Vertical industry applications began to crop up

---

[*] In the interest of full disclosure, the author was one of the angel investors and remains a director of IS&S.

as entrepreneurs all over the world saw the potential to utilize PCs to run applications developed by those who knew the details of each industry very well.

My physician partner and I shared a vision for medical practices and hospital clinics that would be able to instantly access patient information to improve clinical practice and to handle the burdensome financial tasks associated with the complex reimbursement system in the United States. We raised money from angel investors, got enthusiastic initial customer interest, obtained pilot contracts from two large and respected institutions, and hired staff to start writing code.

Typical of most software operations, we began looking for "beta customers"* and also started selling to other potential clients for full installation while software was still being written and debugged. This "beta" stage is crucial in the software business. You hope to find out if the product is really ready from a feature and error standpoint, but you also hope to build credibility with clients who will become enthusiastic references as you go into full sales mode. Two things soon became obvious.

First, we had a lot more to do on the features side. The programming job was bigger than anyone ever imagined, both for the clinical and financial applications. The second, and most surprising, thing we learned was that there was little overlap in the customers who were interested in clinical and financial applications. Those interested in clinical applications tended to be larger organizations (medical schools or large hospitals) that had automated billing systems that were working well. Those interested in the financial systems had no automated billing (smaller individual medical practices) and saw billing and receivables management as the first priority if they were going to computerize at all.

It soon became clear that neither the people nor the financial resources were there to continue work on both the clinical and financial applications. A philosophical rift developed between my partner and myself right along the lines of our training and experience—medicine versus business. Each of us thought our area

---

* Customers who receive a discount or other consideration in exchange for helping to test and evaluate software as it is readied for full deployment.

was the way to business success. Following a few months of arguing about how to make progress on both fronts, the debate reached a head, and a "divorce" was in order.

The physician became a silent partner, retaining his ownership but no longer active in the business. All resources were redirected toward the financial systems side. The business grew, merged with a service bureau to expand the offerings, and was acquired by a larger company after four years.

The reality was that the clinical system was literally ten years ahead of its time and was a precursor to those used in managed care organizations today. It was seen as valuable to those with a vision of the future but was of no value at the time to those customers worried about the present. The product that will sell today is what smaller companies must pay attention to unless they have access to sufficient capital to fund the needs of tomorrow for a long time. This does not mean you never invest in the future, but when you are small, the first priority is staying alive with today's markets, and the second priority is creating future markets. As you grow, that priority will shift.

Both of these examples illustrate a principle that for many years I have called the "conditioned market." A market is "conditioned" when a potential customer sees your product or service offering and instantly knows how it would be used, the value it could add, and has at least a preliminary interest in knowing more about the offering.

If a market is not conditioned, the converse will be true. The potential customer does not understand what the product or service is, what value it will add, and why he or she should even be interested. It is a market that requires education and orientation, something that is always more expensive and time consuming than any entrepreneur can imagine and few can afford.

Unconditioned markets are sometimes associated with regulatory requirements, where a customer may understand the regulation requiring installation of a scrubber on his smokestack to reduce emissions but does not want to and has no incentive, other than regulation, to do so. This is not a good place to expect a quick and effortless sale to an enthusiastic purchaser.

An unconditioned market, regardless of the reason, should be a red flag waving with a warning to revisit the business plan.

Planning Your Mistakes—The Business Plan

Every book, pamphlet, course, and self-help guru will tell you that you have to have a business plan before you start your business. Contradicting this advice are many successes in which there was a business plan, but it never got out of the head of the entrepreneur and onto paper. Compaq Computer's famous "sketch on a napkin" of a portable computer as a business plan was actually better conceived than it sounds. Very experienced engineers saw a need in a rapidly developing market and pounced, but they were not the first there. (Osborne was earlier.) They were the first with a design that worked, was physically tough, had demonstrable software compatibility (Lotus 123), and had an initial marketing partner that was the nucleus of a distribution network (Sears).

A very experienced entrepreneur, an obviously great technology, a hot venture market, or an excess supply of venture money can all lead to funding a business without a detailed plan. This does not mean that mistakes will not be made; it's just that these folks had an easier time raising money.

On the other hand, there are many situations in which writing a business plan causes an entrepreneur or small business owner to engage in a structured thought process that helps to identify some potential mistakes that can be avoided. It is this discipline that is the most valuable part of putting the plan together, not the fact that you have a roadmap—because that will change as the market evolves and the team learns more. The best products do not always win in the startup world. It is usually the organization with the most discipline around product development, timetables, quality control, marketing focus, financial management, talent recruitment, and a range of other issues. A good idea and a disciplined approach will get you to market and success faster than a great idea and little discipline.

These are some of the major business planning mistakes that I have witnessed dozens of times:

- **"Nobody else is doing what we are doing..."** except for about a thousand other entrepreneurs. Even in very complex scientific endeavors that take years, we see research teams that have not collaborated reaching similar conclusions in similar time frames. This happens in most businesses. So much of business and especially technology builds on past experience and supporting discoveries by others that it is logical that many will see opportunities in similar time frames. This, of course, means you need to do as much investigation as possible to find out who competitors really are or might be in the future. It does not mean you stop when you find that you are not the first to think of the idea. It does mean that you should make an informed judgment about how you will get to market and in what time frame. In some ways, it is encouraging to know that others are in the market, helping to educate and condition it.

- **"If we only get one percent of the market…"** We have all seen this kind of projection somewhere in our business lives, and it was made easier by the advent of spreadsheets. It is too easy to back into the market share you need to reach breakeven and then rationalize that it will be easy to get there because it seems like a small number. What is usually missed here is the question, "Does anyone want this product, are they willing to pay a price that we find attractive, and how many highly likely customers are there in the first six months?"

- **"We don't need much capital."** This is something that can be said in error in large or small organizations, but the well is always deeper if you need to go back a second time in larger companies. The best time to raise capital is before you start making any sales in a startup or when things are going well in an established small company. The worst time to raise money is when things are going badly, but many small company executives are so paranoid about giving up equity that they reduce their chances of success by believing they can get by with less money. In my experience, this usually leads to more pain and distraction because capital has to be raised again under less-than-favorable conditions. The real reason that most startups take twice as much money and time as originally planned is a series of bad estimates: time for development, time for marketing and acceptance, and time to get payment from customers. Bad estimates of capital required are rarely because the unit costs of components or activities are not known. They usually result from bad estimates of the time it takes to accomplish important milestones, especially building market acceptance. Experienced people should know the difference between hope and reality. Inexperienced individuals should seek help from experienced business and technical people, especially with their time estimates.

- **"We already have our first customer."** I have made this mistake personally. My first customer pushed me to start the systems business previously described. I was a trusted consultant to a large company on issues only loosely related to the new business idea. I had discussed our concept with some of the senior executives on a number of occasions for over a year. One day a senior VP handed me a company check for $50,000 and said:

> "I'm tired of hearing you talk about this. We believe it's a great idea, so get to work. This should be enough for the first demonstration system. We want it installed in our hospital in Hickory, NC when it's ready, but within the next year."

This is heady stuff—your customer forces you into business—and you make the assumption that everyone else is just as eager to get started. We were eventually successful, but the rest of the world was not as forward thinking as the VP who handed me the check. It took longer than we thought to develop the product and the market to a point where we could make sales, but at least he had pushed us over the precipice, and we started trying to save ourselves. The lesson is to make sure that the customers who are eager are not simply early adopters because, if they are not representative of the larger population, it may be a longer road to success than you realize.

- **"Customer growth will be exponential."** This is a mindset that is close to the "If we only get one percent..." thought. We all want to believe that demand will snowball once we get a few influencers to buy and like the product or service. Webvan believed that and even with $1 billion in investment never got to breakeven. Lots of people believed this about the application service provider (ASP)* market in the late 1990s and have been disappointed.

It rarely turns out as well as expected. Most small businesses, whether established or startup, underestimate the amount of selling that has to occur continuously. Look at large company financial statements and try to understand what goes into SG&A† (selling, general, and administrative expenses) on their income statements.

---

* The "application service provider" concept is essentially "renting" software on the basis of usage.

† Selling, general, and administrative expenses are usually one of the headings in an income statement.

Pure selling expense is not always broken out cleanly, but it is usually a big number and is required. Small companies usually get the bottom of the barrel in terms of sales staff because they are not willing to pay reasonable commissions, cannot afford to pay a retainer plus commission, or hire the sales force before the product is ready to be sold and then lose them when they become unhappy.

- **"Our competitors are big and slow to react."** This is something you should never say out loud and should try to avoid even thinking. That big, slow competitor just may not know you are there yet. When it finds out you are there, it will decide whether it is worth the time to squash you, and there are many legal and ethical ways to do that (and some that are both illegal and unethical but will be seen in competitive markets).

I am aware of a technology-based company that brought an extraordinary new product to market. The entrepreneur found a customer, a Fortune 100 company that liked the product and wanted to order many of them for internal use. A good and well-entrenched competitor offered to give the customer a similar product made by them at no cost as part of a package deal on a wider range of equipment. The customer refused the "free" offer on the basis that the small company offering was better technically and would mean lower life cycle repair costs—and also because they thought it was an unethical offer. This customer was the one who made the entrepreneur's company successful because they were large and well respected in their industry and provided nice sales volume for some time. These situations happen all the time, and you are lucky if you find a customer who believes your product is good enough to do something like this—but you cannot bank on it happening.

- **"Our product is superior."** This is nothing more than an opening line for the small company. There are few customers that will take the chance previously described on a new company that does not have a track record or on even a small, well-established company. Large company purchasing and technical people want security from making mistakes, and do not want to be questioned about why they took a chance on something when there were more established alternatives available. What this usually means is that you have to be able to make a proposition where the value added is so high that it is almost impossible to reject. For technical products or services, this means you have to design to sell at a price where your competitor will lose money. This must be part of the economic business visioning (EBV) process described in the previous chapter. You will get the customer's attention when you have found ways to improve productivity, engineer new designs, reduce maintenance costs, or add so much value in products or services that the customer cannot deny the economic returns. As a small company or new entrant, an undifferentiated entry into a market is the kiss of death.

There are many other ways to build mistakes into the assumptions you make and document in a business plan, but these are some of the most important to avoid. But once you have convinced yourself that you have a plan of sorts, you will naturally be thinking about financing.

Financing—Choose Your Poison

The good news is that lots of startups and small companies raise money every year. The bad news is that the ease or difficulty of raising money from any source is highly cyclical. In case you haven't heard, banks do not take much risk. They like collateral such as receivables, your house, your trucks, or your relatives' signatures backed by assets. They do not lend against patents (unless already generating an income stream), copyrights, or what walks around with you in your head. Obviously, macroeconomic variables affect the picture as well in terms of interest rates and willingness to lend, regardless of risk or collateral.

Other potential funding sources, such as family and friends, angel investors, venture capital, leasing companies, and a variety of high-risk lenders, are available on different terms for different situations.

- **"Friends and family are a great source of startup capital,"** if you really like both pressure to produce for investors and the guilt of worrying about putting your mother in the poorhouse. This is where most small businesses get started though, with a combination of personal savings and family loans or investments. I was pleased to have friends as investors in my company some years ago, but the pressure was worse than if I had taken money from a professional venture capitalist. At least that would have been an arm's length transaction. I valued the friendship of those who invested, which made it harder during the rough times in the business. It also meant that when we sold the company some years later, I sold some of my stock back to my original investors at a discount because I realized that it had been overpriced when we raised the first round of money from them. I would not have felt such compunction with a professional investor at arm's length.

I have now invested in my son's business, but I told him that it would provide him with more guilt than he deserves. I also told him I would invest only what I could afford to lose without caring (not the objective, just a calibration) because that gives him the freedom of doing the right thing without worrying about liquidity or his relationship with me. Money from friends and relatives can be a godsend, but it should be done with care because it is an added source of pressure and guilt.

- **"I don't want to be diluted."** This is the most common reason that business owners wait too long to raise money, and they often pay for it because things have gotten worse. Not only is Bill Gates the richest man in the world, but he and his co-founder, Paul Allen, managed to retain an amazing amount of ownership in Microsoft, even to this day, despite giving away vast sums philanthropically. I do know of another entrepreneur in a technology company who retained about 25 percent of his firm post-IPO, but this is not typical. My philosophy has always been that I would rather own 1 percent of a large company than 100 percent of a hot dog stand. There is no reason to go looking for dilution, but if more money will accelerate growth or bring a product to market a year earlier, it may be worth it in terms of higher market capitalization sooner rather than later.

- **"The VCs have the same objectives we do"**—up to a point. They want to help you make money so that they can make money for their partners, but there are differences. Their objectives and time frames are straightforward: 5 to 10 times their money in 5 to 7 years. They will not hit those numbers on every deal, but those are the objectives. It means that the expectations are high, and there has to be a liquidity event in a reasonable time frame. These expectations limit the deals they will do to a small number of businesses relative to the hundreds of thousands that start each year. Venture capital is a required piece of the infrastructure for growth in a region or a nation, but it is not for every business. They are more likely to choose you than the other way around, but if you have the choice, make sure the objectives and expectations are consistent and achievable. If you have a business that will produce a nice living but is not likely to produce high growth and high profitability fairly rapidly, venture capital is a mistake.

■ **"I refuse to do a 'down round,'"** meaning you have not done as well as you expected and need to sell equity, or debt with a conversion privilege, at a price that is lower than a previous round of financing. This can happen to companies at any stage of their existence, but it is most common for newer companies within the first three years or so. As previously described, it is fairly common to have missed development objectives, have slower-than-planned market adoption, more competition, more pricing pressure, and a variety of other unanticipated events. The firm may not be cash positive and yet still requires more capital. Whether you go back to existing investors or bring in new investors, a "down round" is rarely a pleasant experience. It usually involves loans with warrants to purchase more stock, meaning that if you are successful, you will pay back the debt with interest, and the investors will get a chance to buy more stock at an attractive price for up to ten years. I have seen entrepreneurs fight to avoid this until there was no other choice and then later succeed, with everyone being much happier for the result. I have also seen an entrepreneur lose his company in such a deal, but the controlling group could not turn it around either because of industry conditions.

■ **"We're short of cash; I'll pay the taxes in a couple of weeks."** This is the greatest single mistake a company of any size can make. It is tempting to borrow from the government, but they just are not an understanding creditor. As a board member for a number of smaller companies over the years, I have always required attestation from management that all required taxes have been paid each quarter because directors and officers can be held personally liable for unpaid payroll taxes. Skip paying the management before you skip paying Uncle Sam.

■ **"I can't agree to those terms,"** but while you wait the market may pass you by. This mistake applies to terms that customers demand for sales as well as raising capital. The most common problems have to do with customer payment terms (45 to 60 days when you need it yesterday) and security related to guaranteed performance, delivery, or ability for ongoing service. There are no simple answers here except to remember that once you have lawyers talking to lawyers, you have lost control, and the probability of a happy outcome goes down dramatically. The best way to avoid this problem is to keep looking for the champion inside your customer company that wants you to succeed and try to get him or her to get the legal department to deviate from the standard terms.

Small companies do not want to turn over source code for software in the event of a default and do not want to turn over proprietary designs for technology, but large customers will ask for these kinds of things. If you are producing a physical product, agreeing to license and qualify a second source may provide some satisfaction. Even if you are willing to do things that could potentially shift intellectual or proprietary property to a customer in order to get the business, be very careful about defining what constitutes a default under the agreement. You do not want to lose your company over a nonsubstantive technical default.

- **"An IPO will solve all our problems"**—not in the post Sarbanes-Oxley world of corporate governance. The costs and hassles are extraordinary, and going public might be a mistake if it is just for the ego trip of being able to talk to the analysts and track your stock price each day. Many fairly small public companies are spending $500,000 or more in annual audit and compliance fees. These fees have tripled or quadrupled with the newer, tougher audit and compliance standards of recent years. There are ways other than going public to provide for liquidity, and many smaller companies are looking at sales to larger firms or buyout funds with more interest.

The availability of risk capital is one of the great competitive advantages of the U.S. economy, but there are some great risks for smaller companies who take outside equity capital. You should not take equity capital, other than in the very early stages, if you can only keep the business alive without growth because this is rarely productive. If you do not believe the business has substantial growth prospects, then forms of capital that are more tied to operations (such as SBA guaranteed bank loans) may be more appropriate than equity investment where a liquidity event will be required at some point in the future. Capital formation and operations are not as separate as some think. They are inextricably linked because the type of capital and associated requirements or expectations for return should be linked to the plans for and expected results of operations. While most businesses need capital to start, once successful, the ability to generate free cash flow can make financing issues irrelevant. Just look at Microsoft's balance sheet.

Operations–Implementation Is the Difference

There are many things that have to go well from an execution standpoint to make a business successful, and we have highlighted some of them in looking at mistakes in larger enterprises. There are some operational issues that are somewhat unique to smaller firms, however.

- **"Just a few more tweaks and it will be ready for release."** This is particularly true of anything having to do with software, but it can affect any physical product. Whether it is bugs or adding new features because you have been talking to customers who want more even before there has been a product release, this is a tough problem. The tradeoff with what is called "scope creep" is time to market versus added features or stability. These can be difficult judgments calls, but they have to be made explicitly rather than just letting the development or engineering process drag on. I believe that if the product is stable and breaks new ground with features and capabilities that will excite people, you may lose more by waiting than by freezing development and getting the marketing and deployment started. The challenge is very visible with large, visible companies in which software, a new airplane, or a new auto model are known to be moving along in development but encounter delays. Large companies have sales of other products that produce revenue, and while the delay may be costly, it is rarely life threatening. In small companies, these delays may threaten survival because there is no other revenue.

  In the last couple of years, there have been a number of announcements about new, small (six-passenger) business jets for about $1 million to $1.5 million. This is a barrier not broken before, and it depends on much new development. New companies with names like Eclipse, Saffire, and Adam Aircraft are pushing forward along with established companies like Cessna. First prototypes have begun to fly, though it is clear that development is not done, and a number of companies are going back to change engines or other major design issues that have not turned out as expected. These things happen, but once an idea, category, or concept goes past the tipping point and a market gets excited, the market will not wait for those new entrants who cannot execute. In this case, Cessna has decades of experience in making small jets and, even though higher priced, will find customers to wait for their entry in the new category. For the new entrants, timing and performance are both critical, but the first new entrant to market and then Cessna, as the established player, will set the time frame for everyone else.

Disciplined processes around product development and review, plans for getting into production, procedures for delivering services—whatever the discipline required, small companies have to work more quickly to develop a culture of performance because they will be judged that way by the markets and with less room for error than the established players.

■ **"Nobody around can do anything right except me."** Many small companies are small for a reason, and that reason is often that no one can get along with the entrepreneur. The challenge is that, in the early stages, the entrepreneur may be the most talented person in the firm. Small firms have difficulty attracting employees who need more pay, more security, or better benefit packages than are typical. So in the early stages, for financial and recruiting reasons, the founder may be the jack-of-all-trades. If this persists and the company cannot afford to hire capable people or if the founder or owner is a control freak who cannot let go, then a culture develops that becomes self-fulfilling mediocrity. Sometimes the entrepreneur figures this out and fixes it by hiring sharp people, and sometimes he does not, in which case advisors, venture capitalists, and others will be happy to point it out. The shift from entrepreneurial micromanagement to professional management quality and standards is traumatic for many companies and failure to make this transition is one of the most common obstacles to growth for small companies.

- **"This guy has been with us from day one."** This is a classic loyalty/performance problem. Companies that have grown rapidly but are still fairly young usually have someone who was critical in the early days but whose skills or aptitude are no longer as important, or even relevant, as the company has grown much larger. The person may even be overpaid, have too much responsibility, and have more stock options than others who were hired later at a similar level.

  The problem is loyalty. How can you fire or demote someone who has been with you from the week you started and who stood by you through thick and thin? Most managers eventually realize that they need to make sure that even the most loyal early employees are in appropriate jobs for their skills and personalities. This is a difficult adjustment, but demotion, lateral transfers, or invention of special status jobs with little supervision are often called for in the interest of organizational performance. Ignoring the problem rarely leads to a positive outcome and often drives off better-performing staff.

Stopping the Mistake Sequence in Smaller Companies

Many of the principles we have discussed for larger situations apply to smaller companies, including looking for signals, developing standard procedures, evaluating scenarios and risk factors, and developing an economic business visioning process. But there are a number of specific smaller-company approaches that should be considered as well:

- **An advisory board.** Even a small enterprise needs advisors. A company that is so small that the board is just a technicality with a couple of family members may still want to have an advisory board. The advisory board should be the best you can assemble and should be a mix of individuals who bring relevant experience from a range of skills and backgrounds. A good advisory board will often help see blind spots, push you to do the things you have been avoiding, and generally provide a perspective that is above the minutiae where the average small company leader spends his or her time.

  I watched one successful entrepreneur I know in an advisory board meeting for another company as he listened to the plans for a sales campaign that was going to be launched in about three months. The advisor shifted around in his seat and was clearly uneasy with what he was hearing. He finally blurted out, "What's wrong with selling more tomorrow? Why wait until you refine the plan for another month? Let's simplify the plan, refine it this afternoon, and tell the sales team what they will be held responsible for each week over the next three months. If they miss the target two weeks in a row, they don't get less commission, they get fired. What's wrong with that?" The group sat stunned for a moment, then got into the discussion. The small company launched the program that week and had increased sales by 30 percent within four months, with a dramatic increase in profit. Sometimes an advisor can give you the whack on the head you knew you needed but just had not given yourself.

Customer advisory boards are also important to continue to calibrate your product or service offerings and to test new ideas. Some shy away from brining customers together, fearing they may learn "too much," but if you select customers that you know like you enough to want to be helpful, this is usually time well spent.

- **Get "bigger than life."** Customers may like personalized attention and a friendly relationship with staff, but they do not want to know that you are so small that there is a danger of them not getting service if someone is sick or of you going out of business. The "bigger than life" list is important to help fix this perception. Most of the things that will help are small but contribute to an important perception of size and stability. The list includes:

  - **Use different last names if multiple family members are in the business.** My wife and I did this for a number of years, and after a few years, when the business was larger, there were even employees who did not know we were married.

  - **Spend the money necessary** for professional-looking calling cards, stationery, and a logo.

  - **Develop a Web presence** and provide some information, customer feedback, or other information that changes enough that customers will not simply see a static Web site. Utilize Web ordering if appropriate, but if you do this do it very well; otherwise, you will be swamped with support calls.

- ◆ **Have a local presence** at visible local charity or civic events.
- ◆ **Develop a business philosophy,** customer promise, or something else that is easy to remember and associated with the company.
- ◆ **Develop and enforce dress codes and/or a code of conduct** for those who interface with customers in person or via phone or e-mail.
- ◆ **Find ways to seek feedback and information from customers** on a regular basis via surveys, interviews, or customer-appreciation events.

There are many other "bigger than life" approaches that will work for specific types of businesses or geographies, but the point is that unless the team thinks about these sorts of things as a priority, they will not happen, and you may not control the way you look to your customers.

- ■ **Listen, continue to evaluate the EBV, and change the business plan** as you get new information, advice, input, customer feedback, and response data regarding your offerings. When in the software business, I always told the team that our customers gave us all the answers to what the product needed to do in the future; they just did not know when they were doing it. Develop a disciplined approach to sit down periodically with everyone who touches customers and ask them what they are seeing and hearing. Find ways to synthesize this information and try to figure out what it all means. You will find that a lot of information from different customers and sources often points with some alignment in a direction that helps shape the business.
- ■ **Be open to changing your role.** The most difficult thing a small business person ever does is to ask the question, "Is it time to replace me?" Succession is not just for large companies, and in small companies, it should not be just because you reach retirement age. There are some small business people who grow with businesses that become very large, continue to manage them well, and enjoy the transition. There are others who are terrible at managing a larger organization and hate it. Especially for founders, there is nothing

dishonorable about taking on a chairman or vice chairman role and becoming a trusted advisor to those who have learned to run the business for you.*

■ **Seek professional advice—and take it.** I have watched small company CEOs grudgingly pay auditors, lawyers, and business advisors and generally hate the requirement to have them so much that good advice is ignored. You have to have some of them and probably want to have others. Choose them on the basis of their proven ability to help other companies your size, listen to what they have to say, and think seriously about whether it makes sense and can be applied in your situation. Many men and women in small businesses tell me they do not have enough colleagues with whom to discuss important issues. The advice is often free in CEO affinity groups, chambers of commerce, or other organizations, but you have to make the involvement and exchange a priority.

Small company mistake chains look similar to those in larger companies, and despite all the literature and experience in the market, the learning process for avoiding mistakes is no better. In fact, because entrepreneurs tend to be relatively young and do not have good internal mentoring and support networks, it is more difficult for them to see patters and learn from others' experience. On the positive side, once mistakes are discovered, small business can often react and change more rapidly.

> **Insight #36: Startups and small businesses make mistakes in the same ways that larger organizations make mistakes. However, they usually have fewer resources to avoid or recover and less flexibility to survive mistakes with alternate plans or products.** While the patterns are similar, some mistakes or sequences are unique to small business. These have to do with fundraising and the mechanics of getting things done in the early stages, but many others look similar to what occurs in larger, more established entities.

---

* I should point out that, as a general corporate governance philosophy, I am opposed to former CEOs staying on their board after retiring or assuming a chairman role. The exception to that is a founder of a company who often has a great deal to add as an ongoing member of the board—if he or she can stay out of micromanaging the new CEO.

10

Making M³ Part of Your Culture for Success

> "The greatest challenge in most organizations is not figuring out
> how to fix a problem but recognizing there is a problem
> that needs to be fixed."
>
> —Robert E. Mittelstaedt

Throughout this book, we have explored the idea that training ourselves to identify problems at the earliest possible stage makes economic sense, whether in business or the operation of complex systems. We hear this all the time about medical care—early detection saves lives. But are the diagnostic tools available and effective?

In a number of chapters, we have suggested that lack of information, routine disregard for existing data, failure to communicate, lack of procedures, and just plain not paying attention are common causes of serious business mistakes. When we began to use spreadsheets 20 years ago and mainframe-produced financial reports before that, we began to be overwhelmed with data. Systems vendors continue to look for ways to make their systems produce more useful analytics for users, but figuring out what is relevant and useful across industries, businesses, and individuals is difficult.

In medicine, the diagnostic side of the equation has often outpaced our ability to treat what we find, something that is especially true with many complex conditions like Alzheimer's disease and certain forms of cancer. Diagnostic technologies continue to improve, even more rapidly than the treatment side, as genomic testing gives us greater ability to understand and even predict certain diseases accurately. But everyone does not want or seek the tests that are available, out of ignorance, lack of concern, or perhaps being afraid of what they will find.

The same is true in business. We have more systems, data, and other mechanisms for understanding markets and customers, but when we see some of the business mistakes made by companies discussed in this book, you wonder if they are using any of the tools available to diagnose problems.

Even if problems are diagnosed, business solutions to fixing problems seem a lot like fashion. There always seems to be a hot new trend that leaders and managers eagerly adopt as the latest solution to never-ending challenges of improvement and differentiation. Over the last 15 years, we have witnessed a blizzard of business books and consultants that told us how to make our organizations more efficient, improve quality, improve customer satisfaction, create focus, motivate employees, allocate capital, enhance shareholder value, and develop leaders.

Yet the greatest challenge in most organizations is not figuring out how to fix a problem but recognizing that there is a problem that needs to be fixed. And the greatest economic benefit will come from avoiding problems altogether rather than fixing them.

From the complexity of the space shuttle, to business on a global or small-business scale, to family life—we struggle most to recognize that all is not well as the first and most difficult step in resolving most challenges. Failure to recognize that a problem exists increases the probability that some amount of damage will occur before it can be fixed.

The difficulty is with our cognitive abilities. If we have not seen a situation previously, we may not recognize the need to act or understand the consequences of inaction. The cases, stories, and examples in this book are about problems that led to mistake sequences that were blatantly obvious after the fact. Yet most initial problems and the mistake sequences went unrecognized by experienced individuals or teams for too long to avoid damage. The challenge then is to find ways to help ourselves and others in our organizations to develop cognitive abilities for problem and mistake recognition to improve the chances of avoiding damage.

In this chapter, I offer some suggestions of concepts and structures to help the problem/mistake recognition process. These will work for a single issue or patterns of repeated problems. It is important to realize, however, that learning to avoid the domino effect of multiple mistakes is a mindset—recognition that constant vigilance is required.

Many organizations do this inherently through powerful cultures that support and encourage excellence, even in the face of challenging circumstances without precedent. Other organizations and individuals do not even think about managing mistakes until after they occur, which is the reason they get into trouble and magnify the damage exponentially.

We have discussed many extreme examples of failure to recognize a series of incipient mistakes, from *Titanic* to Enron, that resulted in unforgettable disasters that could have been prevented. Some accidents and disasters occur with little or no warning or in ways that there is little that man can do to stop the damage. But the common thread in a significant number of physical and business disasters has been early warnings in some form or another that were ignored.

We can utilize the "Business flywheel" shown in Figure 10.1 to illustrate what happened in most of these situations where mistakes overcame the potential for success. A flywheel serves a purpose in a variety of machines to store energy and smooth out pulses in systems where power is being generated or used, as in an automobile engine. The energy stored in a rotating object is a function, among other things, of the speed of rotation squared. In physical systems, or our mistake analogy, once momentum is gained it requires energy to stop.

The same kinds of things that are responsible for business success are usually responsible, in the opposite direction, for failures. Organizations usually have vision, strategy, leadership, effective operations, talented people, good customer relationships, and sensing mechanisms or they do not.

Success follows from having these things and using them well, while poor results or even failure follow from their absence. But success or failure is not so discreet. The forces driving one oppose the other. Thus, we might think of the business flywheel as being rotated positively toward progress and success (to the right) and negatively toward mistakes and failure (to the left). Mistakes do not always cause the wheel to move to the left toward complete failure, sometimes they just slow down progress to the right toward success.

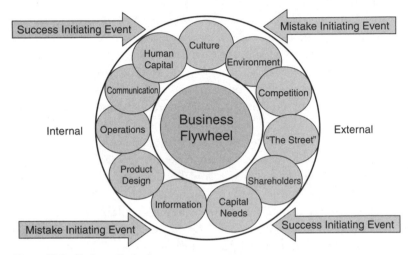

Figure 10.1   Business flywheel.

A friend and a passenger were driving along a busy and complex eight-lane highway one day when the car was suddenly struck by something that hit without warning. It turned out to be a wheel that had rolled from the opposite side of the highway across many lanes of traffic, bounced over a median guardrail, and continued rolling along on his side of the road. The wheel and tire hit with such force that there was substantial damage to the front of the car, and the windshield was shattered. The front-seat passenger escaped injury only because the wheel was still moving in a vertical orientation and was too big to come through the windshield opening.

Shaken, they stopped, looked around, and could not figure out how the wheel came to be rolling toward them. While walking to find a telephone, they passed a car on the other side of the highway that was unable to move because it was missing a wheel. When the accident was reconstructed, it became clear that the energy stored in the rotating wheel had carried it more than a quarter mile before it hit their vehicle, where it still had enough energy left to do substantial damage.*

---

* The driver of the vehicle that lost the wheel reported that she had purchased new tires the day before. The lug nuts on the wheel had obviously not been tightened properly. Multiple mistakes at the tire store—training, failure to follow procedures, and no check process—probably cost them an insurance claim.

To extend what we have said throughout the book to this physical example, initiating mistakes can come from a number of sources, and it often does not matter where it starts. Once the mistake flywheel starts rolling, each mistake adds momentum, making it harder to stop the sequence (flywheel). The initiating event that starts our wheel rolling could be external (Tylenol) or internal (Intel), as we have seen in many examples. Around the wheel are many general issues/areas of concern that could have the effect of slowing or stopping the rotation, offering no resistance at all, or even accelerating the rotation once started.

Martha Stewart was convicted of some serious crimes as a result of a small initiating mistake—a bad decision to sell stock, apparently with inside information. The mistake wheel accelerated for her as she and her broker tried to cover up, destroyed evidence, and conspired on their stories. Once accelerated, it was impossible to stop the wheel without serious consequence, but Ms. Stewart still chose to never "step on the brake" to slow the wheel and break the chain by admitting anything along the way. The wheel kept rolling, she did not try to stop it, and she ended up with a felony conviction and attendant consequences for her business and personal life.

As we have discussed, company culture is the greatest influence on the issue of accelerating or decelerating a move toward a mistake scenario, so we have placed that at the top:

- **Culture** is the often ill-defined set of characteristics of an organization that describes the business norms and values, decision-making processes and criteria, competitiveness, the way people treat each other, and even how individuals dress. As we saw in a number of examples, cultures can help organizations react properly to avoid crisis and stop mistake scenarios through reflexive actions based on strong values (Tylenol) or can escalate the damage from mistakes (Enron).

- **Human capital** is both the most significant source of solutions to problems and the most likely source of mistakes. If we can educate, train, motivate, and broaden perspectives of employees so that they can do more thinking on their own, we will have a better chance of avoiding mistakes. But many of those who were in leadership positions in the organizations we studied here were well educated and trained. The difference is ensuring a thorough understanding of potential outcomes under a variety of scenarios and respect for the importance and value of stopping mistake scenarios early.

- **Communications**, or lack thereof, is one of the factors we saw over and over in escalating mistake chains including *Titanic*, many airline crashes, Coca-Cola in Belgium, Intel, and Firestone. Effective communications to understand danger, customers, and actions of coworkers or competitors and to seek and employ other resources is one of the keys to avoiding mistakes.

- **Operations excellence** goes almost without saying as one of the greatest protections against a mistake chain ever getting started. Standard procedures and training, a focus on continuous improvement, practice for emergencies, and identification of proper metrics are all important in preventing mistakes, as is postmistake analysis of mistakes as a means of avoiding repetition.

- **Product or service design** has the potential to encourage or discourage difficulty in operations. Consumers Union, through its magazine *Consumer Reports*, analyzes many products to provide information for consumers, but their most popular magazine issue is the annual April auto issue. Because their data is drawn from surveys of owners of many vehicles, they are able to draw an accurate statistical picture of the strengths and weaknesses of vehicle models. Strengths and weaknesses of vehicles originate in the design and manufacturing process but affect performance in the field for all types of products and services. Organizations that design for performance rather than skimping on cost, quality, manufacturing, or service-delivery processes usually have fewer mistakes.

- **Information** is critical to any organization or business, especially in rapidly changing situations. Building effective systems that collect and present information in ways that help managers and operators spot trends and detect problems early is crucial. One of the greatest problems with information systems, however, is a lack of compliance around entry of information or use of systems in organizations, thus designing organizations and processes so that staff cannot do their work without the systems will help compliance. For more senior levels, executive information systems (EIS) were spreading by the early 1990s, but there are still many organizations with woefully inadequate means of understanding critical business information on a real-time, or even recent-time, basis. NASA and American Express (Optima) both had plenty of information, but both failed to analyze it or understand its importance enough to find the value that was possible.

- **Environment** often appears simple, but unrecognized complexity creates a climate for mistakes. Kodak faced a changing environment and embraced it with new technologies. While being a leader in digital technology, however, Kodak's embrace was weak because they still devoted far more resources to maintaining the competencies of the past rather than aggressively growing those needed for the future. On a narrower basis, Coca-Cola's delayed and arrogant response in Belgium was a cultural response that was out of synch with its environment in a specific part of the world. NASA also experienced a dangerous interaction of its can-do, but bureaucratic, culture and an environment that demanded proof that progress was being made for continuation of funding.

- **Competition** can often be a stimulus for mistakes, as we saw in AmEx's Optima launch, where the desire to grab a piece of a profitable stream of business from entrenched competitors led to a series of bad decisions that ignored information and facts. Enron's competitive nature, where they defined the entire world as their competitor, led to delusional pursuit of extraordinarily risky strategies. Competition can and should be a stimulus for understanding changes in markets that result in new ideas and directions, but slavish focus on winning against a current competitor can also lead to missing the next game, as Kodak did while being distracted by competing against Fuji Film in the traditional chemical imaging market.

- **"The street,"** and what analysts think of your quarterly earnings, has led many to a seductive mistake scenario, including Enron, WorldCom, HealthSouth, and others. Fear of being seen as losing momentum often leads to a gambler's mentality about risk and ethics that is life threatening to the company that engages in or tolerates the behaviors needed to illegally manage earnings.

- **Shareholders** are supposed to be the focus of the management and board's fiduciary responsibility to create value. Yet in too many businesses we have discussed in this book and elsewhere, this focus has been lost to greed and self-interest on the part of a management team. Yet even honest management teams that attempt to meet their responsibilities find themselves losing to better competitors and destroying shareholder value. We have witnessed this in the U.S. auto industry for some time but especially over the last decade. This always results from a fundamental misunderstanding of the competitive environment, changing customer preferences, changing technologies, and a failure to manage cost and increase productivity.

- **Capital needs** create extraordinary pressure when executives realize they need to invest but do not know how to generate the required funds. Small companies enter into expensive deals for funding or "borrow" from the IRS and find themselves in trouble. Larger firms, such as Enron, put together complex deals to find funds while obscuring the risk.

Obviously, if we make no mistakes, the business flywheel doesn't slow or rotate in the wrong direction. And if we are good at breaking the mistake sequence early, the energy required to resist the adverse force is less, since there is little or no momentum in th wrong direction. The key question is, "How do we break the sequence or stop it before it starts?" There are generally two forms of opportunity for early intervention to stop preventable disasters:

- **Heeding early warnings of specific danger and detecting patterns in operations.** For example:
  - The presence of icebergs (*Titanic*)
  - The 1990 study of the potential for space shuttle heat shield damage from impact with foam insulation
  - Initial customer reaction to Intel's position on its chip flaw
  - The early failure of Firestone tires on Ford vehicles in Saudi Arabia and Venezuela

  In each of these, and many similar cases, ignoring early warnings allowed the mistake forces to slow the business flywheel or to begin rolling and accelerating it in the wrong direction. Mistakes beyond those that caused the accident sequence to begin contributed to increased severity once the disaster scenario was underway, but the initial warning signs were there and were ignored.

- **Detecting dangerous patterns of action, in operations and strategy.** For example:
  - Extreme leverage and high-risk deal structures at Enron
  - Continuing to focus on chemical-based technologies for too long at Kodak
  - Erroneous assumptions at Webvan

In these examples, no single incident can be pinpointed as "the thing" that started the business flywheel moving toward a disaster. Many individual decisions and actions became part of a pattern that was not recognized as dangerous but ultimately created significant damage. The irony is that, in situations where patterns of mistakes are evident, the mistakes are usually things that experienced business people know are wrong when viewed in another context. Yet in the context of their own businesses, managers and executives typically do not recognize the mistake patterns or rationalize them away.

Learning to Evaluate and Believe Early Warnings

On the morning of December 7, 1941, soldiers manning "portable" radar equipment* at Opana Radar Station on the north shore of Oahu, Hawaii tracked a substantial number of aircraft inbound from the north for more than 30 minutes.† An officer on duty believed the targets to be a group of U.S. Army Air Corps B-17 bombers that were expected that morning, so no warning was sounded. The reality was that the aircraft detected with that new crude radar unit were the initial wave of aircraft launched by Japanese carriers to attack Pearl Harbor.[98]

The reaction of the soldiers looking at the radar was understandable given that they were expecting inbound aircraft and that the technology was new. But the operators' minds were conditioned by information that biased their analysis and decision-making. Without realizing it, they assumed they knew the correct explanation (friendly airplanes that were expected) for data they did not fully understand. They had conditioned their minds in a way that completely negated the potential value of the sensor.

How often do we do this in business by classing an individual or source of information as unreliable or unbelievable without fully investigating the data? How often do we explain away something as unimportant because we have seen a similar situation in the past and it was not a danger? On the other hand, it is possible to overreact to information and warnings and become dysfunctional as an organization in the process, reacting to every minor issue as if it were life threatening.

---

* Portable in this case meant four trucks for the generator, antenna, receivers, displays, and spares.

† The original paper plot of the track of those targets, prepared by Private Joseph L. Lockard, is preserved as part of the congressional inquiry into the events of December 7, 1941.

The problem with a warning is that it is not always clear that it is a warning at all or if the source of information can be relied upon. The insights offered with the examples in this book where organizations failed to see the warning signs of danger offer some lessons about how to detect and utilize warnings. Based on these examples and others, here are some situations that should raise red flags and warrant further analysis for the potential for trouble:

- Situations you have not seen before
- Operating experience different than your competitors'
- Unusual or rapidly changing data (about operations or customers)
- Results off plan
- Results on plan through luck
- Constant revision of plan/budget
- Failures of control systems
- Need to retrain significant numbers of personnel because they are not performing
- Frequent operational problems that are not addressed by standard procedures
- Problems caused by communications issues
- Problems where help was available but not utilized

When you do see warning signs, there are some tools you should be ready to employ to stop a mistake sequence before it starts. Some of these tools are shown Figure 10.2, along with the organizational levels where they are likely to be most often used and effective.

If you are going to use any tool effectively, it has to be designed and used at the appropriate level but be reinforced at each appropriate level on a regular basis. Success in application comes down to the ability of the individual on the front line of the organization to understand, internalize, and consistently apply the tools, often with limited supervision.

The differences in typical levels of responsibility for these actions (individual or small team, division or work group, and organization and senior management) are a reflection of the reality of large organizations. Senior executives can set all the policies they like, but unless the systems are in place to carry the philosophy and specific desired actions throughout the hierarchy, there is little you can do from the executive suite.

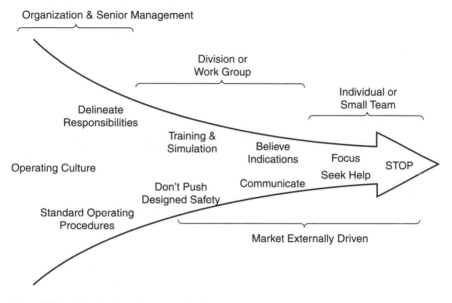

Figure 10.2 Operational tools to stop mistakes.

- **Operating Culture.** The foundation of the arrow is culture, in this case an operating culture that makes everyone in the organization believe that understanding and serving the customer is the highest order priority. As we have discussed, a customer-focused culture does not just happen; it has to be consciously designed and reinforced by senior management if it is to be effective.

  Even if you think you have a productive culture, you have to find ways to make it come alive for each and every individual in the organization—in relationship to his or her job, not in an abstract sense.

  Since job responsibilities are different, it is sometimes tough to have an easily understood common cultural understanding to which everyone can relate, but I have had success in building a culture with a simple mnemonic that is easy to remember. Over the 14 years that I ran Wharton's Aresty Institute of Executive Education, we developed a customer-focused culture that helped us become one of the largest and most successful organizations in the world in our business.

In the early days of my tenure there, we realized that we needed to become market driven rather than supply driven. We came up with something everyone could remember and relate to that we called E^3, which stands for:

- Everyone knows the customer.

- Everyone improves quality.

- Everyone markets (and sells).

  - **Everyone knows the customer,** literally or figuratively. In service businesses, your employee is in direct contact with customers in person or via some communications medium. Figuratively, knowing customers really means understanding their needs and desires, their reason for doing business with you, and the standards by which they judge you.

    Perhaps most importantly, it also means being receptive to the ideas your customers want to let you know about for your current and future operations and products. Because these come through and are filtered by your front-line employees, you will get no benefit from this information if you have not trained your team to look for and welcome this information and know how to move it through the organization so it can be used effectively.

    Knowing the customer is not as easy as it sounds because, in many businesses, the "ownership" of the customer is so diffused by function (sales, manufacturing, service, support) and distance or organizational structure that no one feels any personal responsibility. This is a way to reinforce the need for personal ownership on a continuous basis. By the way, "customer" does not mean just the external end user. In many jobs, you have an internal customer who is very important to serve if the end customer is to receive the expected result.

  - **Everyone improves quality.** This may be literal for someone who sees how to improve his or her job, but it also refers more broadly to the responsibility each of us has to find ways to improve our organization and its products and services and take personal responsibility to do this, teach others how to do it, and/or ensure that information on what needs to be done moves to where it will result in action.

One of the things I learned in the software business is that, while the programmers and technicians are the ones who create the product and fix the problems, they are rarely the ones who discover and diagnose customer-related problems or concerns. This often comes from customers' concerns about bugs or lack of functionality, communicated through installation or support staff. If everyone does not feel a shared responsibility for quality improvement, the sensing and resolution process will not work smoothly.

This concept of shared ownership with different responsibilities applies to most businesses beyond software, especially any technically based business; it is just easier to see the division there. Simple questions to ask here include:

▲ Who is likely to get information we need about quality from a customer?

▲ What should that person do with this information, and why should he or she care?

▲ What mechanism is there to collate and analyze these info bits about how we are doing, and how high up the chain does this need to go for someone to be capable of seeing patterns we need to worry about?

▲ What mechanisms do we have to ensure that improvements result, and how will those be tracked and correlated with the concerns?

▲ How will we let those know who discovered the concerns in the first place that changes have occurred and that their input and attention is valued?

- **"Everyone markets (and sells)."** This will mean different things to individual team members in different jobs, but it is designed to remind each person that his or her livelihood depends in part on the whole organization portraying a positive and effective image and message about the value added by your products and services to individual customers and the marketplace in general.

You can pick out the salesperson in a crowd in about five seconds: outgoing, talkative, interested in finding out about you, and eager to tell you about his or her company, what they do, and why they are good at it. "Everyone markets (and sells)" is not designed to change people or personalities, but it is designed to make everyone realize that they have a role.

One of our most successful senior staff members who sold a lot of customized executive programs for us at Wharton was a woman on her second career. After she had become very successful with us, she told me that all her life she had hated sales. She was uncomfortable selling and said that if I had told her when she was interviewed that selling was going to be a large part of her job, she would not have accepted the position.

What she found out was that much of marketing and selling is just believing in your organization, caring about customers' needs, understanding your ability to deliver, and being honest with potential customers about how you may or may not be able to help them. You do not have to have sales or marketing in your title to be able to do that for your organization. When she realized, "That's all there is to it," she realized she could do it naturally and was fine with selling.

The point is that every person in an organization has the ability to influence customer opinion positively or negatively through his or her job and that will lead to more or less sales and growth for you in the future.

Driving these or other concepts appropriate for your organization on a continuous basis will set a tone within which employees will often surprise you with their own interpretation of how to act or react effectively in nonstandard situations. Regardless of the culture you choose to create, there must be some shared understanding on the part of individuals across an organization of why they are there and what they need to accomplish to succeed.

The desire to be part of something successful is nearly universal, but leaders must provide the context for success to help others achieve. The most effective way to build and use E^3, in my experience, has been through storytelling. People remember stories. A story gives them tangible examples and models of how others handled situations. Set the tone, look for stories, and then use them as tools to spread the learning.

- **Delineation of responsibilities, standard operating procedures, and metrics.** Knowing who has primary responsibility for important tasks or objectives is paramount in avoiding mistakes that lead to accidents, as was evident when Eastern Airlines 401 crashed in the Florida Everglades because the entire flight crew was distracted and no one was flying the airplane. Businesses do this as well when geographic and product or business line structures overall lap with confusing authority. Confusion over responsibilities is compounded when there are not clear metrics for measuring success, failure, or mediocrity. Was Xerox PARC "successful" because things were invented even if they were not commercialized? No one seemed to know, or care.

- **Training, simulation, and designed safety.** Operators at Three Mile Island (TMI) were not able to handle a complex situation they had not seen before, but they should have been able to fall back on some basic principles for guidance. They had bypassed safety systems designed to save them, and so did the pilots of Air Florida 90 before crashing into the Potomac River. Auditors were supposed to catch improper risks, accounting, and fraud, but failed to in Enron, WorldCom, and HealthSouth. Their clients pushed, and the auditors moved the safety limits to accommodate their very important clients.

  One of the most important techniques that should be applied more in business is simulation of complex situations and "can't happen" scenarios. A drug company CEO told me a few years ago that his disaster management team had orders to conduct, at least once a year, a surprise, day-long, realistic disaster drill with a complex scenario, regardless of what was going on in the business or personal lives of the executives on the day the team chose. The realism was extended right down to dummy press releases and reporters with video cameras rolling waiting to catch senior executives for comment. Most businesses are lucky if they can get executives to leave the building during a fire drill, much less participate in a realistic business-mistake simulation.

The military, the airlines, police and firefighters, and many other pubic-sector agencies have all discovered that realistic drills improve performance in real situations. Airlines do this with flight simulators and over the years have added more complex scenarios as a result of events like the United Airlines 232 crash landing at Sioux City.

Navy pilots are observed, videotaped, critiqued, and graded on every carrier landing. The grades are posted for all to see. The " best" grade is "OK-3," meaning that the landing was satisfactory and the plane caught the third wire.* A grade of OK for the desired performance is a reminder that there is little margin for error and lack of competence or overconfidence are both enemies. Training to high levels of performance is rarely a mistake in any business or organization.

- **Believe your indications, never ignore customer data, and communicate.** As a nuclear submarine officer and as a pilot, I have been taught for decades to believe your indications and act on them, even when you do not like what you are being told. The first instinct of most business people is to find a way to explain bad news instead of trying to understand why something is happening as indicated.

Never ignore customer data. My experience is that by the time customer complaints and other bad customer news make it to an executive's desk, you can multiply the problem by ten because your organization's filtering systems are so good at keeping you in the dark. Believe it and act on it—fast—because it probably took a while to get to you.

Appoint a customer advocate, much like an internal auditor, who is responsible for making noise in the organization about the quality of products or services received by customers. This can send an important message that reinforces the fact that you care about customers and expect them to be served well.

Communication of information, whether it is good or bad news, is critical to proper action. It sounds trite to say that this is important, but communication effectiveness depends too much on the

---

* There are four large "wires" across the landing area of an aircraft carrier. The pilot tries to set up the airplane to hit the deck (at 150mph) in a position where the tailhook grabs the third wire to stop the airplane.

personality and preferences of the individuals involved. Standing orders to communicate certain types of information, deviation from metrics, and other guidelines are desirable to build an information culture that broadens the resources available and those involved in decision-making.

- **Mental preparation, focus, and seeking resources.** Training, specific preparation for complex business operations, and analysis of a range of scenarios are all things that managers can and should be taught to think about in advance to improve outcomes. Keeping focus ("fly the airplane") on the objectives and learning to ignore meaningless distractions requires discipline but can often make the difference between success and failure.

   Knowledge about the availability, qualifications, and access methods for resources in any organization are necessary if you are to give front-line management and staff the best shot at producing a satisfactory result in unusual situations. J&J clearly knew how to do this with their impressive handling of the Tylenol situation, but there are probably many other companies that have systems and mechanisms just as effective that you never hear about because they have a culture of managing multiple mistakes.

- **STOP.** This is your last line of defense, and it is usually the place where the executives and senior management have done all they can do and those on the front lines are on their own. This is the point where all the training, preparation, procedures, and cultural development becomes the context for an individual to make decisions in a situation where he or she may be confused by information and not sure what action to take.

   This is where you hope that your front-line employees will remember that there is some action they can take to slow the situation down or put it on hold while they get help to achieve final resolution. This might mean approaching a much more senior individual to let them know you think the organization is in the process of making a big mistake, as Sherron Watkins did at Enron. It does not always work, but you should train your team to understand that they have a responsibility to exercise this option when the situation warrants it.

One case where nearly everything outlined in Figure 10.2 was present and worked well was with Pepsi-Cola North America in 1993. Pepsi was the victim of a product tampering hoax in June 1993 that began when an 82 year old man in Tacoma, Washington claimed his can of Diet Pepsi contained a syringe. This claim obviously received media attention and was followed by hundreds of copycat claims.

Pepsi-Cola North America and their local bottler's combined response included all the right steps:

- Immediate acceptance that the problem was real until proven otherwise;
- A focus on customer safety and confidence;
- Clear definition of roles and responsibilities and broad internal involvement;
- Seeking outside assistance all the way up to the Food and Drug Administration (FDA);
- Rapid public investigation of manufacturing processes and procedures;
- Continuous open internal and external communication; and
- Aggressive customer thanks and confidence building once the crisis was past.

Within a few days Pepsi confirmed, with the assistance and endorsement of the FDA, that the situation was a hoax and arrests were made. Their response had been immediate and effective for all the reasons above, but more importantly they saw the situation as a learning opportunity. Pepsi published a booklet called "The Pepsi Hoax: What Went Right?" to help their employees understand what had happened and how to learn from the crisis. The incident and the focus on learning from it continue to reinforce Pepsi's priorities, values and culture for immediate and appropriate action.

Learning to Detect Dangerous Patterns and Strategic Blunders

Problems at Xerox PARC, Motorola, and Kodak evolved quietly over long periods of time while each of these companies was lauded for its amazing success. As discussed in Chapter 6, "Cultures that Create

Accidents," we can argue that Kodak did "everything right" for nearly a century and yet has still fallen from the lofty perch of one of the world's most respected companies.

Patterns of mistakes that go beyond individual incidents are difficult to spot and troubling when discovered. Patterns of similar operational problems are not just red flags, but flags, lights, and sirens saying, "Look at me."

Mistake patterns are often strategic in origin, but the warning signals and tools for preventing and dealing with broad strategic mistake patterns are different from the signals and tools in the operational arena. Here are some situations and warnings that should raise red flags about strategic trouble:

- Operational patterns
  - Repeated problems of the same type, at similar locations, involving the same individuals or others with similar characteristics, with an identifiable frequency or an increasing rate of occurrence
  - Similarities in root causes
  - Failures that have similarities but are unexplained
- Strategic patterns
  - Margins that are too high or too low for your industry
  - Employees don't understand the growth or the strategy
  - "Surprise" competitors
  - "Surprise" competitive products
  - Need to look outside for growth and/or technology
  - Growth coming only from industry consolidation
  - Market shifting to new technologies
  - Core competencies in declining demand and undifferentiated
  - Need for a different skill set (for example, shift from regulated to deregulated business)
  - Loss of pricing power on flat or declining volume
  - Customers expect more bundled add-ins without price increases
  - No returns on R&D
  - Declining P/E and financials

Although these signals usually indicate strategic trouble, there may be underlying operational causes that have been escalated to strategic issues because of frequency and severity. This was the case with Korean Air when they had one of the worst safety records in the free world through the 1990s. We could argue that their crashes were operational in nature, but in fact they indicated a culture that lacked discipline around problem solving, failed to adopt proven accident-reduction techniques from other carriers, and disregarded customer and crew safety.

Manufacturers whose productivity and quality do not keep up with industry or competitors in other geographies will show similar patterns. Operational problems will become strategic mistakes if not dealt with in sufficient time. Dealing with these kinds of mistakes requires not just new ideas but organizational transformation. Some approaches to building the capability to recognize and deal with such patterns are illustrated in Figure 10.3.

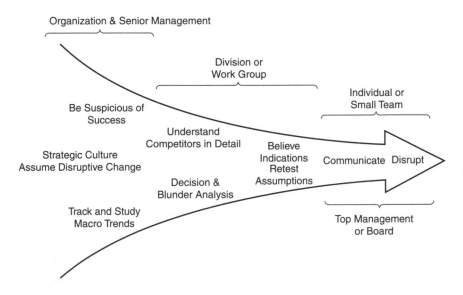

Figure 10.3 Organizational tools to stop mistakes.

- **Strategic culture/assume disruptive change.** Operations are the difference between success and failure in the short run, but in the long run, organizations that think only about operations may be left out as an industry changes. Sending this message to the rest of the organization is important so that others can be sensors, but it must be done with care so that operations are not disrupted while looking for a future that may be a few years away.

- **Be suspicious of success.** The time to worry most is often when you have the best results. Having the financial and organizational flexibility to consider options for the future is when you want to ask the question, "What does reinvention look like?"

- **Track and understand macro trends** because the clues to the future often lie outside the established competitors. The computer industry has shifted, especially during the 1990s, from a focus on hardware to being solutions providers with a much broader set of competencies. A company caught off guard when market preferences change may never recover. Look at Gateway, selling TVs and other consumer commodities after becoming marginalized in the PC business. Having someone in the business that is good at synthesizing events, facts, and information that may appear unrelated to try to identify trends and issues before the changes put an organization in a defensive posture is important.

- **Understand competitors in detail.** Over the years, I have been stunned by the number of companies that do not understand their competitors in detail. To compete effectively, you need to know not just what their products and prices are but what competencies and capabilities distinguish your competitor.

  The real danger here, though, is that we often ignore substitute products or new competitors, instead focusing too narrowly on yesterday's definition of competition. For example, most of the land-line telephone companies have fought AT&T for years to try to get a piece of the long-distance business. While these companies were distracted fighting with each other, long distance calls began shifting to mobile phones where the cost was packaged. The next trend, of course, is the trend for consumers to use a mobile phone as their only line or to shift to the Internet telephony (VOIP) provided by young startup companies and not the traditional telephone companies.

  USAA, one of the most respected insurance companies in the United States, some years ago put together a team and sent them off to a different building for a couple of years with the charge to "figure out how to put us out of business." Sometimes this is the only way you will see the new competitors that you refuse to look at in the normal course of business.

- **Decision and blunder analysis.** Concurrent or retrospective analysis of decisions and decision-making processes is an important part of learning from past mistakes and at least not making the same mistake more that once. It is important to examine both the quality of the decisions we make and the process by which we reach a decision, yet few organizations practice this discipline. Was a decision "good" on the basis of all that was known and possible to know at the time? Are there flaws in the decision process (for example, lack of data, incomplete analysis, bad assumptions), and if so, do the same flaws come up repeatedly?

- **Believe your indications.** This applies in the strategic and pattern context just as it did when we discussed it in relationship to evaluating operations. The difference is where you get the information. In a strategic context, it may be tougher to know that you are looking at an "indicator," much less believe it. This may come in the form of new competitors, new technologies, changing pricing structures, and new channels of distributions that tend to be dismissed in the early stages.

- **Test and retest assumptions.** Many of the mistake scenarios illustrate this weakness. Market conditions do not always change precipitously. The problem is often that the changes seem small and subtle until you wake up and find yourself at a competitive disadvantage. Burger King started letting customers make minor changes to the product (hold the mayo, extra ketchup, and so on) for years while McDonald's stuck with production efficiency as the primary driver of the business. Over time, McDonald's found they were behind, not just on the little things but with an outdated menu that was losing market share.

An interesting exercise to test the assumptions upon which a business is based is to ask the question, "How do we make money?" I have found a surprising lack of knowledge in most companies on this subject. This is not an issue of understanding what business the company is in, but understanding which portions of the company's business produce what portion of the revenue and profit, and what symbiotic relationships exist among the products, services, or segments. If there is a shift in the origin of revenues and profits or a change in the relationships, what does this tell you about the future?

Additionally, techniques such as scenario planning are important here, not to test assumptions factually but to ensure that you have a broad set to analyze. There are times (for example, 9/11) when you cannot predict specific events that will affect you, but if you have thought about a range of scenarios and situations and planned for those that will help or protect you the most, then you have a better chance of surviving difficult challenges.

HIP, a large New York City HMO, had done very detailed disaster planning for their IT operations, including actually rehearsing an offsite shift to backup systems. After 9/11, despite being located just blocks from ground zero and having their IT operation totally shut down (for lack of power), the organization was up and running in a few hours at an alternate site with little or no disruption in authorizing care, filling prescriptions, or delivering other vital health services that had to go on regardless of, and sometimes in support of, the tragedy.

- **Communications.** This is once again the key here as it was in operations. The reason it is at the tip of the arrow is that, when things begin to fail, if we can just train people to speak up, identify what is happening, and seek help and advice, we can often interrupt a mistake sequence.

- **Disrupt.** The last line of defense if an organization has failed at the things beneath the tip of the arrow is the ability of those on the front line to save you. Have you built a questioning culture that will, when confronted with a tough situation, somehow find a way to save the day? It is dangerous to rely on this, but it does happen. It is visible in physical disasters at an operating level. It can be observed at an operating level in business as well. Do you see line managers speak up, push back, or launch local products that become successful and are picked up elsewhere in an organization?

The last line of defense is different in different businesses. For retail businesses, it is usually the salesperson, cashier, or customer service agent. In physical situations, it may be an operator of a plant or some other technician or technical professional. In other service businesses, it may be a nurse, a pilot, an auditor, or a classroom teacher.

The difficulty in business is that, although change needs a champion if the problem to be solved is large, it has to be a champion with substantial power or access to power in the organization. In fact, I spoke with a former Kodak middle manager who told me that she and her colleagues tried, unsuccessfully, to push the culture more aggressively toward a digital future in the mid-1990s. They saw the mistake sequence and understood the scenarios that were unfolding but felt powerless to stop the sequence because the culture and mindset were dominated by those who understood the huge current profit stream from chemical-based imaging.

Operating management may try to stop a mistake sequence that is operational, but the last line of defense when it comes to strategic matters is top management and the board of directors. If top management does not see the pattern of strategic mistakes or is part of the problem, then the board is the last hope. As we saw in Enron, if the board fails to detect the problem sequence, it may literally doom the entire enterprise.

Most people want to do a good job, and many people can manage mistakes instinctively because they have superior cognitive abilities. But overwhelming them by making them the only line of defense is the biggest mistake of all. You can avoid or manage mistakes, but it takes discipline and requires thought, planning, and reinforcement. If your last line of defense is not backed up by culture, procedures, analysis, preparation, and training, you are taking more risks than you realize.

> **Insight #37: Do you want to trust "saving the business" to your last line of defense?** That is what you will do if you do not develop systems for detecting and correcting mistakes before there is any damage of consequence.

The Need for Mistakes

If you do not make any mistakes, you may not be taking enough risk. I firmly believe this as an operating business principle. However, this concept should not be extended to flying airplanes in commercial passenger service, operating manufacturing plants, selling new medicines, or driving your automobile.

We need experiments to learn, and where possible you want experimentation under controlled conditions, both to minimize danger and to collect data and information in a structured environment that will maximize the learning. Aircraft designers want to make their mistakes in wind tunnels. Test pilots confirm expected performance or deviations and identify problems that could not be confirmed in other ways. Ship captains and airplane pilots use computer-driven simulators to learn and refine their ship-handling or flying skills. Medical researchers conduct animal tests and limited human trials before drugs are approved for broad use.

When it comes to normal operations, though, we seek stability and perfection or as close to it as we can mange. Six Sigma and other quality programs adopted by thousands of companies are built on the belief that stopping mistakes saves money—large amounts of money both directly with improved efficiency and indirectly through improved product quality and customer satisfaction. The suggestions in Figures 10.2 and 10.3 offer some ways to identify mistakes as they occur or to prevent them in advance. If we put together the ideas suggested in both the operational and strategic areas, we can keep the "business flywheel" moving in the right direction as shown in Figure 10.4.

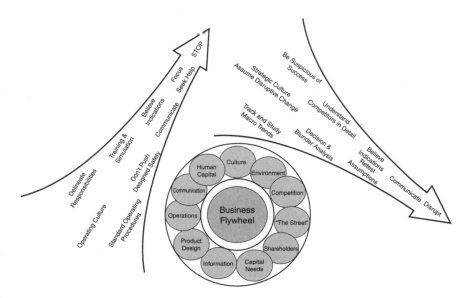

Figure 10.4 Moving the flywheel forward.

The extreme would be to stop all mistakes, but that may well stop not only the mistakes but also the whole engine that drives a business. There is an approach to decision-making called "mini-max regret." This means that one makes decisions in a way that the worst possible outcome is avoided at all costs. The problem is that this may also limit the potential for positive results. This is equivalent to deciding to spend your entire life without ever leaving the safety of your cave to avoid being struck by lightning. The action accomplishes a specific objective but limits the potential for other accomplishments.

Businesses do use a variety of techniques to reduce risk and gather information prior to making significant commitments. Market research, test marketing, limited production runs, joint ventures, alliances, and a variety of other techniques and structures are used for this purpose.

So we do want risk, but wherever possible we want to experiment under conditions in which we control risk and evaluate results. There are some areas in business where the only way to find out what you need to know is by taking significant risk. This is particularly true when bringing out a new product or product category, entering new geographies where taste or culture may affect acceptance, or bringing a new high-cost technology to market where timing and acceptance may be questionable.

Think about the following:

- Mobile phone systems using 3G (third-generation) technology caught on like wildfire in Japan, but there has been much less interest in Europe and the United States. The costs and risks of adopting such technology are huge for the wireless companies, so the risks of misjudging consumer response are great, but if successful, the rewards may be significant.

- When Microsoft entered the game console market, it began by losing money on every Xbox it sold, but it did so with the belief that this is a market with huge potential where it wants to be a major player.

- Numerous biotechnology companies were formed in the 1980s, but only a few survived and prospered the long product development cycle to stability.

There is a difference between gambling and investment. Taking calculated and thoughtful business risks that may or may not succeed is rarely a mistake, even when the risk leads to a failure. Repeatedly taking such risks without any rationale for doing so and failing would likely be classified as a mistake or pattern of mistakes. Webvan fits this description, and Philips Electronics has been accused of such a high risk/low payoff strategy in the United States for years.

Failing to take any risks at all may be the most dangerous type of mistake that a business can make. There are businesses that become so risk averse over time that they doom themselves to failure because innovation by others will render them irrelevant. This is why we characterized Kodak as a company that "did everything right" but still made huge mistakes. The mistakes were more of omission than commission. Large high-cost airlines ignored discounting and struggled as a result. The small druggist, hardware store owner, or grocer is usually nearly powerless in the face of big box retailers and discounters. The common mistake across these industries and companies is not finding a way to be differentiated that customers care about—or exiting the business profitably before the opportunity passes.

Risk is part of growth in a capitalistic system, and most organizations think about ways to take risks while minimizing exposure. There are classic stories about companies that have taken "bet the company" type risks, such as Boeing developing the 747 in the 1960s, and in these cases, the importance of minimizing mistakes is greater than ever.

Mistakes will occur because there are imperfections in human judgment and performance, but failing to take risks in fear of making mistakes is a recipe for failure. Free markets will tolerate mistakes at some level but will not tolerate them indefinitely or in great quantity. Learning to identify mistakes in an analytic and timely fashion is often the difference between success and failure.

Insight #38: If you do not make any mistakes, you may not be taking enough risk, but failing to take any risks at all may be the most dangerous type of mistake that a business can make.

Summary of Insights

Summarized here are the insights associated with the accidents, incidents, and successes examined in the book. They are offered with the caution that slavishly adhering to them in the hope of avoiding all mistakes will not necessarily lead to success, because success is different than a lack of failure, which might lead to mediocrity.

Despite the caution that success requires more than avoiding mistakes, these are powerful insights into the ways that many have "snatched defeat from the jaws of victory." The patterns are similar and have shown themselves repeatedly over and over again in a variety of industries, countries, and businesses.

Additionally, if we are honest we can see similarities to the things that drive or hinder our personal success in school, careers, sports, and social relationships. Consider these guidelines for most situations, personal or business, and look not only for their occurrence individually, but in patterns that serve as warnings for analysis and action.

From Chapter 1:

Insight #1: Mental preparation is critical because organizations and individuals are rarely good at learning by drawing parallels. They need to be taught to recognize types and patterns of mistakes and learn to extrapolate implications from other situations into their own.

From Chapter 2:

Insight #2: "Fly the airplane." It is easy to get distracted, and there are times when you need to have a stern talk with yourself and ask if you are spending your time on the most important things.

Insight #3: You cannot afford even a whiff of an ethical lapse. Issues of trust are serious and strategic in today's world, largely because there have been so many ethical lapses that consumers do not trust the actions of corporate executives. The slightest sense of uncertainty or lack of openness creates suspicion that mushrooms into a lack of confidence that can cost a great deal.

Insight #4: Execution mistakes can be generated through a lack of resources or knowledge. Even a good strategy will fail without adequate resources, training, and discipline around implementation.

Insight #5: Establish and enforce standard operating procedures. Aviation knows how to do this, complex manufacturing operations know how to do this, but management teams do not like it because they believe not everything can be made routine. There is some truth to this, but you need to look for everything that can be standardized and make the procedures known, train for them, and hold those accountable who do not follow them.

Insight #6: Make responsibilities clear. Whether it is Coca-Cola Belgium or one of the airline crashes, mistakes are more likely to be caught and stopped if you know who is responsible for what and who should be providing additional oversight and advice.

Insight #7: Seek advice and seek to understand assumptions. In a number of cases, we saw a disconnect between the views of customers and those of insiders or a lack of sensitivity to regional cultural and political views. In other cases, we saw outright disregard for data provided by others (Air Florida) or easily available data (Webvan or AmEx). Failure to seek and use advice and direct disregard for data on customer behavior is a significant cause of mistakes of all types.

Insight #8: If something does not make sense or feels confused, STOP and figure out what's going on. In most of the cases throughout the book, there was evidence of confusion or lack of information at some point that troubled those involved. Calling a "timeout" in one way or another to understand what is happening is a useful practice.

Insight #9: People are usually at the root of the problem. Looking at mishaps as system problems is the only way to move toward perfection. Multiple causes are far more likely than single causes, but multiple causes almost always means some set of mistakes that were directly people related. An analysis that looks for simple answers, blaming only one cause or only a physical cause, will likely yield an inadequate understanding of the problem and lead to repetition of the problems that caused the accident. It is critical to focus on people-related issues of process, training, and knowledge-building that will allow them to think their way through when technology or process fails.

From Chapter 3:

Insight #10: A significant portion of execution-related mistakes occur because criteria for measuring progress and performance have not been identified and/or communicated explicitly. This includes the need to understand not only what the measures are, but how frequently they should be checked and what the priorities and actions should be when an out-of-specification condition occurs.

Insight #11: Failure to analyze data points and ask what they mean is a major source of mistakes. This seems obvious, but we block our interest and ability to be analytic with time pressures, distractions, and cultures that are not curious. The question, "I see it, but what does it mean?" may be the most important thing you can ask to begin to break a mistake chain. The answer will not always be obvious, but starting the inquiry process is a necessity.

Insight #12: Ignoring data is dangerous—ignoring or misinterpreting customer data can be catastrophic. Intel initially ignored customer concerns, whereas in the Tylenol case J&J never lost sight of its responsibility to its customer. Coca-Cola did not adequately test the depth of its data with hard-core users of its product.

Insight #13: Across industries and situations, ineffective communications can accelerate deterioration of a mistake chain. Conversely, effective communication is one of the keys to breaking a mistake chain.

Insight #14: Spending time and money to build a culture that takes mistakes seriously may have the highest ROI of anything you can do as a manager. This is something that paid off for the airline industry in improving safety and for Intel, J&J, and Coca-Cola.

Insight #15: Look for the opportunity for an accident or even a major success to be a rallying cry for change and transformation. This is a unique opportunity that should not be ignored. This is the silver lining in an accident—your ability to identify some greater benefit that comes from the learning.

From Chapter 4:

Insight #16: A very successful business can blind you to opportunity. This is because you will make comparative judgments on the basis of current business criteria that may not last, while underestimating the potential of new businesses that have not yet grown far enough to show their full potential. Being successful also raises, often inappropriately, your confidence in your own decision-making.

Insight #17: Your competitors are not who you think they are. Until recently, Xerox did not realize that the biggest threat to the copier business in smaller market segments was not Canon or Minolta but Hewlett-Packard and the laser printer that Xerox invented.

Insight #18: Sometimes a mistake is not a mistake. If a mistake is a wrong action, then we have to make some judgment about whether a strategic business decision is "right" or "wrong," and that may not be obvious as quickly as we think. This reinforces the importance of continuing analysis of decisions after the fact and potential future scenarios.

Insight #19: Even companies that have successfully reinvented themselves have to work hard, perhaps even harder, to understand when it is time to do so again. Motorola reinvented itself when it was early to the new TV market and when it sold Quasar and committed everything to communications and semiconductors. It made a huge leap from older communications products based on single sideband technologies to cellular communications. A number of strategic blunders that no one expected from a company with that history caused it to stumble as the twentieth century closed.

Insight #20: With disruptive technology, prices usually drop and value shifts to customers. This is a normal part of the economic cycle for new technologies that you should anticipate and use proactively to advantage. Ignore this phenomenon at your peril.

Insight #21: Some changes happen without your permission. Learn to recognize the signs and get on board early.

Insight #22: Many more industries and companies will see the value continue to shift from hardware to software and services. Even companies like Motorola and Kodak, which at one time thought they were primarily manufacturers, are likely to move more deeply into services for growth.

From Chapter 5:

Insight #23: Test and retest assumptions—until proven beyond a doubt. Assumptions are at the core of mistakes in physical systems and business. The problem is that we often make assumptions and draw what we think are conclusions on the basis of limited data, and then if nothing bad happens, we begin to view the assumptions as truth. *Titanic* was assumed to be unsinkable. Three Mile Island was assumed to be failsafe under all conditions.

NASA assumed that since foam had been coming off the center fuel tank for more than 100 launches and had never caused any serious damage, that it could not cause serious damage. Yet in the investigation of the *Columbia* accident, it did not take long to show that a piece of foam moving at over 500 mph relative to the shuttle wing could do enough damage to bring the shuttle down—but only if it hit in just the right place. This is the problem with assumptions; they are just that—and have limitations that we may not realize. Once we believe them, we have closed doors of understanding, killing curiosity and analysis.

Insight #24: Push or ignore engineered safety at your peril. Engineers and designers that build systems of all types build in features designed to enhance the ability of the system to perform the intended function, but they also include features to minimize the chance of damage in the event of partial or full failure. This is true for physical systems from airplanes to zoos and is also important in today's more complicated business world where "systems" include complex human—software—process systems in a wide range of businesses. Do airline reservation systems, manufacturing control and supply chain systems, credit card billing systems, and billing and receivable systems for most businesses have anything in common with physical disasters? Absolutely—the same opportunity to damage a business is there because of the complexity of the design and operations interface of man and machine.

Although designers try to anticipate adverse conditions that threaten the success of the system, they will not always successfully design for every circumstance, and even if they do, human intervention can often overcome the most rigorous safety design. Understanding that built-in safety features are there for a reason should be a cause for understanding limits. Pushing such systems to their limits or ignoring threats that test or evade safety systems should be undertaken only with the greatest care and understanding of the extreme risk involved. *Titanic*, TMI, *Challenger*, and *Columbia* all pushed engineering limits and lost.

Insight #25: Believe the data. "Believe your indications" is something all of us in the nuclear Navy learned. The failure to believe information that is staring you in the face is one of the most common causes of catastrophes. In *Titanic*, TMI, and at NASA, operators had warnings of danger and did not heed them. In the case of *Titanic*, the warnings were well in advance and could have easily been acted on if minds had been receptive. At TMI, damage could have minimized if warnings that were part of the recovery process had been observed. With NASA, the warnings were repeatedly offered in advance and were analytically sound but were dismissed just as routinely as the captain of *Titanic* ignored the warnings he received. Data were also available in all the business situations discussed in the book and had been ignored in the disaster situations.

Insight #26: Use available resources. Captain Smith of *Titanic* ignored available resources, other than consulting the ship's designer after the collision, who told him exactly how long it would take the ship to go down. When it was clear the ship would sink, Smith began to seek rescue help.

At TMI, it was two hours before the team on watch seriously sought outside help, apparently believing mistakenly until then that they could handle the situation. Some of the help literally wandered in the door as the next shift reported for work. Others, such as the Babcock & Wilcox (B&W) representative, were sought out, and still others, such as the NRC and Pennsylvania government and regulatory officials, were required notifications.

NASA engineers repeatedly asked their superiors to use Department of Defense (DOD) capabilities to get close images of Columbia on-orbit and were denied. The debate will go on forever about whether anything could have been done to save the crew, but the opportunity was missed, not once but repeatedly.

Insight #27: Train for the "can't happen" scenario. Those involved with *Titanic, Columbia*, and TMI all thought many things could not happen or at worst were very remote. This mindset is obviously dangerous, but so is an overly conservative "If I don't go outside the sky can't fall on me" attitude. You obviously train for known situations in operating any device from a car to the space shuttle. But thinking about how you would handle something "they" say "can't happen" may be more important than an idle intellectual game.

Insight #28: Open your mind past your blinders. This is extremely difficult. How do you know that your response has been conditioned by the context of your experiences? Perhaps the only defense is to play "what if" games with yourself and your colleagues. Regardless of the business or physical context, these are useful exercises. If you find yourself in a confusing situation, perhaps the proper question when you have exhausted all avenues is "What's the other right answer?" This question often opens the mind to looking at whether there is another answer by discarding what you have already thought about without success.

From Chapter 6:

Insight #29: Culture is powerful—what creates success may kill you. The cultures of American Medical International (AMI), Ford, Firestone, and Enron worked for and against them. There are many examples, typically in the early stages of successful companies, where culture helps organizations see things in markets that others miss, get past survival challenges, grow faster, and weather competitive threats. The same powerful, but hard to define, force that binds an organization together for success can also be a catalyst, or even a cause, of failure.

From Chapter 7:

Insight #30: Culture is powerful, but be sure you understand where to extend it. As McDonald's found out, its core culture is built around attention to detail, standardization, and discipline in operations and marketing. This is a tremendous strength, but it cannot be extended easily to other businesses or even other food businesses. Other food businesses are different enough that extending the same detailed procedures did not work well. This was predictable because the McDonald's culture thrives on standardization with minimal adaptation. Going into new businesses requires rapid learning and adaptation. This is not to say that McDonald's cannot get results in other food areas, but it will do so less efficiently or will have to develop teams with different competencies.

Insight #31: Rapid culture change designed to obliterate mistakes in supercritical areas is possible, but sharp focus, extra diligence, and continuous training are necessary for success. The difficulty is that if you do not have a history of being a high-performance organization, you can rarely invent this capability on demand. These standards cannot be relaxed if you wish to maintain performance.

Insight #32: Most cultures develop by accident—those that are designed to accomplish a purpose are more effective. Whether we look at McDonald's, Southwest Airlines, the Navy's submarine force, or IBM, when you see successful organizations, you find strong cultures with teams that understand what they need to focus on and reinforce it over and over again. Successful companies design cultures through consistent priorities and behaviors. This does not mean that priorities remain unchanged, but when they do change, the changes take place in a considered and deliberate fashion and are communicated very well.

From Chapter 8:

Insight #33: Economic forces and laws are real, and industry changes are real. They are not as unexpected as most people believe—it is usually only a matter of the timing. The mistake chain where entire industry changes occur is driven by a failure to recognize the need to make fundamental changes in a business model early enough to avoid being consumed by the natural laws of economics.

Insight #34: Being #1 or #2 really does matter. This is not because it was the much-heralded rallying cry at GE, but because it is a reflection of the laws of economics that will bite if you are not a leader in your field. Having a vision that includes an understanding of the forces at work and the time you have available is a must.

Insight #35: Economic business visioning (EBV) is not optional. However, few companies, except perhaps pure commodity businesses, factor such a process into their planning. The usual set of assumptions in most planning cycles revolves around a range of economic assumptions from "a little better" to "a little worse," with "a lot better" and "a lot worse" thrown in to make the set look complete, but with little belief that either will occur. For both the short and the longer term, designing a process for analysis and spending time understanding the shifts in the industry economic issues will help avoid mistakes that are deadly.

From Chapter 9:

Insight #36: Startups and small businesses make mistakes in the same ways that larger organizations make mistakes. However, they usually have fewer resources to avoid or recover and less flexibility to survive mistakes with alternate plans or products. While the patterns are similar, some mistakes or sequences are unique to small business. These have to do with fundraising and the mechanics of getting things done in the early stages, but many others look similar to what occurs in larger, more established entities.

From Chapter 10:

Insight #37: Do you want to trust "saving the business" to your last line of defense? That is what you will do if you do not develop systems for detecting and correcting mistakes before there is any damage of consequence.

Insight #38: If you do not make any mistakes, you may not be taking enough risk, but failing to take any risks at all may be the most dangerous type of mistake that a business can make. This does not mean you should seek mistakes for the sake of making them, but the lack of mistakes (perfection) does not always correlate with the highest level of success. Risk-reward is an economic principle that underlies our whole business system.

References

1   Bossidy, Larry and Ram Charan. *Execution—The Discipline of Getting Things Done.* Crown Business, 2002.

2   Collins, James C. and Jerry I. Porras. *Built to Last: Successful Habits of Visionary Companies.* HarperCollins, 1994, page 3.

3   Perrow, Charles. *Normal Accidents.* Princeton University Press, updated edition 1999.

4   Drucker, Peter. "The Five Deadly Business Sins." *The Wall Street Journal*, October 21, 1993.

5   Wallace, James. "Unlike Airbus, Boeing lets aviator override fly-by-wire technology." *Seattle Post-Intellingencer Reporter*, March 20, 2000.

6   "Aircraft Accident Report, Eastern Airlines, Inc., Lockheed, L-1011, N310EA, Miami, Florida, December 29, 1972." National Transportation Safety Board, NTSB-AAR-73-14.

7   Treanor, Jill. "Coca-Cola Loses Some of Its Fizz." *The Guardian*, July 14, 1999.

8   Horne, Thomas A. "Trial by Takeoff." *AOPA Pilot*, December 1982, pages 24-30.

9   Carley, William M., "Crisis Aloft" *Wall St. Journal*, December 12, 1984, page 1.

10   Ibid.

11   "Intel's chip of worms?" *The Economist*, December 17, 1994, page 65. ©1994 The Economist Newspaper Ltd. All rights reserved. Printed with permission. Further reproduction prohibited.

12   Corcoran, Elizabeth. "The Glitch That Stole Intel Corp.'s Christmas; Pentium's Flaws Shake Company." *The Washington Post*, December 19, 1994, page A1.

13   Courtesy of Johnson & Johnson from www.jnj.com/our_company/our_credo/index.htm.

14   "Aircraft Accident Report, United Airlines, Inc. McDonnell-Douglas, DC-8-61, N8082U, Portland, Oregon, December 28, 1978." National Transportation Safety Board, NTSB-AAR-79-7.

15   Ibid, page 19.

16   "Crew Resource Management Training." US Department of Transportation, Federal Aviation Administration Advisory Circular 120-51D, February 8, 2001.

17   Hiltzik, Michael A. *Dealers of Lightning: Xerox PARC and the Dawn of the Computer Age.* HarperBusiness, 1999.

18   Motorola Web site: www.motorola.com/content/0,,115-110,00.html.

19   Kodak.com: www.kodak.com/US/en/corp/researchDevelopment/facts.shtml.

20   2002 Kodak Annual Report, page 12.

21   Bandler, James. "As Kodak Eyes Digital Future, A Big Partner Starts To Fade." *The Wall Street Journal*, January 23, 2004.

22   Christensen, Clayton M. *The Innovator's Dilemma: The Revolutionary National Bestseller That Changed the Way We Do Business.* HarperBusiness, 2000.

23   "Motorola's Symphony Digital Radio Chipset Delivers Breakthrough AM/FM Reception and Performance—Christmas 2003 Radios Will Receive More Stations and Sound Notably Better." www.motorola.com/mediacenter/news/detail/0,,1573_1221_23,00.html.

24   Columbia Accident Investigation Board, Report Volume 1, August 2003, page 198, U.S. Government Printing Office.

25   Lord, Walter. *The Night Lives On: The Untold Stories & Secrets Behind the Sinking of the Unsinkable Ship* Titanic. Avon 1998.

26   Scripophily.com, Eastern Steam Navigation Company 1851—Great Eastern Ship. http://store.yahoo.com/scripophily/eassteamnavc.html

27   Brander, Roy. "The RMS Titanic and its Times: When Accountants Ruled the Waves." Elias Kline Memorial Lecture, 69th Shock & Vibration Symposium, October 12-16, 1998, Minneapolis, Minnesota.

28   Lord, page 21.

29   "Birth of Titanic." RMS Titanic, Inc. Web site: www.titanic-online.com.

30 "Titanic's Provisions and Linen" Titanic-Titanic.com. http://www.titanic-titanic.com/

31 "Cable & Wireless: A History" Cable & Wireless Web site. http://www.cwhistory.com/

32 "Titanic Tragedy Spawns Wireless Advancements." marconiusa.org Web site.

33 "Passengers and Crew." www.titanic-online.com.

34 "The Voyage." RMS Titanic, Inc. Web site: www.titanic-online.com.

35 "Titanic Tragedy Spawns Wireless Advancements." The U.S. National Marconi Museum, marconiusa.org Web site.

36 "The Ice Warnings." Titanic-Titanic.com

37 "Titanic's Collision with the Iceberg" Titanic-Titanic.com. http://www.titanic-titanic.com/

38 Brander, Roy. "The RMS Titanic and its Times: When Accountants Ruled the Waves." Elias Kline Memorial Lecture, 69th Shock & Vibration Symposium, October 12-16, 1998, Minneapolis, Minnesota.

39 The Molly Brown House Museum, Web site: 1912, http://mollybrown.org/1912.asp.

40 Beesley, Lawrence. *The Loss of the SS Titanic, Its Story And Its Lessons*. Houghton Mifflin Company, 1912.

41 *Three Mile Island, Volume 1, a Report to the Commissioner and to the Public*. Nuclear Regulatory Commission Special Inquiry Group, 1980.

42 *The Accident at Three Mile Island*. President's Commission on The Accident at Three Mile Island, Washington, D.C., October 1979, page 91.

43 *Three Mile Island, Volume 1, a Report to the Commissioner and to the Public*. Nuclear Regulatory Commission Special Inquiry Group, 1980, page 17.

44 Paté-Cornell, M. Elisabeth and Paul S. Fishbeck. "Risk Management for the Tiles of the Space Shuttle." *Interfaces*. The Institute of Management Sciences 24:1, January-February 1994, page 81.

45 Ibid, page 64.

46 Columbia Accident Investigation Board, Report Volume 1, August 2003, U.S. Government Printing Office, page 101.

47 Ibid, pages 37-38.

48 Ibid, page 36.

49 "Pushing Back—Bridgestone Boss Has Toughness, But Is That What Crisis Demands?" *Wall Street Journal*, September 12, 2000, page 1.

50   "A Crisis of Confidence." *Business Week*, September 18, 2000, page 31.

51   "Testimony of Bridgestone/Firestone, Inc. Before the Senate Commerce Committee." September 12, 2000, page 6.

52   "Testimony of John Lampe, Executive Vice President, Bridgestone/Firestone, Inc. Before the Senate Commerce Committee." September 12, 2000.

53   Greenwald, John. "Inside the Ford/Firestone Fight." *Time*, May 29, 2001.

54   "2004 Consumer Ratings for Passenger Vehicle Tires." United States Department of Transportation, National Highway Traffic Safety Administration.

55   "Testimony of Bridgestone/Firestone, Inc. Before The Senate Commerce Committee." September 12, 2000, page 9.

56   "Statement of U.S. Secretary of Transportation Rodney E. Slater Concerning the Senate Commerce Committee Hearings on the Bridgestone/Firestone Recall." U.S. Department of Transportation Press Release, September 12, 2000.

57   Krueger, Alan B. and Alexandre Mas. "Strikes, Scabs, and Tread Separations: Labor Strife and the Production of Defective Bridgestone/Firestone Tires." Princeton University, January 2003.

58   Greenwald, John. "Inside the Ford/Firestone Fight." *Time*, May 29, 2001.

59   Swartz, Mimi with Sherron Watkins. *POWER FAILURE: The Inside Story of the Collapse of ENRON*. Doubleday, 2003, page 13.

60   "Consistently Right About Enron." *Pennsylvania Gazette*, Volume 100, No. 4, March-April 2002.

61   McLean, Bethany. "Is Enron Overpriced?" *Fortune*, March 5, 2001.

62   Swartz, Mimi with Sherron Watkins. *POWER FAILURE: The Inside Story of the Collapse of ENRON*. Doubleday, 2003, page 114 (picture).

63   McLean, Bethany. "Why Enron Went Bust." *Fortune*, December 24, 2001.

64   Swartz, Mimi with Sherron Watkins. *POWER FAILURE: The Inside Story of the Collapse of ENRON*. Doubleday, 2003, page 282.

65   "Report of Investigation by the Special Investigative Committee of the Board of Directors of Enron Corporation." February 1, 2002, page 69.

66   Ibid, page 4.

67   Ibid, page 148.

68   Gantz, John and Jack Rochester. *The Naked Computer*. Morrow, 1983.

69   Leung, Shirley. "CEO Cantalupo's Focus on Improving Food, Service Sparks a Turnaround." *The Wall Street Journal,* January 28, 2004.

70   Treacy, Michael E. and Frederick D. Wiersema. "Customer Intimacy and Other
      Value Disciplines." *Harvard Business Review*, January 1993.

71   "Statement of Rear Admiral Paul E. Sullivan, U.S. Navy Deputy Commander For
      Ship Design, Integration and Engineering, Naval Sea Systems Command before The
      House Science Committee on the Subsafe Program." October 29, 2003.

72   Ibid.

73   Johnson, Stephen. "A Long And Deep Mystery—Scorpion Crewman Says Sub's '68
      Sinking Was Preventable." *Houston Chronicle,* May 23, 1993.

74   DiMercurio, Michael. "How Did The Scorpion Really Sink?" www.ussdevilfish.com/
      newsletter/news14.htm.

75   "Statement of Rear Admiral Paul E. Sullivan, U.S. Navy Deputy Commander For
      Ship Design, Integration and Engineering, Naval Sea Systems Command before The
      House Science Committee on the Subsafe Program." October 29, 2003.

76   FAA data from Aircraft Owners and Pilots Association (www.aopa.org) Web site.

77   *Annual Review of Aircraft Accident Data, U.S. Air Carrier Operations Calendar Year
      1999.* National Transportation Safety Board, NTSB/ARC—02/03.

78   "FAA Historical Chronology 1926–1996." Federal Aviation Administration Web
      site, www1.faa.gov/aboutfaa/History_Chron.cfm.

79   *Business & Commercial Aviation*, McGraw Hill ,April 8, 2003.

80   "Controlled Flight Into Terrain, Korean Air Flight 801." NTSB # AAR-00/01,
      Adopted January 13, 2000

81   Haynes, Al. "Eyewitness Report: United Flight 232." AirDisaster.com.

82   "Aircraft Accident Report, United Airlines, Inc. McDonnell-Douglas, DC-10-10,
      N1819U, Sioux City, IA, July 19, 1989." National Transportation Safety Board,
      NTSB-AAR-90-06.

83   Quintanilla, Carl. "USAir Taps Former General to Oversee Safety, Commissions
      Independent Audit." *The Wall Street Journal*, November 21, 1994, page A4.

84   Ban, Linda. "The Automotive Industry: On the Road to On Demand." IBM Executive
      Strategy Reports, www-1.ibm.com/services/strategy/e_strategy/demand_road.html.

85   Flint, Jerry. "Tearing Down the 'For Sale' Sign." *Forbes*, February 26, 2004.

86   J.D. Power and Associates 2003 Initial Quality Study.

87   Michaels, Daniel. "A British Survivor Goes from Nuts to Aerospace Push." *The Wall
      Street Journal*, March 16, 2004, page 1.

88   U.S. Government, Department of Transportation data compiled by the Air
      Transport Association, "Annual Revenue and Earnings—U.S. Airlines, All
      Services," with charts by the author.

89   Airline Handbook, Chapter 4, "Airline Economics," Air Transport Association, 2001.

90   National Business Aircraft Association Fact Book 2004, page 25.

91   Branson, Richard. "A Letter from Lindbergh to Trippe: September 15, 1933." Juan Trippe (1899–1981) biography, www.charleslindbergh.com/plane/trippe.asp.

92   U.S. Census Bureau, Statistical Abstract of the United States, Table No. 716. Employer Firms, Establishments, Employment, and Annual Payroll by Enterprise-Size: 1990-1999, page 483.

93   "Small Business Share of Economic Growth," United States Small Business Administration, Office of Advocacy, Small Business Research Summary No. 211, January 2002, page 1.

94   U.S. Census Bureau, Statistical Abstract of the United States, Table No. 700. Number of Returns and Business Receipts by Size of Receipts: 1990-1999, page 471.

95   Micklethwait, John and Adrian Wooldridge. *The Company: A Short History of a Revolutionary Idea*. The Modern Library, 2003, page 3.

96   Keay, John. *The Honourable Company: A History of the English East India Company*. Macmillan Publishing Company, 1994, page 25.

97   Klein, Karen E. "What's Behind High Small-Biz Failure Rates? Flawed Statistics May Make Entrepreneurs' Prospects Look Worse Than They Are." Business Week Online, September 30, 1999, www.businessweek.com/smallbiz/news/coladvice/ask/sa990930.htm.

98   "The Original Radar Plot of Detector Station Opana December 7, 1941." Records of the Joint Committees of Congress (Record Group 128), National Archives and Records Administration, www.archives.gov/records_of_congress/features/day_of_infamy.htm.

Index

consumers, 23-25, 27, 45, 64-65, 76, 82, 84-87,
141-143, 146-147, 202, 205-206, 211, 224,
227, 231, 266, 281, 290
coordination, 21, 39, 62-64, 191
Credo, 56-57
crew resource management (CRM), 34, 39, 58,
63-64, 66, 183, 187, 191
culture, xviii, xxi, 3, 5, 9-11, 30, 44, 48-50, 67,
72, 89, 120-121, 123-125, 128, 133, 136,
140, 147, 149, 151, 153, 158, 160-161,
163, 165-168, 173, 177-179, 185-186, 191-
192, 194-199, 205, 209-210, 227-228, 233,
239, 256, 261, 265, 267, 271, 274, 277,
280, 283-284, 286, 292, 296
curious, xix, 48, 67, 101, 220, 291
customer service, 11, 75, 163, 227, 283
customers, xix, 5, 10-11, 16-17, 23, 28-29, 41-
43, 45, 50, 53-58, 64-67, 70, 75, 80-82, 85,
87-90, 97, 142-143, 147-149, 163-166, 168,
178, 194-195, 197-198, 207, 209-210, 217-
219, 221-230, 232-236, 243-246, 248-251,
253-256, 258-259, 262, 266, 268, 270-274,
276, 280, 282-283, 285, 287, 290-293

D

damage, xviii, xx, 5-8, 10, 14-16, 21, 27, 33,
38-39, 50, 52-53, 66, 68-69, 92-93, 101-
102, 106, 109-110, 113-116, 118, 125-127,
129-130, 132-133, 136, 149-150, 155, 159,
161, 172, 187, 189-190, 192, 241, 262-265,
268-269, 284, 293-294, 298
data, 16, 20, 33, 36-37, 39, 43, 45, 54-55, 57,
67, 70-71, 75, 84, 117, 126, 129, 132, 141-
143, 163, 170, 173, 224, 234, 238, 240,
259, 261-262, 266, 269-270, 276, 282, 285,
291-293, 303
decision-making, xx, 15, 33, 69, 73, 90, 106,
123, 132-133, 269, 277, 286, 292
Dell, 75, 89, 134, 168, 215, 217-220, 222-
223, 228
demand, 17, 42, 79, 142, 147, 201, 203-204,
206, 208, 211-212, 214, 221-222, 249,
253, 279, 303
differentiation, 3, 226, 262
Diners Club, 27
disasters, xvii-xviii, xx-xxi, 2, 5-6, 8, 14, 16, 18,
22, 35, 44, 49, 52-53, 68, 91-92, 94, 107,
121-122, 124-125, 128-129, 131-132, 135-
136, 164, 173, 183, 186, 191, 263, 268-
269, 275, 283, 294

disbelief, xx, 68
disruptive, 84, 280
Drucker, Peter, 9, 73, 299

E

e-Commerce, 40
E³, 272, 274
Eastern Airlines, 17, 20, 229, 275
economic, xviii, xxi, 13, 16, 25, 148, 155, 158,
201-204, 206, 208, 211-217, 220-224, 227,
229, 231, 233-235, 239, 251, 261-262, 297,
303
economic business visioning (EBV), 220-225,
257, 227-233, 235-236, 251, 259, 297
EDS, 75
Enron, xvii-xix, 8, 22, 150-160, 263, 265,
267-268, 275, 277, 284, 296, 302
Ethernet, 72
ethical, 27, 45, 250, 290
evaluate, 15-16, 48-49, 133, 220, 242, 245, 286
execution, 3, 9-11, 17, 30, 45, 47, 290, 299
exponential, 4-5, 101, 136
Exxon, 72, 203

F

failures, xix, 3, 6, 8, 38, 79, 141-143, 146-147,
160, 164, 173, 183, 220
Firestone, xix, 135, 141-149, 160, 210-211, 266,
268, 296, 301-302
fly the airplane, 22, 39, 189-190
focus, 4, 7-8, 21-22, 34, 42, 46, 50, 55, 58, 61-
65, 70, 73-75, 78, 82, 86-87, 97, 101, 115,
121, 147, 177, 183, 187, 191, 197, 209,
212, 216, 247, 262, 266-268, 277, 281,
291, 296, 302
Ford, 4, 70, 140-149, 160, 165, 203, 206, 208,
210-213, 240, 268, 296, 302
forecasting, 47-48, 219

G

GE, 70, 235, 297
Germany, 9, 23
Gimli, 35, 37-39
GKN plc, 215
groceries, 40
growth, 4, 71, 249, 279, 304